THOSE GRAND OLE
Country Music Stars

In Art and Story

❈

DAVID LIVERETT

Other books by David Liverett:

When Hope Shines Through

Faith for the Journey

Love, Bridges of Reconciliation

Light from the Barn
A collection of stories and art refecting country life

This Is My Story
146 of the World's Greatest Gospel Singers

They Called Him Sparky
Friends' Reminiscences of Charles Schulz

Just Beyond the Passage
Life's Changes in Art and Story

and

Oh, to be in Miss Collier's class again!
Christie Smith Stephens and David Liverett

Chinaberry House
P.O. Box 505
Anderson, Indiana 46015-0505
www.2Lights.com
Cover photo by Dale Pickett

ISBN 978-0-615-26176-8
Printed in the United States of America

DEDICATION

Monroe William Liverett,
my dad, who always loved playing country music.

"Country music is three chords and the truth."

— Harlan Howard

TABLE OF CONTENTS

INTRODUCTION

The only time I was in the Ryman Auditorium was in the summer of 1950. I was still six and had just finished the first grade in Austinville, (Decatur) Alabama. My family had been to see Rock City earlier that day, and then we traveled to Nashville to see the Grand Ole Opry. I don't remember exactly what happened but there was a question about whether we would be able to see the show since we were arriving late. I remember Dad telling the person at the box office that if there was anyway we could still see the show, we would be much obliged. After some discussion, we did get to see the show. The other memory I have of the event was being seated under the balcony and someone above spilt a Coca-Cola onto our pew. Mom soaked up the puddle with her handkerchief. The only thing I can remember about the show was Minnie Pearl's trademark greeting of "Howdee! I'm just so proud to be here..."

Years later I got to see the Grand Ole Opry again—in the new auditorium. Judy Nelon, my friend in Nashville, got backstage passes and I was able to watch the show from the stage—behind the performers. Some of the same pews from the Ryman were available for guests to sit in while watching the show. A highlight of the evening was getting to meet Little Jimmy Dickens after the show.

My dad loved playing country music and would gather with his buddies, O. T. Terry and Buford Brewer, on our front porch and play their guitars. I remember that Dad rigged up a holder for his harmonica so he could play it at the same time he was playing his guitar. The music from those days is still fresh in my mind.

Each day at about the time I arrived home from school, Eddy Arnold's radio show would be coming on with his signature song "Cattle Call." I loved to hear him yodel.

As a teenager, I tended to prefer the folk music of the Kingston Trio or rock music from Buddy Holly. After graduation from college in 1968, I was exposed to another genre of music. I was hired by the Gaither organization to design custom album jackets at their new recording studio. Most of the clients were gospel singers. For the next twenty years, I spent much of my life hearing various gospel groups. In 2004 I compiled a gospel music book that featured my pen and ink drawings of 140 gospel singers. The book was called *It All Started with a Song*. It had been released only a month when the publisher from Thomas Nelson asked to publish it. Thomas Nelson changed the name to *This Is My Story—146 of the World's Greatest Gospel Singers*. The book in its new format was released in 2005.

My dream of a book that features country singers started in late 2006. Now over two years later I have drawn some of the singers that my dad loved. I have also included the more recent artists who have arrived on the scene since my dad passed away in 1991. Each drawing takes about twelve hours to complete. Most of the drawings are done with dots in the pointillism style. I realize that this is not a complete list of very deserving country singers, but I have included 217 artists who have had an impact on me. The essay that accompanies each drawing is just a brief glimpse of the artist's story.

David Liverett
December 7, 2008

"Country music is the people's music. It just speaks about real life and about truth and it tells things how they really are."

— Faith Hill

ROY **ACUFF**

SEPTEMBER 15, 1903 - MAYNARDVILLE, TENNESSEE - NOVEMBER 23, 1992

Known as the "King of Country Music," Roy's recordings of "The Great Speckled Bird" and "The Wabash Cannonball" made him a superstar.

Legendary may be overused to label famous performers of all music genres. In the case of Roy Claxton Acuff, the title most certainly fits. As a young boy, he dreamed of a professional baseball career but after suffering sunstroke while fishing, he gave up the idea and picked up his dad's fiddle. Roy played for a while with a traveling medicine show before he formed his own band, the CRAZY TENNESSEANS, and began auditioning at WSM for the Grand Ole Opry in 1934. His recording of GUY SMITH's "The Great Speckled Bird" made Acuff famous in 1936. He renamed his band the SMOKY MOUNTAIN BOYS and decided to stay with a traditional country sound. He even returned to his roots of singing in church by adding religious songs to his repertoire. During the 1930s and 1940s, Acuff sold more records than any other country performer.

By the 1940s, Roy had recorded such classics as "The Wreck on the Highway," "The Precious Jewel," and "Beneath That Lonely Mound of Clay." He even published his own songbook and sold 100,000 copies. Roy collaborated with FRED ROSE to form Acuff-Rose Publications in 1942. Some of the most popular songs and their writers became the property of their company during the next couple of decades.

In 1948 Roy ran unsuccessfully for governor of Tennessee. He campaigned for TEX RITTER in 1970 when Tex ran for the U.S. Senate from Tennessee. In 1962 Roy was the first living person to be elected a member of the Country Music Hall of Fame®. In 1987 he was presented with the Grammy Life Achievement Award for his contributions in the music industry. He also has a star on the Hollywood Walk of Fame.

In declining heath in the late 1980s, Roy built a home near the Opry to greet his fans. He passed away November 23, 1992, leaving a legacy that will forever shape country music.

TRACE **ADKINS**

JANUARY 13, 1962 - SPRINGHILL, LOUISIANA

Beginning with his debut album, Dreamin' Out Loud in 1996, Trace keeps bringing on the hits such as "Honky Tonk Badonkadonk."

Not far from the Arkansas state line, Tracy Darrell Adkins was born into a musical family. His dad taught him to play the guitar at an early age. His first singing experience was in a gospel quartet while he was still in high school. At Louisiana Tech Trace played football and studied music. In the early 1990s, he decided on a solo career singing in honky-tonk bars in Louisiana and Texas until 1992 when he moved to Nashville. For three years he worked in construction and sang in bars at night. SCOTT HENDRICKS of Capitol Records heard him one night and signed him to a record contract. The rest, as they say, is history.

"Every Light in the House," "(This Ain't) No Thinkin' Thing," "I Left Something Turned on at Home," and "The Rest of Mine" are some of his early hits. From the album *Songs About Me*, "Honky Tonk Badonkadonk" was a major crossover hit for Trace in 2005. His unmistakable baritone voice-over can be heard in television commercials and documentaries. Trace has played at the White House, appeared in the center square on the game show, *Hollywood Squares*, and on the NBC television series, *The Celebrity Apprentice*.

Trace accepted his membership to join the cast of the Grand Ole Opry from LITTLE JIMMY DICKENS in 2003. It required a stepladder for the 4'-11" Jimmy to look face to face into Trace's 6'-6" height. Trace commented, "The country music fans at the Opry are the best and they've always made me feel like I'm home, no matter how many times I perform there. I've been blessed with a career that I enjoy and being an Opry member is just an awesome honor."

The town of Sarepta, Louisiana, can be proud of this former gospel singer, oil driller, and star football player turned country music star.

GARY **ALLAN**

DECEMBER 5, 1967 - MONTEBELLO, CALIFORNIA

Following in his dad's footsteps, Gary formed his own band in the style of the Bakersfield Sound. He was a seasoned musician from the age of twelve.

Gary was born Gary Allan Herzberg. He was reared in La Miada, California, the son of Harley and Mary Herzberg. Mary insisted that the family guitar be visible at all times. Gary played in honky-tonk joints with his dad's band before he was twelve. The stage had been set by MERLE HAGGARD, BUCK OWENS, and others for what is known now as the Bakersfield Sound. Gary brought his own band, the HONKY TONK WRANGLERS, to the same bars to perfect his style. In 1993 Gary was introduced to BYRON HILL, a songwriter and producer. Two years later, Byron and Gary began working on four songs at Javeline Studios. Mercury, RCA, and Decca all seriously considered signing them to a contract.

Gary signed with Decca Records in 1996 after turning down record deals while he was still in high school. His recording of "Her Man" from his album, *Used Heart for Sale,* appeared that same year. MCA picked up Gary's contract after Decca folded in 1999. His album, *Smoke Rings in the Dark*, was released later that year and included a honky-tonk version of DEL SHANNON'S "Runaway."

In 2003 Gary was nominated for the Country Music Association's Horizon Award which is given to an individual or group that has demonstrated the most growth in overall chart and sales activity and media recognition.

Tragedy struck in 2004 when Gary's wife took her life. Gary decided not to retreat but to release his next album called *Tough All Over.* "Best I Ever Had" became a Top Ten hit and was considered the best song of his career. In 2006 Gary toured with RASCAL FLATTS.

The New York Times has described Gary's music as "elegant, often deadpan songs [that] tend toward manly understatement."

DUANE **ALLEN**

APRIL 29, 1943 - TAYLORTOWN, TEXAS

Lead singer for the Oak Ridge Boys since 1966, Duane was trained in both operatic and quartet styles of singing.

Besides being the lead singer and co-producer for the Oak Ridge Boys, Duane is a smart business-man. Each year the OAK RIDGE BOYS try to schedule 150 concert dates. Duane also serves as a fundraiser and advocate for many civic and charitable causes such as Feed the Children, the Boy Scouts of America, and the National Committee for the Prevention of Child Abuse.

Duane and his wife, Norah Lee, have reared two children, Jamie and Dee. He enjoys spending time with his four grandchildren, March, Kell, Tallant, and Texas LeeAnn.

Affectionally known as "Ace," Duane is a collector of antique cars who owns two dozen classics. The collection is housed in a museum called "Ace On Wheels." Duane's farm in Hendersonville, Tennessee, includes beef cattle, horses, and burros. He tries to stay in good physical shape by walking twenty to thirty miles a week and shooting some hoops when he has a chance.

The Oak Ridge Boys are known for their uplifting songs. Duane says, "You don't hear us singing 'cheating' or 'drinking' songs, but 'loving' songs, because we think that will last."

"Elvira" is probably the best known song associated with the group. It won them a Grammy Award for Best Vocal Performance by a Group or Duo, Country in 1982. They have won numerous awards including four other Grammy Awards between 1971 and 1979. They have also won seven Dove Awards and Duane was inducted into the Gospel Music Hall of Fame in 2000 as a member of the Oak Ridge Boys.

Duane says, "After forty years of singing lead for the Oak Ridge Boys, I still love what I do...It's likely that one day my tombstone will say: 'He never had a real job — he just played and sang music and here rests a very happy man.'"

REX **ALLEN**

DEC. 31, 1920 - MUD SPRINGS CANYON, ARIZONA - DEC. 17, 1999

Known as the "Last of the Silver Screen Cowboys," Rex starred in nineteen movies for Republic Pictures. His big hit song was "Crying in the Chapel."

Rex Elvie Allen was born forty miles from Willcox, Arizona, on a ranch in Mud Springs Canyon. He learned to play a Sears and Roebuck guitar while his dad played a fiddle. Rex sang in the church choir until he was thirteen. By the late 1930s, he had graduated from high school and was on the rodeo circuit. WTTM in Trenton, New Jersey, hired Rex as a singer and billed him as "Cactus Rex." By 1945 he was hired at WLS in Chicago to perform on the *National Barn Dance*.

Rex married Bonnie Linder in 1946 and that same year signed a recording contract with Mercury Records. Rex Allen, Jr. was born the following year. Rex had two other sons, Curtis and Mark, and a daughter, Bonita.

Republic Pictures had launched their singing cowboy movies with stars such as ROY ROGERS and GENE AUTRY and now was the time for Rex Allen. In 1949 *The Arizona Cowboy* was released. In the movie, Rex sang two songs that he had written, "Arizona Waltz" and "I Was Born in Arizona." Television put an end to big-screen Westerns and Rex was branded as the "Last of the Silver Screen Cowboys." *Phantom Stallion*, released in 1954, was the last of his nineteen Westerns. His beloved horse, Koko, was featured in many of his movies as were his sidekicks, BUDDY EBSEN and SLIM PICKENS.

Rex's distinctive voice can be heard narrating more than eighty Disney movies. For Hanna-Barbera, he provided the narration for the animated version of *Charlotte's Web*. In 1958 Rex starred in the television series, *Frontier Doctor*.

It can be said that Rex Allen, the clean-cut western hero that we all loved seeing in the movies or whose soothing voice we listened to, was truly an American hero.

Kenny **Alphin**

NOVEMBER 1, 1963 - CULPEPER, VIRGINIA

Known as Big Kenny, he is one-half of Big & Rich. His credentials are varied from carpentry to running a logging crew to songwriting and performing.

William Kenneth Alphin's "overnight" success took a decade. His parents, Bill and Mary, have always supported Kenny's dream. He says, "My parents love me...without their support, I don't know where I would be." Growing up on a farm, he recalls that when equipment is broken, you learn to fix it.

Kenny's career started with a dare to sing in a club in northern Virginia. During his solo career, he went by the name Big Kenny Rocks. Later he became the lead singer for luvjOi (pronounced Love Joy). Meeting CHARLEY PRIDE and PORTER WAGONER on his first trip to Nashville in 1993 was an exciting time.

Kenny met and became friends with JOHN RICH in 1998. Their mutual love for singing and songwriting has sustained their friendship. BIG AND RICH blends country music, rock, and hip-hop. The first song they collaborated on was "I Pray for You."

A weekly Tuesday night jam session ensued known as MuzikMafia (Musically Artistic Friends In Alliance) at the Pub of Love. *Horse of a Different Color*, their studio album, was released in 2004. From that album, "Save a Horse (Ride a Cowboy)" has become one of their signature songs. They have had much success lately with 120 dates in less than five months. They employ sixty-five people with nine buses and four or five tractor-trailers.

Kenny is one of the most authentic persons in a world that needs hope. He and his wife, Christiev wanted to made a difference. They flew to Akon, Sudan, in 2007 and brought medical and school supplies. Musical instruments, clothing, and building tools for the Kunyuk School for Girls, were included. His roots of singing in the Culpeper Baptist Church have stayed with William Kenneth Alphin and made him truly a big man.

BILL **ANDERSON**

NOVEMBER 1, 1937 - COLUMBIA, SOUTH CAROLINA

He's known as "Whispering Bill" for his of style of singing. As a songwriter, Bill is credited with such hits as "City Lights" and "Mama Sang a Song."

Bill Anderson is one performer you dare not pigeonhole. First of all, he is a composer extraordinaire. In addition he has been a country singer, game show host, actor, and author. After learning to play the guitar, Bill formed his own band at age twelve. After graduating from college with a degree in journalism, he was hired by the *Atlanta Constitution*.

At the age of nineteen, Bill wrote the song "City Lights." RAY PRICE recorded the song in 1958 and it topped the country charts. When Decca Records signed him to a contract, Bill moved to Nashville. He had his own Top Ten two years later with "Tip of My Fingers."

BMI named Bill Anderson the first country music songwriting icon. His songs have been heard on recent works from VINCE GILL, LORRIE MORGAN, KENNY CHESNEY, and SARA EVANS. No other composer had four songs in the Top Twenty Country Songs from 1960 to 1995. "City Lights," "Still," "Once a Day," and "Mama Sang a Song" were the songs that *Billboard* reported in this milestone.

Bill hosted the ABC-TV game show *The Better Sex* in 1977, and for three years he was a regular on the daytime soap opera, *One Life to Live*. For six years he hosted the game show *Fandango* for the Nashville Network as well as *Opry Backstage*. He co-produced *You Can Be a Star*. In addition Bill has appeared on a variety of talk and game shows, including *The Tonight Show*, *The Today Show*, *Family Feud*, and *Hee Haw*. Since 1961, he has been a member of the Grand Ole Opry and performs there regularly.

"Whispering Bill" became his nickname in 1966 for his soft approach to singing. He has said that "if you want someone's attention, whisper." Bill has lived with that philosophy for his adult life. His autobiography, *Whispering Bill*, details his life and career in show business.

KEITH ANDERSON

JANUARY 12, 1968 - MIAMI, OKLAHOMA

Keith's debut album, Three Chord Country and American Rock 'n' Roll, *featuring "Pickin' Wildflowers," scored gold in 2006.*

In a small town in the northeast corner of Oklahoma, Keith Anderson grew up in a deeply religious family. He considers his folks "angels on earth." Because his parents, LeRoy and Janice, cared for foster children, he remembers there were always lots of kids around the house. Keith learned to play the drums while his brother Brian played the guitar in church.

In college Keith played baseball and was approached by the Kansas City Royals. An injured shoulder ended his hopes for a professional baseball career. He earned a degree in engineering with a GPA of 3.9 (first in his class) from Oklahoma State University in 1990. He accepted an engineering position in Dallas after graduation, but it wasn't long before he started writing songs and taking guitar lessons from his brother. He auditioned and was accepted at the Grapevine Opry, a steppingstone to performing for Six Flags Over Texas. Keith was experiencing financial problems but all the while enjoyed what he was doing. He was accepted into a physical therapy program but music, his first love, was calling him back.

In the spring of 1998, Keith arrived in Nashville. He became a waiter in a restaurant on Music Row. It wasn't long until he became friends with songwriter GEORGE DUCAS. The two of them began collaborating on some songs in the fall of that year. Building his confidence, Keith started writing with other well-known writers.

By 2002 GARTH BROOKS and GEORGE JONES recorded a hit duet "Beer Run." The song was co-written by Keith and four others, including his friend George Ducas. Two years later, GRETCHEN WILSON recorded Keith's song, "The Bed," on her debut album. Keith's hit single "Pickin' Wildflowers" from his debut album was certified gold in 2006.

LYNN **ANDERSON**

SEPTEMBER 26, 1947 - GRAND FORKS, NORTH DAKOTA

In 1971 "(I Never Promised You A) Rose Garden" made Lynn Anderson an international star. In the top 500 Greatest Country Songs it is 120.

Besides being a superstar in the country music world, Lynn has won seven hundred trophies at horse shows. She won the title of California Horse Show Queen in 1966.

By the time Lynn was six, her songwriting parents, Casey and Liz Anderson were encouraging her to sing. In the mid-1960s, she left the equestrian circuit to pursue a recording career. After her recording of "Ride, Ride, Ride" made it into the Top Forty, Lynn became a regular on *The Lawrence Welk Show* in the 1967-1968 season, becoming the only country artist featured weekly on national television at that time. She went on to secure a few more Top Ten hits by the late 1960s such as "That's a No No," "Rocky Top," and "Promises, Promises."

By 1971 Lynn's signature song, "Rose Garden," sent her to international stardom and she won a Grammy Award for Best Female Country Vocal Performance. Twice Lynn has earned the Academy of Country Music Award for Top Female Vocalist as well as a CMA Award for Female Vocalist of the Year. To her credit she has earned eight number one records, eighteen Top Tens, and over fifty Top Forty hits plus seventeen gold albums. "Rocky Top" is now one of Tennessee's official state songs, the other being, "The Tennessee Waltz."

Lynn Anderson has been called "The Great Lady of Country Music" and has performed for the Queen of England as well as five U.S. presidents. She was proud to be asked to sing for JIMMY CARTER'S seventy-fifth birthday celebration in 1999.

The American Rose Society created a hybrid rose in cream, finely edged with pink, and named it the Lynn Anderson. This champion horsewoman, mother of three, and international recording star has certainly made an impact on the world.

19

EDDY ARNOLD

MAY 15, 1918 - HENDERSON, TENNESSEE - MAY 8, 2008

Known as the "Tennessee Plowboy," Eddy's "Cattle Call" and "Make the World Go Away" made him a country music icon.

Eddy's father died when Eddy was only eleven, forcing the family farm to be sold at auction. Before that his father had set aside funds to buy Eddy a guitar. After chores his mother tutored him on the instrument.

Eddy had his radio debut on Jackson, Tennessee's WTJS in 1936. In 1940 he was a regular with PEE WEE KING'S GOLDEN WEST COWBOYS which gave him exposure at the Grand Ole Opry. Three years later, he emerged as the TENNESSEE PLOWBOY and hosted a radio program on WSM. "Cattle Call" became his theme song. With COLONEL TOM PARKER as his manager, Eddy signed a contract at RCA.

Eddy began to dominate the country music world in the late 1940s, having six number one hits and thirteen in the Top Twenty. With his smooth, "country Perry Como" voice, Eddy appeared on the *Milton Berle Show* as well as the *Ed Sullivan Show*. In the mid-1950s, he recorded a pop-oriented version of his signature song, "Cattle Call," with the HUGO WINTERHALTER ORCHESTRA. This broadened his exposure to a wider audience. By the mid-1960s, Eddy's "Make the World Go Away" gave him a second run of sixteen hits. At that time he shifted to other venues such as Hollywood's Coconut Grove and sold-out engagements in Las Vegas, in addition to two sold-out performances at Carnegie Hall.

Eddy was inducted into the Country Music Hall of Fame® in 1966. He is the only artist to receive the CMA Entertainer of the Year Award, the ACM Pioneer Award, and the President's Award from the Song Writers Guild. From his first record in 1944 until his 2005 release of "After All These Years," Eddy Arnold has sold over eighty-five million records. He has had an incredible twenty-eight number one hits on *Billboard's* Country Singles chart. In 2003 Arnold ranked number twenty-two in CMT's 40 Greatest Men in Country Music.

ERNIE **ASHWORTH**

DECEMBER 15, 1928 - HUNTSVILLE, ALABAMA

Ernie's number one hit, "Talk Back Trembling Lips," stayed on the country charts for forty-two weeks. He wrote "I Wish" for Paul Anka.

I t isn't far from the cotton fields of north Alabama to NASA's guided missile operations at Huntsville, Alabama's Redstone Arsenal. Ernest Bert Ashworth has made the journey with a little detour to the Grand Ole Opry.

Ernie was writing songs before he could play the guitar. By the time he was twenty, Ernie had formed his first band, the TUNETWISTERS and was appearing on the local radio station WBHP. In 1949 he tried his wings as a staff writer for the Acuff-Rose Publishing House. WESLEY ROSE was instrumental in landing a record contract for him at MGM. Ernie had already composed several songs that were making other artists rich, including LITTLE JIMMY DICKENS, CARL SMITH, JOHNNY HORTON, and even pop singer, PAUL ANKA. After a disappointing first attempt as a country singer, Ernie headed back to Huntsville to work on guided missiles. Three years later in 1960, Wesley called Ernie back to Nashville to sign a contract with Decca Records.

The 1960s were very good for Ernie with twelve singles in the Top Ten on the country charts. "Talk Back Trembling Lips" went to number one and stayed on the country charts for over eight months. The song is believed to be one of the first records to crossover to the pop charts. Some of Ernie's hits were "Each Moment Spent with You," "You Can't Pick a Rose in December," and "Forever Gone." In 1963 and 1964, *Billboard*, *Cashbox*, and *Record World* acclaimed Ernie as the Most Promising Male Artist. Also in 1964 his dream of induction into the Grand Ole Opry was fulfilled. Ernie appeared in the movie *The Farmer's Daughter* in 1965. His work has also made an impact in Europe where he was voted the most programmed independent artist in 1999. He was inducted into the Alabama Music Hall Fame in 2008. Ernie still performs at the Opry and says, "It's a lot more fun than the cotton field."

CHET **ATKINS**

JUNE 20, 1924 - (NEAR) LUTTRELL, TENNESSEE - JUNE 30, 2001

Known as "Mr. Guitar," Chet earned thirteen Grammy Awards, more than any other country artist, and became the most recorded solo instrumentalist.

Chester Burton Atkins was reared in a musical family. His mom played the piano; his dad gave piano lessons and sang with touring evangelists. His parents were divorced when he was six. Because of his asthmatic condition, he moved Georgia to be with his dad and music became his passion. Chet first took up playing the ukulele before mastering the fiddle and guitar.

In 1942 Chet dropped out of high school and was hired to play the fiddle and guitar at Knoxville's WNOX radio station. Three years later, Chet moved to Cincinnati and went to work for WLW, where MERLE TRAVIS had worked. For years he had admired Travis' style of playing the guitar using the thumb for the bass and index finger for the melody. Chet developed the "Atkins Style" of picking with his first three fingers and using his thumb for the bass.

Chet auditioned for RED FOLEY and won a spot on the Grand Ole Opry in 1946. STEVE SHOLES of RCA signed Chet in 1947. After unsuccessful sales of his first recordings, he stayed on playing in studio sessions that year but relocated back in Knoxville to work with HOMER AND JETHRO. A year later he moved to Springfield, Missouri, to play for the CARTER FAMILY at KWTO. By 1950 Chet had moved back to Nashville where he played in recording sessions and performed at the Grand Ole Opry. His first hit, "Mr. Sandman," was followed by "Silver Bell" with HANK SNOW.

Sholes moved to pop music production in 1957 and Chet was placed in charge of RCA's Nashville division. As a producer, he signed notables such as WILLIE NELSON, DOLLY PARTON, and PORTER WAGONER.

Chet Atkins is among the most influential musicians in music history and was the youngest person ever inducted into the Country Music Hall of Fame® in 1973.

RODNEY **ATKINS**

MARCH 28, 1969 - KNOXVILLE, TENNESSEE

In 1997 Rodney released his first album, In a Heartbeat. *"If You're Going Through Hell" went to number one as a* Billboard *country single in 2006.*

Rodney Atkins was asked in 1994 by his new record label to change his last name because it was too close to CHET ATKINS and TRACE ADKINS. He refused to consider this request. Twenty-five years earlier he had been put up for adoption at the Holston Methodist Home for Children in Greenville, Tennessee. Because of a bad case of colic and a severe infection, two couples tried to adopt him but called it quits, and after several sleepless nights, returned him to the facility. It took Allan and Margaret Atkins to stick it out. They weren't afraid to take him home, and they didn't bring him back to the orphanage.

It wasn't until he was in high school that Rodney began playing the guitar. His hometown of Cumberland Gap, Tennessee, began to hear from this rising star. It was at Tennessee Tech University that Rodney had the opportunity to perform in Nashville. In 1997 he signed with Curb Records and his first single made it to the *Billboard* country charts. In 2002 his "Sing Along" was a Top Forty single. Two years later, Rodney landed his first Top Five hit with "Honesty (Write Me a List)." In 2006 *Billboard* declared his first number one single with "If You're Going Through Hell (Before the Devil Even Knows)."

Since then Rodney has built a studio at his home and can lay down all his vocals while still spending time with his family. He has said, "This could be the most inexpensive record Curb has ever done, because there was no engineer and no studio clock ticking away. I'd just go in whenever I felt like singing and it made the process for me that much better."

Rodney understands that family is one of the most important things in life. Because of his background, he believes that the love of the family has healing powers. He has turned out to be one of the happiest kids in eastern Tennessee.

GENE **AUTRY**

SEPTEMBER 29, 1907 - TIOGA, TEXAS - OCTOBER 2, 1998

Known as "The Singing Cowboy," Gene was the first movie star to use the television medium. He co-wrote over three hundred songs.

Orvon Gene Autry, the oldest child of a poor tenant farmer, was taught by his grandfather to sing at the age of five. His grandfather wanted him to perform in the local Baptist church and at other town events. Gene loved hearing cowboy songs. At twelve, he paid eight dollars for his first guitar from Sears and Roebuck. At fifteen, Gene was playing at the local cafe and anywhere else that would have him, in and around Tioga, Texas.

By the time he was twenty, Gene was working at the local telegraph office in Chelsa, Oklahoma. His shift was four to midnight and to pass the time, he would sing and play his guitar. Just by chance, WILL ROGERS came into the office and heard him singing. Rogers encouraged him to go to New York and pursue a singing career. On October 9, 1929, Gene was at RCA in New York cutting his first record. This was the first of six hundred and thirty-five recordings, including more than three hundred songs that he wrote or co-wrote, that sold more than a hundred million copies.

Gene's songs for children, "Here Comes Santa Claus," "Peter Cottontail," "Frosty the Snowman," and "Rudolph the Red-Nosed Reindeer" are among his biggest sellers. From 1940 to 1956, on his weekly radio show, *Melody Ranch*, one could hear his signature song, "Back in the Saddle Again." His popularity grew and during a public appearance tour he became the first performer to sell out Madison Square Garden.

From his days as the "Oklahoma Yodeling Cowboy" and as a featured artist on the *National Barn Dance* in Chicago, Gene Autry became one of the most beloved country western singers of all time. He is the only performer with five stars on the Hollywood Walk of Fame covering radio, records, motion pictures, television, and live stage performances. He was inducted into the Country Music Hall of Fame® in 1969.

DeFord **Bailey**

DECEMBER 14, 1899 - CARTHAGE, TENNESSEE - JULY 2, 1982

The first African-American star of the Grand Ole Opry, DeFord appeared in the first year and played his harmonica in forty-nine of the first fifty-two shows.

Known from the early days of the Grand Ole Opry, DeFord was the "harmonica wizard." He was given that nickname by the Opry's first announcer, GEORGE HAY.

DeFord suffered from polio as a child and was left with a deformed back. He was taught to play the guitar, fiddle, banjo, and the harmonica by his father and an uncle. By the time DeFord was fourteen, he had become a professional musician. He moved to Nashville in 1925 and soon met DR. HUMPHREY BATE. Besides being a physician, Dr. Bate was a respected harmonica player. Being impressed with the talent of DeFord, the doctor opened the doors for him to become a regular cast member at the Grand Ole Opry.

DeFord had an association with the show's name, "Grand Ole Opry." Originally the Opry was known as The Barn Dance. In December of 1927, NBC's national opera program ended their show preceding The Barn Dance with the imitation of a locomotive. George Hay was looking for a segue, and before DeFord played *his* train song, "Pan American Blues," George said, "For the past hour, we have been listening to music largely from Grand Opera, but from now on, we will present "The Grand Ole Opry."

DeFord was paid only five dollars for each performance but he contributed to the format of the show. Not only he was the first African-American to perform at the Grand Ole Opry, but he was also the first solo star. The public never knew that he was African-American for it was never mentioned on the air. During his fifteen years on the show he had a secure contract in addition to recording in the late 1920s on Columbia, Brunswick, and Victor Records. After sixteen seasons, in 1941, Deford left the show and never returned until the old-timers' show in 1974. In the meantime, he polished shoes at a stand he opened with his uncle in 1933.

PHIL **BALSLEY**

AUGUST 8, 1939 - STAUNTON, VIRGINIA

Known as the "Quiet One," Phil was one of the original members of the Statler Brothers.

Philip Elwood Balsley was born and reared in the beautiful Shenandoah Valley. As is the case for many country singers, young Phil's earliest memories were of singing in his hometown church choir. He attributes his biggest influences in life to his mom and dad plus George Sergeant, his music teacher. His musical tastes always leaned toward gospel music.

When Phil was sixteen years old, he and some friends formed a group called the FOUR STAR QUARTET. The members included Phil, HAROLD REID, JOE MCDORMAN, and LEW DEWITT. Joe arranged their first appearance at the Methodist Church in Lyndhurst, Virginia, in 1955. The group was not paid for their efforts, but the forty people who showed up seemed to have enjoyed their singing by the applause they gave.

The quartet changed its name to the KINGSMEN before eventually becoming the STATLER BROTHERS. When Joe left around 1961, Harold's younger brother DON joined the group. Lew DeWitt passed away in 1981 with complications from Crohn's Disease and JIMMY FORTUNE became the newest member. In 1964 the "Brothers" got a big break when JOHNNY CASH hired them as an opening act on his television show.

Before Phil joined the Statlers, he kept the books for his dad's sheet metal factory. With his knack for numbers, he was responsible for overseeing much of the day-to-day business for the Statler Brothers. Phil was not known for his contributions in songwriting but his rich baritone voice was essential for the quartet's harmony. Phil is known as the "Quiet One" because of his quiet and humble presence on stage. He says about being a Statler, "It's all of us, even though I don't write songs. We're friends with each other, and more than anything else, we are friends with our fans and they seem to consider us friends, too."

BOBBY **BARE**

Bobby's "The All American Boy," "Detroit City," and "500 Miles from Home" made the country and pop charts during the 1950s and 1960s.

Bobby grew up poor in southern Ohio. His mother died when he was five and since there was not enough income, his father split up the family. Bobby spent time on a farm and working in local factories until he began making his own music. By the time Bobby was nineteen, he had built his own guitar and was playing with bands in the Springfield, Ohio, area. By 1958 Bobby had moved to California and recorded his first "talking" song, "The All American Boy." When the song was finally released in 1959, it became the second biggest hit on the country charts, peaked on pop charts at number three, and reached number twenty-two in England.

After a stint in the armed forces, Bobby gave pop music a try. He roomed with WILLIE NELSON and toured with ROY ORBISON and BOBBY DARIN. In 1962 Bobby turned back to his roots in country music and signed with RCA Records. His "Shame on You" was one of the first country songs to feature horns. The next year Bobby recorded his hit, "Detroit City," which scored big on both pop and country charts. "500 Miles from Home" continued the hits in both genres. Bobby also tried his hand at acting, appearing in the movie, *A Distant Trumpet.*

Also influenced by BOB DYLAN, Bobby explored American folk music while touring in England. In 1970 on the Mercury label, Bobby recorded such hits as, "How I Got to Memphis," "Please Don't Tell Me How the Story Ends," and "Come Sundown." In 1973 Bobby was back at RCA and a double album of SHEL SILVERSTEIN's songs, *Bobby Bare Sings Lullabys, Legends and Lies,* was released. The album fit in with the outlaw movement of the 1970s. His first number one hit, "Marie Laveau," came the next year. Another album of Silverstein songs, *Drinkin' from the Bottle, Singin' from the Heart,* was released in 1982. Bobby came out of retirement in 2005 and released *The Moon Is Blue.*

DIERKS **BENTLEY**

NOVEMBER 20, 1975 - PHOENIX, ARIZONA

Dierks' debut album produced three major hits; his second included the number one hit, "Modern Day Drifter."

The standout first name of this new artist comes from his maternal grandmother's maiden name. Dierks was born in Phoenix, Arizona, but spent his teenage years in Lawrenceville, New Jersey. Neither location is considered a hotbed of country music. In fact it wasn't until Dierks moved to Nashville in 1993 to attend Vanderbilt University that he had any interest in country music. After hearing HANK WILLIAMS JR.'S "Man to Man," Dierks said, "That moment really changed my whole perspective. Everything just clicked. I just knew I loved country music."

Hired as a researcher for The Nashville Network (TNN), Dierks studied the history of country music. After self-financing a demo recording, he had gotten a gig at Market Street when VINCE GILL and AMY GRANT came through the door. As it turned out, Vince, with his mandolin, jammed with Dierks for almost an hour and a half. Says Dierks, "I thought that if my music dreams never went any further, that would be all right because I got to share the stage with Vince Gill."

When his independent demo had been heard around Music Row, Dierks acquired a publishing deal with Sony/Tree Publishing as a full-time songwriter. Then he met MIKE DUNGAN at Capitol Records and "knew immediately that was where I wanted to be."

Since 2003 Dierks has soared to the top of the country charts with hit singles, "What Was I Thinkin'," How Am I Doin'?," and "My Last Name." In 2005 he received the CMA Horizon Award and on October 1, 2005, he was elected to the Grand Ole Opry (the youngest member at that date). He says, "The Opry is such a huge part of American history. It's bigger than just country music. It's a big reflection of our country." Dierks takes every opportunity he can to come back and play his favorite stage, the Grand Ole Opry.

CLINT **BLACK**

FEBRUARY 4, 1962 - LONG BRANCH, NEW JERSEY

Although Clint was born in New Jersey, he grew up in Texas, and is considered to be one of America's neo-traditional country music singers.

Because his dad loved COLE PORTER, Clint was almost named Cole Black. His dad thought he would be teased and so he was named Clint Patrick Black. By the age of thirteen, Clint had a passion for music. He learned to play the harmonica, guitar, and bass. While in his teens, Clint started playing in Houston nightclubs. He tried to sound like some of his favorite singers, among them MERLE HAGGARD AND WILLIE NELSON. To support himself, he worked in construction.

In 1987 Clint met guitarist HAYDEN NICHOLAS who soon joined his band. Producer BILL HAM saw Clint and his band perform and asked if he wanted to be star. Less than six months later Clint had signed a contract with RCA Records. His first single, "A Better Man," made it to number one on the country charts. His debut album, *Killin' Time,* also became number one, its songs having been written by Clint and Hayden. The album went platinum eight months later. 1991 was a big year for Clint. He began touring with ALABAMA, joined the Grand Ole Opry, and was chosen by *People* as one of their "50 Most Beautiful People in the World." That same year, he married LISA HARTMAN of *Knots Landing* fame. They have a daughter, Lily Pearl.

On television Clint has appeared on *Wings, Hope and Faith*, and *Hot Properties*. On the big screen his credits include *Maverick* and *Anger Management* with JACK NICHOLSON. Clint has a star on the Hollywood Walk of Fame for his contribution to the recording industry.

In 1998 Clint's hit single, "Same Old Train," earned him a Grammy. His duet partners have included MARTINA MCBRIDE, STEVE WARINER, and one of his heroes, ROY ROGERS.

In late 2003, Clint parted ways with his longtime record label RCA and started recording under his own label, Equity Music Group.

Joe Bonsall

MAY 18, 1948 - PHILADELPHIA, PENNSYLVANIA

Joe has been a member of the Oak Ridge Boys since 1973. He is an avid songwriter and has authored the Molly the Cat *series of children's books.*

Besides singing tenor with the OAK RIDGE BOYS, Joe loves writing about his five cats. The *Molly the Cat* series has taken on a life of its own. His love for writing is noted also in a tribute to his parents. The book, *G.I. Joe and Lillie,* tells the tale of his dad, Joseph Sr., a decorated hero of Normandy, and his mom. When his parents met, his mother was in the Women's Army Corps. The story deals with the hard times before WWII, as well as with aging parents. The book includes his family tree and his folks interment in Arlington National Cemetery.

When Joe was fifteen, his dad suffered a debilitating stroke and the teen had to become the man of the house. His mother was always his encourager and taught him to trust in God.

Growing up in Philadelphia, Joe was always around sports and music. He loved both. Joe found a kindred spirit in RICHARD STERBAN who also loved Joe's favorite style of singing, southern gospel. They began singing together in a group called the KEYSTONES.

The OAK RIDGE BOYS have been around since about 1943 and were originally founded by WALLY FOWLER in Knoxville, Tennessee. In 1973 Joe replaced WILLIE WYNN as tenor for the OAKS, a year after his friend Richard replaced NOEL FOX. It wasn't until 1977 that they branched out into the crossover market and produced their first music video, "Easy." The group sang back-up for PAUL SIMON's hit song, "Slip Slidin' Away" and recorded with other country greats: GEORGE JONES, JOHNNY CASH, BRENDA LEE, BILLY RAY CYRUS, and ROY ROGERS. 1981 was the year they recorded the novelty song, "Elvira," which became a Grammy Award winning smash hit.

With all the great music that has come from Philadelphia, Joe marvels that his name appears in the Philadelphia Music Hall of Fame.

BOXCAR **WILLIE**

SEPTEMBER 1, 1931 - STERRATT, TEXAS - APRIL 12, 1999

Famous for his original hobo-style music, Boxcar Willie is known for "Wabash Cannonball" and "Lonesome Whistle Blues."

Lecil Travis Martin was born in a small railroad shack alongside the KD (Keokuk and Des Moines) Railroad in Sterratt, Texas. As the son of a farm and section hand, Lecil spent his childhood in a three-room toolshed provided by the railroad and placed about six feet from the first set of tracks. As a child, he loved the railroad and ran away often to ride the trains. Growing up, he also loved country music. Favorites were ERNEST TUBB, JIMMIE RODGERS, and ROY ACUFF.

Lecil left home in 1949 to join the air force. He was trained as a pilot and during the Korean War was assigned to the B-29 super fortress. While still in the military, Lecil had a television show in Lincoln, Nebraska, and was a radio disc jockey. Lecil's professional name was MARTY MARTIN. His group was known as MARTY MARTIN AND THE RANGERS. The idea for a stage name came when he was waiting at a train crossing in Lincoln. As the train rumbled by, he saw a man sitting in a boxcar who resembled his boom operator, Willie Wilson. Lecil pulled his car to the side and wrote the song, "Boxcar Willie."

Lecil was playing a club in Boise when a lady named Lloene Davis Johnson came in and sat in front of the band. She caught Lecil's eye. She wasn't into country music and hadn't heard of Lecil, but he must have made an impression for the two fell in love, were married, and had four children. Lloene was a huge supporter of Boxcar Willie's career.

While on a trip to California, Lecil entered a contest as BOXCAR WILLIE and won the $150.00 first prize. He was slow to catch on with the country music crowd. When he was playing in Grand Prairie, Texas, GEORGE JONES' agent asked Boxcar to play at George's club in Nashville.

In May of 1986 the Boxcar Willie Theater opened in Branson, Missouri, where he performed successfully though 1998.

GARTH **BROOKS**

FEBRUARY 7, 1962 - LUBA, OKLAHOMA

Garth has one of the most celebrated music careers in popular music history with seventy hits and sales of over 123 million albums.

Growing up in a musical family, Troyal "Garth" Brooks inherited his ability to please an audience from his famous mother, COLLEEN CARROLL. Her strong sweet voice was featured on "Red Foley's Ozark Jubilee" during the 1950s.

Garth's passion in high school was sports. He attended Oklahoma State University on a track scholarship. He tried out for the San Diego Padres pro-baseball team in the spring of 1999, but was not successful.

Garth may have earned a degree in advertising, but country music flowed though his veins. He worked as a bouncer in a Stillwater nightclub after his first attempt as a country singer. By 1987 he had met his future manager, BOB DOYLE. A year later, Capitol Records released his first album, *Garth Brooks,* and with the help of singles, "Much Too Young," "If Tomorrow Never Comes," and "The Dance," it rose to number four on the country charts. Garth's second album in 1990, *No Fences,* sold over thirteen million. The controversial video from this album depicts an abused wife. By the late 1990s, Garth was the highest selling male country singer, but his future was about to take a turn. Brooks played a tortured rock star named CHRIS GAINES in the film, *The Lamb.* He further tried to become the character with his release of the album, *The Life of Chris Gaines.* Although the recording made it to number two on the pop charts, it was considered a commercial disappointment. Many of his loyal fans thought they were going to lose the real Garth Brooks. About this same time, his wife, Sandy, filed for divorce and Garth retreated into retirement.

In 2005 Garth married his long-time friend, TRISHA YEARWOOD. That same year, he announced that he would not tour or record any new material in the near future. Today Garth is considered to be the greatest bestselling male artist in U.S. history, even surpassing ELVIS PRESLEY.

Kix **BROOKS**

Brooks and Dunn have won more Country Music Association awards than any other act in the history of country music.

Leon Eric Brooks III discovered country music from a neighbor, famed country singer, JOHNNY HORTON. After Kix graduated from the Sewanee Military Academy, he briefly attended Louisiana Tech University. He decided to work on the oil pipeline with his dad in Alaska, but after only one summer, he moved back to Ruston and finished his degree at LTU. He spent some time in Maine writing ad copy for his brother-in-law's company in addition to performing at ski resorts.

Kix moved to Nashville in the early 1980s after his dad urged him to pursue a music career. He was hired by Tree Publishing as a staff songwriter. When his first solo single didn't made the charts, Kix returned to songwriting. Capitol signed him to a record contract in 1989 and by 2000 he had won six BMI awards.

Kix Brooks and RONNIE DUNN enjoy a full range in writing music, from gospel to ballads to rock. It was a natural blend as songwriting, singing, guitar playing, and the love of country music came together. Brooks and Dunn joined efforts and were off and running with their 1996 hit, "My Maria." The song was number one for three weeks on the country charts. The hits kept coming with a REBA MCENTIRE collaboration, "If You See Him (Her)" that rose to number one in 1998. For six weeks, the duo's 2001 album, *Ain't Nothing 'Bout You,* stayed at number one. After September 11, 2001, "Only in America" became a healing anthem for the nation. Both men write, sing, and play the guitar, but on stage it is Dunn who does most of the singing while Brooks plays the guitar. The duo has sold over thirty million records and earned more Country Music Association awards and Academy of Country Music awards than any other act. In 2006 Kix became the new host of *American Country Countdown*, a weekly radio show.

LUKE **BRYAN**

JULY 17, 1976 - ALBANY, GEORGIA

Not forgetting his southern roots, Luke's "We Rode in Trucks" honors his hometown of Leesburg, Georgia. He also co-wrote "Good Directions."

Thomas Luther (Luke) Bryan's biggest music supporters by far are his mom and dad. On trips into town his mom would encourage young Luke to sing along with GEORGE STRAIT on the radio. At fourteen his parents bought him an Alvarez guitar. Luke played in several bands while in high school and gained some experience by singing and playing with local country singers at Skinner's, a nearby club.

When Luke was still in high school, he was invited to meet twice-a-week with two other local songwriters at a nearby church for writing sessions. After graduation, Luke became convinced that he should move to Nashville. He had packed his car for the move, but tragedy struck. His older brother Chris, whom Luke had considered his best friend and supporter, was killed in an automobile accident. Luke changed his mind about Tennessee and enrolled in Georgia Southern University. He continued to perform and recorded the first album of material he had composed almost entirely himself. Luke found comfort in writing down his feelings in songs.

After graduating from college, Luke had planned to move back to his hometown of Leesburg, Georgia, to continue working on the farm and helping his dad in the peanut and fertilizer business. His dad told him to either go to Nashville or stay at home and get fired! Luke arrived in Nashville on September 1, 2001. By November he had signed with a publishing company owned by ROGER MURRAH.

Luke's debut album, *I'll Stay Me*, was released by Capitol in August 2007. In early 2008, a second single topped the charts with "We Rode in Trucks." He has been nominated as the Top New Male Vocalist by the Academy of Country Music.

Luke and his wife Caroline have a son "BO" born in 2008.

GLEN **CAMPBELL**

APRIL 22, 1936 - DELIGHT, ARKANSAS

Glen made history by winning a Grammy in both country and pop categories with "Gentle on My Mind" and "By the Time I Get to Phoenix."

Growing up in a small town, the Campbell family made up over ten percent of the population. Wesley and Carrie Campbell reared their twelve children near Billstown, Arkansas. Wesley encouraged his youngsters to develop their talents and bought them a five dollar Sears and Roebuck guitar. By age ten, young Glen had mastered the instrument without learning to read music. At sixteen he left school to follow his dream of a full-time career in music.

At twenty-four Glen moved to Los Angeles and was soon recognized as a fine studio musician. In 1964 and 1965, he became a regular member of the BEACH BOYS when BRIAN WILSON was having health issues. He can be heard on the famous *Pet Sounds* album. Not long after that Glen's solo career took off. "Gentle on My Mind" became his first major hit in 1967. A string of JIMMY WEBB city songs, "By the Time I Get to Phoenix," "Wichita Lineman," and "Galveston" gave Glen a chance to record some of his biggest hits.

By the late 1960s, Glen had his own weekly variety show, the *Glen Campbell Goodtime Hour*. He also filmed the movie, *True Grit*, with JOHN WAYNE, which earned him a Golden Globe nomination. With ROBERT CULP, he co-starred in *Strange Homecoming*. Not giving up on his recording career, he released three more hits, "Rhinestone Cowboy," "Southern Nights," and "Sunflower" in the 1970s. Throughout the 1980s, Glen recorded "Faithless Love," "A Lady Like You," as well as, "The Hand That Rocks the Cradle" with STEVE WARINER.

In 1994 Campbell's autobiography, *Rhinestone Cowboy*, was published. The book deals with the rise and fall in his career.

Glen Campbell ranked twenty-ninth on the CTM's 40 Greatest Men of Country Music in 2003.

Mary Chapin **Carpenter**

FEBRUARY 21, 1958 - PRINCETON, NEW JERSEY

Mary Chapin earned the CMA Female Vocalist Award in 1992 and 1993 and has received six Grammys. Her album, Come On, Come On, *has sold five million copies.*

Born in Princeton, New Jersey, Mary Chapin Carpenter is the daughter of a *Life* magazine executive. Her growing up years were spent in Princeton, Japan, and Washington, D.C. Mary Chapin loved contemporary pop music in her early years, but since her mother listened to Judy Collins and Woody Guthrie, Mary also had an interest in country and folk music. By the time she was in second grade, Mary Chapin had learned to pick out chords on an acoustic guitar. Her father encouraged her to perform at talent nights, and by 1986 she had won five Washington Area Music Awards.

During her college years at Brown University, she performed at a campus coffeehouse. After her 1981 graduation with a degree in American civilization, Mary Chapin became a regular on the Washington bar scene. She covered songs by artists such as Bonnie Raitt, Billie Holiday, and James Taylor. When late nights and hard drinking took their toll, she found a job with the R. J. Reynolds philanthropic organization. It was then that she began to concentrate on songwriting.

Mary Chapin's debut album, *Hometown Girl,* in 1987 for Columbia Records did not produce any hits. However, her second attempt in 1989, *State of the Heart,* had four Top Twenty hits, including "Never Had It So Good" and "Quittin' Time." This was followed in 1990 by *Shooting in the Dark* with "Down at the Twist and Shout." In 1990 her album, *Come On, Come On,* sold five million copies. It was rated triple platinum in 1992.

Future albums have failed to produce any Top Ten hits, but she has been a consistent favorite on the road. Her five albums have been critically acclaimed and she has won six Grammys during her career. The ACM honored Mary Chapin with its Best Female Vocalist Award in 1989. She received the CMA Female Vocalist of the Year Award in 1992 and 1993.

A. P. CARTER

DECEMBER 15, 1891 - MACES SPRINGS, VIRGINIA - NOVEMBER 7, 1960

A.P. was inducted into the Nashville Songwriters Hall of Fame in 1970 and his image appeared on a U.S. postage stamp in 1993.

Alvin Pleasant Delaney Carter was born in an area called Poor Valley in a town not on most maps. Maces Springs, Virginia, is about twenty miles north of Bristol, Tennessee. A. P. was the son of Robert and Molly Carter. At twenty-three he married SARA DOUGHERTY and they had three children, Gladys, Janette, and Joe.

A.P. worked as a carpenter and storekeeper before fulfilling his dream of establishing a singing group that would spread some hope in hard times. A.P. traveled across the Blue Ridge Mountains collecting songs, especially Appalachian and African-American melodies. "Keep on the Sunny Side," "The Meeting in the Air," and "Wildwood Flower" were three of his best-loved songs.

No one could imagine the impact on the world of music when on August 1, 1927, three people walked into a recording studio in Bristol, Tennessee. It was a simple audition that A.P., his wife SARA, and her first cousin MAYBELLE, made for RALPH PEER, talent scout for the Victor Talking Machine Company. Actually, a fourth person was signed by Peer the same day, JIMMIE RODGERS.

Three hundred country songs and gospel hymns were recorded by the CARTER FAMILY in the next seventeen years. These recordings cover Appalachian folklore like nothing else. Their music spread hope to a country going through the darkest days of the Great Depression.

A. P. recorded his first solo, "The Cannonball," in 1931. A year later he recorded with Jimmie Rodgers in Louisville, Kentucky. In 1943 the Carter Family disbanded. A. P. returned to his roots in Poor Valley and opened a country store at the foot of Clinch Mountain. He passed away on November 7, 1960. In 1993 A.P.'s picture appeared on a U.S. postage stamp honoring the Carter Family.

37

MAYBELLE CARTER

MAY 10, 1909 - NEAR NICKELSVILLE, VIRGINIA - OCTOBER 23, 1978

Maybelle was an original member of the Carter Family and was the mother of June Carter Cash.

Maybelle Addington was twelve years old when she had mastered the skills of playing the guitar, the banjo, and the autoharp. She had developed a unique sound on the guitar by using her thumb to play the melody on the bass strings while keeping the rhythm on the treble strings. This method of playing was later known as the "Carter scratch" or "Carter lick."

Barely five feet tall, the petite Maybelle was sixteen when she married EZRA CARTER, brother of A.P. CARTER. She began singing in 1927 with her first cousin, SARA, wife of A.P., making up the famous CARTER FAMILY singing group.

Maybelle was pregnant with her first child when the trio auditioned for record producer, RALPH PEER, in Bristol, Tennessee. For every song the group recorded, they were paid fifty dollars. Peer made arrangements for the three to travel to New Jersey in 1928 to record some favorite songs including, "Keep on the Sunny Side," "Will the Circle Be Unbroken," "Wabash Cannonball, " and "Wildwood Flower." Those songs are still considered country classics. When the group disbanded in 1943, Maybelle formed her own group with her three daughters, known as MOTHER MAYBELLE AND THE CARTER SISTERS.

During the 1950s, Maybelle's new group was a regular fixture at the Grand Ole Opry and on the *Old Dominion Barn Dance* radio show. Maybelle stayed with the Opry until 1967. She continued making appearances at the *Newport Folk Festival* and on the *Johnny Cash Show*. She performed with the NITTY GRITTY DIRT BAND on their album, *Will the Circle Be Unbroken.*

Maybelle was inducted into the Country Music Hall of Fame® in 1970 as part of the Carter Family. They are considered the "First Family of Country Music."

SARA **CARTER**

JULY 21, 1898 - COPPER CREEK, VIRGINIA - JANUARY 8, 1979

Sara married A.P. Carter in 1915, and in 1927 she became an original member of the singing group, the Carter Family.

Sara Dougherty was born and reared in Russell County, Virginia. The story has been told that while A.P. CARTER was selling trees, he saw his future bride playing and singing "Engine 143" on her front porch. She had learned to play several instruments including the guitar, autoharp, and banjo. With this common love of country music, they fell in love and were married on June 18, 1915. She was sixteen; A.P. was twenty-three. They settled in the rural community of Maces Springs, Virginia. The couple started performing at local socials with Sara singing alto. In July 1927, they read about a talent search to be held in Bristol, Tennessee. The ad informed them that fifty dollars would be paid for every song recorded. With plenty of doubt, it was reported that Sara said, "Ain't nobody gonna pay that much money to hear us sing." Sara was wrong.

RALPH PEER from the Victor Talking Machine Company liked what he heard and they recorded six songs, including "Singing Girl," "Married Girl," and "The Wandering Boy." The group was offered a long-term contract and their records sold well. They also signed with a few radio stations in Texas, including a twice daily show at Del Rio's XERF.

During the Great Depression, Sara and A.P.'s marriage began to fall apart and they separated in 1932, only seeing each other during recording sessions. They eventually were divorced in 1939. Sara later married A.P.'s cousin, Coy Bays, and moved to California in 1943. In 1952 Sara and A.P. reunited the CARTER FAMILY, adding their grown children, Janette and Joe, for a concert in Maces Springs. Throughout the mid-1960s, Sara and Maybelle played at several folk music festivals.

In 1970 the Carter Family were the first group to be inducted into the Country Music Hall of Fame®.

JOHNNY **CASH**

FEBRUARY 26, 1932 - KINGSLAND, ARKANSAS - SEPTEMBER 12, 2003

Singer, songwriter, actor, and author, Johnny ranks number one in the 40 Greatest Men in Country Music. He won a total of eight Grammy Awards.

"**H**ello, I'm J. R. Cash" doesn't quite have the same sound as his signature greeting. It wasn't until he joined the air force in 1950 that he had to change his name to John R. Cash. Five years later, he auditioned for SAM PHILLIPS at Sun Records in Memphis. Johnny chose mostly gospel songs. Sam told him to "go home and sin and come back with a song I can sell." He did come back to record "Cry, Cry, Cry" and "Hey Porter." Soon after, he changed his name to Johnny Cash.

In 1958 Johnny signed with Columbia Records to record songs that he had heard as child on the radio. With help from the TENNESSEE TWO, LUTHER PERKINS and MARSHALL GRANT, he recorded *That's Enough*. His second recording, *Hymns By Johnny Cash,* included his original song, "It Was Jesus," as well as "The Old Account," and "Swing Low, Sweet Chariot."

Johnny went through a rough period of time in the early 1960s. JUNE CARTER and other friends and family convinced him to get some help for his drug addiction. Johnny and June were wed on March 1, 1968. By then their personal performances had become a gospel concert.

In 1986 Johnny returned to Memphis to record *Class of '55* with ROY ORBISON, JERRY LEE LEWIS, and CARL PERKINS. Throughout the 1980s and 1990s, he toured with the HIGHWAYMEN. The group included KRIS KRISTOFFERSON, WAYLON JENNINGS, and WILLIE NELSON.

During his fifty years in show business, Johnny recorded over 1500 songs and sold more than fifty million records. His classic recordings included his signature song, "I Walk the Line," plus "Ring of Fire," "Folson Prison Blues," and "A Boy Named Sue."

Johnny and HANK WILLIAMS are the only artists who have been inducted into the Rock and Roll, Songwriters, and Country Music Halls of Fame®. He ranks number one of the 40 Greatest Men in Country Music.

JUNE CARTER CASH

JUNE 23, 1929 - MACES SPRINGS, VIRGINIA - MAY 15, 2003

June joined the Carter Family singers in 1939 at the age of ten. She was Johnny Cash's second wife.

Perhaps Valerie June Carter got her middle name because she was born in the sixth month. She was the second daughter of MOTHER MAYBELLE of the famous CARTER FAMILY. June picked up the autoharp first and later learned the guitar. By the time she was ten, June and her sisters were singing with the Carter Family.

Comedy became June's forte because she thought her voice was not the strongest. Her comedy act centered around a character she called Aunt Polly. In 1949 she joined the comedy duo, HOMER AND JETHRO, to record a parody of the song, "Baby It's Cold Outside." After a four-year marriage to CARL SMITH had ended, she considered a career in acting. She studied acting with ELIA KAZAN and LEE STRASBERG in the mid-1950s and became friends with ROBERT DUVALL and JAMES DEAN.

With COLONEL TOM PARKER as her manager, June toured with ELVIS PRESLEY in the mid-1950s and was introduced to the music of Johnny Cash. She began working with Johnny after a backstage meeting at the Grand Ole Opry.

In 1962 she co-wrote "Ring of Fire" during the time she was falling in love with Johnny Cash. Their recording of "It Ain't Me Babe" made it into the country and pop charts in 1964 and their country hit "Jackson" earned them a Grammy in 1967. They were married on March 1, 1968, and June appeared on the *Johnny Cash Show* between 1969 and 1972. The two shared a second Grammy for "If I Were a Carpenter." June's *Press On* won a Grammy in 1999 for Best Folk Album.

Johnny writes in his autobiography, "…our Christian faith strengthened the bond between us. She is wife, lover, friend, and my biggest critic." June ranks number thirty-one in CMT's 40 Greatest Women in Country Music.

ROSANNE CASH

MAY 24, 1955 - MEMPHIS, TENNESSEE

Rosanne is the daughter of Johnny Cash and has produced eleven number one hits. "Seven Year Ache" became her signature song.

Although Rosanne is the daughter of JOHNNY CASH and has her own musical career including many country hits, she doesn't think of herself as a country singer. She has tried to avoid the label that was been placed on her from her birth. Her first memory of home was living in California. When she was three, Johnny and Rosanne's mother, Vivian (Liberto), bought JOHNNY CARSON'S house in Encino. Her parents were divorced when Rosanne was eleven and she continued to live with her mother until she moved to Nashville to study drama at Vanderbilt University. After a year in London working for CBS Records, Roseanne recorded her debut album with Ariola Records in 1978. The record, *Right or Wrong,* was produced by RODNEY CROWELL whom Roseanne married in 1979. Although it wasn't a mega success, the album did have three memorable hits, "No Memories Hangin' Round" with BOBBY BARE, "Couldn't Do Nothin' Right," and "Take Me, Take Me."

Three years later, Rosanne wrote and recorded *Seven Year Ache.* The pop/country album struck gold and the title track was the first of eleven number one hits. Her *King's Record Shop* in 1985 produced a Grammy winning song, "I Don't Know Why You Don't Want Me." That same year Roseanne was divorced from Crowell.

Billboard named Roseanne Top Single Artist in 1988. The eleven songs on Rosanne's *10 Song Demo* album, released in 1996, included "The Summer I Read Colette" and "If I Were a Man." The record is a meditation on things lost. Her *Black Cadillac* album was nominated for a Grammy for Best Contemporary Folk/Americana Album in 2006.

Rosanne lives in New York City with her husband John Leventhal. Her four children are Caitlin, Chelsea, Carrie, and Jakob.

42

RAY CHARLES

SEPTEMBER 23, 1930 - ALBANY, GEORGIA - JUNE 10, 2004

Ray's classic recording of "Georgia on My Mind" became his home state's official state song in 1979. His country album sold over a million copies.

Known as "the genius," Ray Charles Robinson was born into extreme poverty and became completely blind at the age of seven. He once said, "Even compared to other blacks, we were on the bottom of the ladder looking up at everyone else." Ray was sent to the St. Augustine School for the Deaf and Blind in Florida where he learned to read and write music in Braille. He became proficient at playing the piano, organ, sax, clarinet, and the trumpet. Ray listened to the band leaders of the day, such as DUKE ELLINGTON, ARTIE SHAW, and COUNT BASIE. Other influences were the classical compositions of FRÉDÉRIC CHOPIN and Jean SIBELIUS, as well as gospel and the blues. And on Saturday nights there were the melodies from the Grand Ole Opry.

As his career began to take shape in the late 1940s, Ray dropped his last name to prevent confusion with the boxer SUGAR RAY ROBINSON. He made three recordings in Tampa, Florida, in 1947. By the time he moved to Los Angeles in 1949 with a record contract in hand, Ray had begun to pattern his musical style after NAT KING COLE. Of his style Ray said, "When I started to sing like myself—as opposed to imitating Nat Cole...it had this spiritual and churchy, this religious or gospel sound."

Ray's breakout hit came in 1953 with "The Things That I Used to Do." Two years later, he had a number one hit, "I Got a Woman." His signature song came at the end of the decade with "What'd I Say." Ray's album, *Modern Sounds in Country and Western Music*, stayed at number one on the *Billboard* pop charts for three and a half months. Ray earned twelve Grammys, was nominated for three Emmys, and was honored at the Kennedy Center. He had duets with country greats, including GEORGE JONES and HANK WILLIAMS JR., as well as a number one hit with WILLIE NELSON, "Seven Spanish Angels," in 1984.

KENNY **CHESNEY**

MARCH 26, 1968 - KNOXVILLE, TENNESSEE

Kenny's first Billboard *number one single was "She's Got It All." The song spent three weeks at the top of the country charts in 1997.*

Kenneth Arnold Chesney was reared in Luttrell, just northeast of Knoxville, Tennessee. While in college, his first gigs were playing folk, jazz, and rock in eateries around Johnson City, Tennessee. He traveled to Bristol, Virginia, to record his own songs at the Classic Recording Studio. He was able to sell all one thousand of those records at his concerts.

After graduation from East Tennessee State in 1991, Kenny headed to Nashville to spread his wings. He became a regular playing at the Turf before he got a songwriter's contract with the Opryland Music Group in 1992. "The Tin Man" was the beginning of what would become a string of hit recordings from his own pen. BNA Records, an affiliate of RCA, bought the master copy of "The Tin Man" from Capricorn Records.

Kenny had now hit the big time. The album *All I Need to Know,* his first with BNA, came out in 1995. The song "Me and You" went gold in 1996, "I Will Stand" went platinum, and the album *Everywhere We Go* was certified double platinum. "She Thinks My Tractor's Sexy" could be heard on jukeboxes across America starting in 1998. He earned two number one hits on the country charts in 1999 with "How Forever Feels" and "You Had Me From Hello."

Kenny's album, *No Shoe's, No Shirt, No Problem,* had two big hits, "Young" and "The Good Stuff." The latter stayed at number one for seven weeks in 2002 and earned the Academy of Country Music Award for Song of the Year.

By 2006 Kenny had sold twenty-five million albums and earned the Entertainer of the Year Award from the ACM. His first album, *In My Wildest Dreams,* had been released way back in 1994. At the 2008 CMA Awards Kenny won Entertainer of the Year for the third straight year.

Mark Chesnutt

SEPTEMBER 6, 1963 - BEAUMONT, TEXAS

Mark got his start in honky-tonks in Beaumont, Texas. By winning the CMA Horizon Award he attracted the attention of George Jones.

Mark Nelson Chesnutt played the drums and guitar in his dad's band when he was fifteen. He recorded his first album *Doing My Country Thing* on San Antonio's Axbar label. He paid his dues playing in the honky-tonks around Beaumont while fine-tuning his skills. Mark's dad had made several trips to Nashville to record and now it was time for his son to get a chance at a country music recording career.

Record producers in Nashville began paying attention to this singer with raw talent. MCA Nashville signed him to a record contract in 1989. "Too Cold at Home" was his first single and with that release he earned the CMA Horizon Award. GEORGE JONES had been a mentor of Mark and when Jones introduced him as "a boy from Beaumont, Texas, who is the real deal," that truly was a real deal.

During the 1990s, *Billboard* rated Mark as one of the Ten Most-Played Radio Artists. "Bubba Shot the Jukebox" and "I'll Think of Something" demonstrated the range of his voice. Mark's heart and soul can be heard in "Blame It on Texas" and "Old Flames Have New Names." Some of his other hits include "Old Country," "It Sure Is Monday," "I Just Wanted You to Know," "Going Through the Big D," "It's a Little Too Late," and "Brother Jukebox." Being heard on the jukebox is great but Mark prefers performing live on stage. He has said "I've got to be out there on stage making it."

Not only has Mark made it big in the U.S. country market but after touring in Europe, he has many fans who love his honky-tonk country sound. His "That Good, That Bad" made it to number four in the European Country Music Association radio charts.

Mark and his wife Tracie are the parents of three sons.

ROY CLARK

APRIL 15, 1933 - MEHERRIN, VIRGINIA

Roy is best known for hosting the first nationally televised country variety show, Hee Haw, *and for his signature song, "Yesterday, When I Was Young."*

As is true of most country stars, the parents of Roy Linwood Clark were a big influence. Both his mom and dad were amateur musicians and young Roy developed his talent at a young age. He mastered the banjo and mandolin in addition to playing the guitar in his dad's band at age fourteen. It wasn't long before he won the National Banjo Championship, twice. This honor got the attention of the Grand Ole Opry and he made his debut at the age of seventeen. Roy had considered boxing and professional baseball, but country music won out.

Roy had had some musical exposure on radio, in local clubs, and on local television shows by the mid-1950s. JIMMY DEAN invited him to appear on his television show, *Country Style.* When Jimmy left the show, Roy became its host and earned a reputation as a great entertainer. From 1969 to 1992, Roy and BUCK OWENS hosted the ever-popular television show, *Hee Haw. Rowan and Martin's Laugh In* had been the inspiration, but *Hee Haw* was centered around a theme that Roy loved, country humor and country music. He was the first country music artist to guest host Johnny Carson's *Tonight Show.*

Roy's best-known hits include "Yesterday, When I Was Young" and "Thank God and Greyhound." In the 1970s, as a popular TV personality, he had a string of Top Ten singles, "I Never Picked Cotton," "Somewhere Between Love and Tomorrow," and "If I Had It to Do All Over Again." Roy recorded an inspirational album in 2005, *Hymns for the Old Country Church.*

Roy Clark's musical career goes back to touring with HANK WILLIAMS. He hosted a network television show that reached thirty million fans weekly and has been a member of the Grand Ole Opry since 1987. Roy and his wife Barbara live in Tulsa and breed race horses.

TERRI **CLARK**

Terri has three platinum albums to her credit and is considered to have one of the most unique voices in country music.

Terri Lynn Sauson took her professional last name from her stepfather, Peter Clark. Her mother, LINDA (SAUSON) CLARK was a folk singer; her grandparents, RAY and BETTY GAUTHIER were country singers from Québec who opened for JOHNNY CASH, GEORGE JONES, GRANDPA JONES, and LITTLE JIMMY DICKENS. Terri was reared about as far from the heart of Music City as one could be, in Medicine Hat, Alberta, Canada. She knew as a young girl that she wanted to be a country songwriter and performer. With her mother's encouragement, she moved to Nashville in 1987. Her first paying gig was playing at the famous honky-tonk bar, Tootsie's Orchid Lounge.

In her mid-twenties Terri signed a deal with Mercury Records. Her debut album, *Terri Clark*, included songs she had composed. Four Top Ten hits by 1996, including "When Boy Meets Girl," "Better Things To Do," "Poor, Poor Pitiful Me," and "If I Were You," earned Terri the title of Top New Female Country Artist from *Billboard*. In 1996 she won three awards from Canadian Country Music, the first of many in the coming years.

On June 12, 2004, one of Terri's childhood dreams came true when she became the first Canadian female to be inducted into the Grand Ole Opry. After twelve years and seven albums with Mercury Records, Terri signed with BNA Records in 2007. Recording her first BNA album, *In My Next Life,* was a difficult time for Terri. Her mother was diagnosed with cancer. Terri said about her experience recording "Never Say No," "I didn't know if I could get through it."

With her guitar and cowbell, Terri Clark enjoys getting dressed up in a cowgirl outfit and performing for her fans; it is her passion. As she says, "I'm such a ham and I love to entertain."

PATSY CLINE

SEPTEMBER 8, 1932 - WINCHESTER, VIRGINIA - MARCH 5, 1963

In 2001 Patsy was voted by the country music industry as number one on the list of the 40 Greatest Women of Country Music.

Virginia Patterson Hensley became superstar "Patsy Cline" after she married Gerald Cline in 1953. Called "Ginny" most of her life, Patsy was encouraged by BILL PEER to change her name to "Patsy" when at twenty, she performed with Bill and his MELODY BOYS. Peer was instrumental at the beginning of Patsy's musical career.

Patsy began singing at age three for the neighbors and could be heard ten years later in the choir at the local Baptist church. In 1945 after a bout of rheumatic fever, she developed a life-threatening throat infection which left her with a much stronger, booming "Kate Smith" voice.

On the *Arthur Godfrey Talent Show* in 1957, Patsy first gained national exposure. She had recorded "Walkin' after Midnight" in 1956, but it wasn't released until after she won on the talent show.

After her divorce from Gerald Cline, Patsy married Charlie Dick on September 15, 1957. They had two children, Julie and Randy. Just six months after giving birth to Randy, Patsy was almost killed in a head-on collision on June 14, 1961. Because the accident had broken some ribs, she had difficulty reaching the high notes of her signature song "Crazy." That same year, she became a member of the Grand Ole Opry.

Hits kept coming with "She's Got You" and "Leavin' on Your Mind." "I Fall to Pieces" ranked number one on country charts, number twelve on pop charts, and number 107 on the Recording Industry Association of America's list of Songs of the Century. *Patsy Cline's Greatest Hits* is listed in the *Guinness Book of World Records* for staying on the musical charts longer than any other female of any music genre in history.

Patsy is considered number eleven on the VH1 listing of 100 Greatest Women of Rock and Roll and CMT rates her at number one on its 40 Greatest Women of Country Music.

JEFF COOK

AUGUST 27, 1949 - FORT PAYNE, ALABAMA

As one of the founding members of the group ALABAMA, *Jeff played lead guitar, keyboard, and fiddle in addition to doing vocals.*

Known as "Mr. Musician," Jeff Cook fits the title as a multi-talented performer. Jeff has mastered the keyboard, bass, banjo, mandolin, and drums. After ALABAMA had its farewell tour in 2004, Jeff has continued to follow his dream with his ALLSTAR GOODTIME BAND.

Jeffrey Alan Cook, at fourteen, started working for a local radio station as a disc jockey. He had recently received his broadcast license.

Back in the late 1960s, Jeff began making music with his cousins RANDY OWEN and TEDDY GENTRY, calling themselves YOUNG COUNTRY. While they were still in high school, the group won a trip to the Grand Ole Opry. After Jeff graduated from college, the three cousins moved to Anniston, Alabama. While keeping their day jobs, they played in clubs at night. By 1972 they had changed the band's name again to WILDCOUNTRY and began writing their own songs.

A year later, they gave up their day jobs and played the clubs in the coastal area of South Carolina. In 1979 they added MARK HERNDON and changed their name to ALABAMA. JOE GALANTE of RCA heard them at the New Faces Show at the Country Radio Seminar in 1980. On April 21, 1980, they signed with RCA. That summer they recorded "My Home's in Alabama" as well as their number one hit, "Tennessee River."

Today Jeff owns and operates one of the finest recording studios, Cook Sound Studio, in his hometown of Fort Payne, Alabama. He has created the studio as a kind of pay back to help young musicians follow their dreams as ALABAMA was helped along the way.

Jeff was inducted into the Country Music Hall of Fame® in 2005 as a member of ALABAMA. ALABAMA has earned the Recording Industry Association of America's title of "Country Group of the Century."

COWBOY COPAS

In 1943 Cowboy Copas achieved national fame when he replaced Eddy Arnold as a vocalist for Pee Wee King's Golden West Cowboys.

Lloyd Estel Copas picked up the fiddle and had mastered playing it by the time he was fourteen. He entered a talent contest on a dare and played on WLW and later WKRC in Cincinnati. In 1940 at twenty-seven, he was performing on WNOX in Knoxville, Tennessee, with the band, GOLD STAR RANGERS. Three years later, PEE WEE KING asked Cowboy to join his GOLDEN WEST COWBOYS, replacing EDDY ARNOLD. This gave him the chance to be on the Grand Ole Opry for the first time. Cowboy recorded his debut single, "Filipino Baby" in 1946. It reached number four on the country charts. With this success he secured a regular position playing at the Opry. During the late 1940s and the early 1950s, Cowboy had a string of hits including "Candy Kisses," "Signed, Sealed and Delivered," "Tennessee Moon," "Tennessee Waltz," and "I'm Waltzing with Tears in My Eyes." He became known as "The Waltz King of the Grand Ole Opry."

Cowboy's contract with King Records expired in 1955 and although he continued playing at the Opry, his career seemed to be fading. It wasn't until signing with Starday Records in 1960 that Cowboy had his biggest hit with "Alabam." The song stayed at number one for three months. Success continued with other hits, among them "Flat Top" and a remake of "Signed, Sealed and Delivered."

On March 5, 1963, RANDY HUGHES, Cowboy Copas' son-in-law, and PATSY CLINE'S manager, was piloting a Piper Comanche with Cowboy, HAWKSHAW HAWKINS, and PATSY CLINE on board. The plane crashed en route to Nashville from a benefit show in Kansas City and all on board perished that night.

Ironically, a month after Cowboy's death, his last single, "Goodbye Kisses," hit the Top Fifteen on the country charts.

50

FLOYD **CRAMER**

OCTOBER 27, 1933 - SAMTI, LOUISIANA - DECEMBER 31, 1997

Floyd became the busiest studio musician in the industry, playing the piano for Elvis Presley, Brenda Lee, Patsy Cline, Roy Orbison, and others.

Although Floyd Cramer was born near Shreveport, Louisiana, he grew up just across the state line in Huttig, Arkansas. He was playing the piano by ear at the age of five but objected to taking lessons. In 1951 after high school, he moved back to Shreveport where he joined the *Louisiana Hayride*, a country radio show. Next on his journey was playing in WEBB PIERCE's band and as a session player for JIM REEVES and HANK WILLIAMS.

Arriving in Nashville in 1955, Floyd became the hottest session piano player in town. He played for the greats, including ROY ORBISON, PATSY CLINE, PERRY COMO, BRENDA LEE, and the EVERLY BROTHERS. HE played for ELVIS PRESLEY's first album, recorded at RCA. Elvis asked Floyd to go on tour with him but Floyd declined; he was hoping to become a member of the Grand Ole Opry someday. MGM Records signed Floyd in 1957, but soon after CHET ATKINS brought him to RCA where he enjoyed great success.

Floyd was known for a distinctive piano style that he developed called "bent note" or "slip note" in which two notes were struck in a manner that made a slurred sound. In 1960 he recorded his own composition, "Last Date," an instant hit that climbed the country charts to number two. "On the Rebound" and "San Antonio" also made the Top Ten. He won a Grammy for Best Country Instrumental in 1979 for "My Blue Eyes." It was Floyd's unique piano style and Chet Atkins' smooth production, along with others that helped to create the Nashville Sound.

Floyd Cramer's memorable piano sound can be heard on Elvis Presley's "Heartbreak Hotel," Patsy Cline's "Crazy," Roy Orbison's "Only the Lonely," and Brenda Lee's "I'm Sorry."

In 2003 Floyd was inducted into both the Rock and Roll Hall of Fame and the Country Music Hall of Fame®.

BILLY RAY CYRUS

AUGUST 25, 1961 - FLATWOODS, KENTUCKY

Known for his hit single, "Achy Breaky Heart," Billy Ray starred in TV's Doc *and in 2006 joined daughter, Miley, in Disney's* Hannah Montana.

Billy Ray Cyrus was born near the banks of the Ohio River in Flatwoods, Kentucky. His grandfather was a pentecostal preacher and at age four Billy Ray got his first chance to sing for the congregation.

As a high school student, both music and sports captivated his interest. Offered a baseball scholarship to play for Georgetown College, Billy Ray soon decided that baseball was not the direction he wanted to take. Music won when he and his brother formed the band SLY DOG. Within the year, the group had a regular gig playing for a club in Ironton, Ohio, just across the river from his hometown. Two years later in 1984, after a fire destroyed the club, Billy Ray moved to Los Angeles.

In 1990 HAROLD SHEDD of Mercury Records signed a record contract with Billy Ray after seeing his opening act for REBA MCENTIRE. Billy Ray's debut album, *Some Gave All,* did more than release a major hit single with "Achy Breaky Heart," it renewed the popular line dance. By the time his blockbuster song dropped off the top of the country charts, it had sold nine million albums. It was not only number one on the country charts for five weeks, it was also on top of the pop charts for seventeen weeks.

Acting came naturally for Billy Ray. In the TV series *Doc,* he played a small town doctor in the big city. He has also had parts on shows, such as *The Nanny, Diagnosis Murder,* and *The Love Boat.* In 2005 Billy Ray, with his daughter, Miley, began starring on Disney's mega hit, *Hannah Montana.*

Billy Ray Cyrus has proved that he is more than a one-hit wonder with a mullet hairstyle. On country charts his six Top Ten singles include "Could've Been Me" and "Busy Man." "Southern Rain," from *We the People,* became the campaign song for GEORGE W. BUSH. Billy Ray has received several humanitarian awards for his work with children.

CHARLIE **DANIELS**

OCTOBER 28, 1936 - WILMINGTON, NORTH CAROLINA

Charlie won the Grammy Award for Best Country Vocal Performance in 1979 for "The Devil Went Down to Georgia."

As a child, Charles Edward Daniels loved the music he heard from Nashville. He was also hearing the music from the local pentecostal church. By high school graduation in 1955, he had mastered the three main instruments of a good country music band – the guitar, fiddle, and mandolin. Later Charlie would gain experience on the banjo. Charlie's band, the MISTY MOUNTAIN BOYS, had just begun to make money when Charlie's family moved and he with them.

In 1959 Charlie was playing in a rock and roll band called the JAGUARS. On their way to Los Angeles, they stopped in Fort Worth, Texas, and there met BOB JOHNSTON, a well-respected record producer. The band signed with Epic Records and released their first album. Charlie was also writing songs. With Johnston he co-wrote "It Hurts Me," recorded by ELVIS PRESLEY on the back of "Kissin' Cousins."

By 1967 Johnston had joined CBS Records in Nashville and he encouraged Charlie to come to Nashville. Tired of playing all the clubs, Charlie decided that session work would be a good break. His first hit came in 1973 with "Uneasy Rider" from the album, *Honey in the Rock*. Epic Records signed Charlie in 1976 in the category of rock. "The Devil Went Down to Georgia" was a mega hit in the summer of 1979. The song topped both country and pop charts and won a Grammy for Charlie. He continued to play in sessions including three of BOB DYLAN'S projects. Charlie also produced two YOUNGBLOOD albums from 1979 through 1980. His first Christian album, *The Door,* earned him a Grammy nomination as well as a Dove Award in 1994.

Twice voted Touring Band of the Year by the ACM, the CHARLIE DANIELS BAND continues to tour and bring a little bluegrass, gospel, and just plain country to the delight of his many fans.

JIMMIE **DAVIS**

SEPTEMBER 11, 1899 - BEECH SPRINGS, LOUISIANA - NOVEMBER 5, 2000

Jimmie was elected to two terms as governor of Louisiana. His song "You Are My Sunshine" ranks 73rd on CMT's 100 Greatest Songs.

James Houston Davis was born in Jackson Parish, Louisiana, near the small community of Beech Springs. His family was what has been called "dirt poor," living in a shotgun shack. The two-room home was shared by parents, grandparents, and ten siblings. It was Jimmie's dad who instilled in his children the importance of a good education.

Jimmie left home after graduating from Beech Springs High School and earned his bachelor's degree from Louisiana College in Pineville in 1927. He supplemented his income by singing on street corners and by washing dishes. A year later, he earned a master's degree from Louisiana State University. The following year he taught history at a college in Shreveport and sang on the local radio station KWKH.

In 1929 Jimmie signed a record contract with Victor Records. He recorded almost seventy singles but none sold very well. The Great Depression had hit just as he was getting started in his music career. Jimmie had a better response with record sales when he signed with Decca in 1934. "Nobody's Darlin' but Mine" and "It Makes No Difference Now" were his first two major hits. He has been credited with writing "You Are My Sunshine" after a rainy day in Louisiana. Jimmie said, "I carried 'You Are My Sunshine' around but…I couldn't get anyone else to record it." He decided to record the song in 1940, and in 1999, RIAA named it one of the Songs of the Century. It ranks number seventy-three on CMT's list of 100 Greatest Songs in Country Music.

This man with such humble beginnings, known as the "Singing Governor," had a career in country music that spanned eight decades. He was inducted into the Country Music Hall of Fame® in 1972. After living through the entire 20th century, Davis died at 101 leaving his widow, Anna, who had been a member of the CHUCK WAGON GANG.

SKEETER **DAVIS**

DECEMBER 30, 1931 - DRY RIDGE, KENTUCKY - SEPTEMBER 19, 2004

Skeeter is best known for her crossover pop hit song "The End of the World," recorded in 1963.

Mary Frances Penick's grandfather nicknamed her "Skeeter" because as a child she had so much energy. With a love of music, Skeeter began harmonizing with her childhood friend, BETTY JACK DAVIS. They called their duo, the DAVIS SISTERS. That is the origin of Skeeter's new last name. The girls traveled about fifty miles south to appear on WLAX in Lexington, Kentucky. This was a springboard to other venues in Detroit, Cincinnati, and Wheeling, West Virginia.

By 1953 the "sisters" had earned a record contract with RCA and had a hit with "I Forgot More Than You'll Ever Know." It ranked number one on country charts and eighteen on the pop charts. On August 23 of that year, the young women were in a serious car accident in which Skeeter was critically injured and sadly Betty Jack died.

After more than a year of recovery, Skeeter briefly toured with Betty Jack's sister, GEORGIA. She began her solo career within the year and worked with EDDY ARNOLD and ELVIS PRESLEY. In the mid-1950s, there was a trend toward what was called "response" or "answer" songs. CHET ATKINS recorded "Lost to a Geisha Girl" and Skeeter answered with "Geisha Girl." HANK LOCKLIN recorded "Please Help Me I'm Falling" and Skeeter responded with "I Can't Help Falling Too." She became a regular member of the Grand Ole Opry in 1959 and was married to RALPH EMERY of WSM fame for four years in the early 1960s.

During the 1960s, Skeeter had her best years with RCA. Her signature song, "The End of the World," ranked number two on both country and pop charts. It was also a hit in England for over three months.

In the late 1960s and early 1970s, Skeeter recorded albums of tribute to both BUDDY HOLLY and her friend DOLLY PARTON. In 1997 she co-wrote a children's Christmas book based on her life entitled *The Christmas Note.*

JIMMY **DEAN**

AUGUST 10, 1928 - PLAINVIEW, TEXAS

Today Jimmy is best known as the founder of the Jimmy Dean Food Company. He rose to fame for his country crossover hit, "Big Bad John."

Jimmy Ray Dean's mother began giving him piano lessons at age ten. His love for music led him to play other instruments as well. It wasn't long before young Jimmy had also mastered the guitar, harmonica, and accordion. Growing up poor, he could only imagine where music might take him.

At sixteen Jimmy joined the Merchant Marines. Two years later, he was stationed near Washington, D.C., with the U.S. Air Force. He began to perform with a band called the TENNESSEE HAYMAKERS in venues around Washington. In 1948 after leaving the military, he formed the TEXAS WILDCATS and signed a record contract with 4-Star Records.

Jimmy's first hit was "Bummin' Around" which reached country's Top Ten in 1953. During the mid-1950s, he was a pioneer in the broadcasting of country music on television, hosting *Town and Country Time* on WMAL-TV in Washington. Two years later, he had his own show on CBS. From 1963 to 1966, *The Jimmy Dean Show* was picked up again, this time on ABC-TV. On his highly visible show, Jimmy introduced future country music stars PATSY CLINE, ROY CLARK, and ROGER MILLER and is remembered for his sketches with JIM HENSON'S muppet, Rowlf the Dog.

Probably Jimmy's biggest surprise occurred in 1961 when he recorded the song "Big Bad John." It was a song he wrote and on which he mostly spoke the words. It became his biggest hit going to number one on both country and pop charts. The song earned a Grammy for Best Country and Western Performance. It was followed by "PT-109," honoring JOHN F. KENNEDY, and "The First Thing Every Morning."

Jimmy Dean's autobiography is titled *Thirty Years of Sausage, Fifty Years of Ham*, a fitting title for the "Sausage King" who has brought so much musical entertainment to his fans since the late 1940s.

ALTON DELMORE

DECEMBER 25, 1908 - ELKMONT, ALABAMA - JUNE 8, 1964

Alton was lead singer of the Delmore Brothers. The composer of over a thousand songs, his "Beautiful Brown Eyes" was recorded by Bing Crosby.

Eighth child of ten, Alton Delmore was born on Christmas Day. His brother Rabon would be born eight years later. This team of brothers would become one of the biggest influences in country music as early as the mid-1920s. Although they were sons of a tenant farmer, they dreamed of becoming professional musicians. With their smooth harmony and original compositions, the brothers became regular performers on several radio stations. Alton usually sang lead but would sometimes switch parts with Rabon in the middle of a song.

Between 1932 and 1938, the DELMORE BROTHERS were a regular feature on the Grand Ole Opry. In 1944 they signed with King Records and created an innovative expansion of full-band backup with the increased tempo of boogie-woogie. Alton composed over a thousand songs, many of which were written down by Rabon while Alton was driving the car. He milked the boogie theme with such songs as "Hillbilly Boogie," "Mobile Boogie," "Steamboat Bill Boogie," "Freight Train Boogie," and "Pan American Boogie." They recorded other tunes such as "Blues Stay Away From Me" for which they were best known.

During the early 1940s, they recorded "When It's Time for the Whippoorwill to Sing" on Decca Records, but stopped touring due to gas rationing. They continued singing on the radio with GRANDPA JONES and MERLE TRAVIS, and in 1943, they teamed up as the BROWN'S FERRY FOUR. Merle always credited Alton as being a key influence on his music.

In a tribute to her father, Debby Delmore writes: "My Daddy quit performing professionally in 1952, the year I was born and sadly the year Susan [his sister] and Uncle Rabon died. My family eventually settled in Huntsville, Alabama. My mom started working as a waitress and my daddy was making a living from his royalties and giving music lessons."

RABON **DELMORE**

DECEMBER 3, 1916 - ELKMONT, ALABAMA - DECEMBER 4, 1952

With their close harmony, Rabon and his brother Alton were a big influence on the Louvin Brothers of the 1940s and the Everly Brothers in the 1950s.

By the time Rabon was ten years old, he was playing the guitar and harmonizing with his big brother, Alton. Rabon first mastered the fiddle and guitar until Alton brought home a four-string tenor guitar. Softer and sweeter, it became a natural for Rabon to play. The act included the regular six-string and the four-string guitars, a unique combination. With their close harmony, the DELMORE BROTHERS began winning fans, which led them to a successful music contest in 1930 at Athens, Alabama. Their professional music career began when Rabon was seventeen, after a successful audition for the Grand Ole Opry. The brothers were invited to become members in 1932.

Rabon's versions of pop tunes, such as "Baby It's Cold Outside" and "Stormy Weather," pleased crowds with his jazz-style playing on the six-string guitar. Not only did their concerts include instrumental pieces, but also humor and gospel songs. Their style of singing influenced many other brother duos that followed later, including another from Alabama, the LOUVIN BROTHERS. Later in the late 1950s, the EVERLY BROTHERS credited the Delmores in part for their success. Rabon and Alton were considered the first country rockers.

Although Alton wrote ten times as many songs as his brother, Rabon's contribution was recognized and included in their induction into the Nashville Songwriters Hall of Fame in 1971. The Delmore Brothers were also inducted into the Country Music Hall of Fame® in 2001. Delmore Days are held in July at Athens State University near their birthplace of Elkmont, Alabama.

In the *Chicago Tribune*, November 10, 1985, BOB DYLAN was quoted: "The Delmore Brothers,...I really loved them! I think they've influenced every harmony I've ever tried to sing."

JAY **DeMARCUS**

APRIL 26, 1971 - COLUMBUS, OHIO

Jay sings harmony with his second cousin, Gary LeVox, and Joe Don Rooney in the group Rascal Flatts.

Stanley Wayne DeMarcus Jr. was brought up in a musical family. At an early age, Jay remembers family jam sessions where he learned to play the guitar, bass, mandolin, and keyboard. Jay graduated from Tree of Life Christian School in Columbus, Ohio, and moved to Cleveland, Tennessee, to attend Lee College.

In the early 1990s, Jay played keyboard for two Christian music groups, NEW HARVEST and EAST AND WEST. Soon he became the band leader for country singer, CHELY WRIGHT with JOE DON ROONEY on the guitar. At this time, Jay was also playing at Nashville's Printers Alley with his second cousin, GARY LEVOX. Jay had convinced Gary to leave his job in Ohio and follow his dream as a musician. Jay remembered Joe Don and asked him to join the trio one night when their guitarist failed to show up. They knew the chemistry was right with the music they made that night. They recall adjusting the harmony and deciding who would sing which part. Jay had been singing the high part above Gary. He was glad that Joe Don could reach the high notes. The magic began that night. RASCAL FLATTS, the Grammy Award winning country and pop group, was born. DANN HUFF heard some rough demos of the group and was very impressed. He called DOUG HOWARD, senior vice-president of A&R. Less than a week later, Rascal Flatts signed a record contract with Lyric Street Records, which is part of the Disney family.

Jay has also become a record producer. While still singing and playing with Rascal Flatts, he has found the time to produce records for JO DEE MESSINA and MICHAEL ENGLISH. In 2006 Jay produced a record for the rock group CHICAGO, titled *Chicago XXX*.

On May 15, 2004, Jay married ALLISON ALDERSON, Miss Tennessee 1999 and Miss Tennessee USA 2002.

JOHN DENVER

DECEMBER 31, 1943 - ROSWELL, NEW MEXICO - OCTOBER 12, 1997

By 1971 John was a superstar with "Sunshine On My Shoulders;" "Take Me Home, Country Roads;" and "Rocky Mountain High."

Henry John Deutschendorf Jr., at twelve, was given a 1910 Gibson f-hole acoustic jazz guitar by his grandmother. The family had moved to Tucson, Arizona, due to his dad's job with the U.S. Air Force. They moved from state to state often and John found that playing the guitar was his way to meet new friends. After a move to Fort Worth, Texas, while he was in high school, John ran away to California but returned to finish school. While attending Texas Tech in Lubbock, he started playing at the local clubs. John dropped out of college in 1964 and moved back to California where he started playing with the CHAD MITCHELL TRIO. When RANDY SPARKS of the NEW CHRISTY MINSTRELS suggested that his last name wouldn't fit on a marquee, John changed it to "Denver" to honor an area of the country that he greatly loved.

In 1969 John's debut album at the start of his career was not a big hit. It did contain, however, one of his best compositions, "Leaving on a Jet Plane." It was another two years before he struck gold. *Poems, Prayers and Promises* introduced "Rocky Mountain High," "Take Me Home, Country Roads," and "Sunshine On My Shoulders." In the mid-1970s, as America's bestselling singer, John was offered a co-starring role in the movie, *Oh God!*, with GEORGE BURNS. As a frequent guest host on the *Tonight Show*, he used the expression "far out" so many times that it became a catch phrase associated with him.

In 1975 John Denver received the Country Music Association's Entertainer of the Year Award. That same year, his popularity peaked. Denver achieved fourteen gold albums and eight platinum albums in the U.S. alone. He is one of the top-selling recording artists in the industry.

John lost his life on October 12, 1997, when his Long-EZ experimental aircraft ran out of gas and crashed off the California coast.

LITTLE JIMMY **DICKENS**

DECEMBER 19, 1920 - BOLT, WEST VIRGINIA

Jimmy recorded several novelty songs including "Take an Old Cold Tater," "Country Boy," and "A-Sleeping at the Foot of the Bed."

J ames Cecil Dickens was the thirteenth child of a farming family from West Virginia. Listening to the radio, he dreamed of someday becoming a Grand Ole Opry star. While attending the University of West Virginia in the late 1930s, Jimmy began singing on the local country radio station. Using the stage name Jimmy the Kid, he soon left college to sing full time. Jimmy had traveled all over the Midwest when the turning point in his career happened in Saginaw, Michigan. ROY ACUFF heard Jimmy singing on WKMX and invited him to come to Nashville to sing on the Grand Ole Opry. In 1949 Jimmy with his rhinestone suits, Stetson hat, and dwarfed by his large Gibson J-200 guitar, became a permanent member of the Grand Ole Opry.

Also in 1949, Jimmy signed a record contract with Columbia Records and began to use the name LITTLE JIMMY DICKENS. His first release was one his biggest hits. "Take an Old Cold Tater (and Wait)," a Top Ten hit, introduced a series of novelty songs. After that song, HANK WILLIAMS gave Jimmy the nickname "Tater." Jimmy has "Tater" written in rhinestones on his guitar strap. Jimmy had a dry spell with only one hit in the 1950s, "Out Behind the Barn" in 1954. Memorable novelty songs include "I'm Little but I'm Loud" and "A-Sleepin' at the Foot of the Bed." In 1965 "May the Bird of Paradise Fly Up Your Nose" became his only number one hit. Humorous songs sometimes overshadowed Jimmy's renditions of ballads, among them "Life Made Her That Way" and "A Violet and a Rose."

Jimmy remembers the good times traveling on package tours with ROY ACUFF, BILL MONROE, and HANK WILLIAMS. When asked to highlight something from his long career, he commented, "Three trips to Vietnam and thirteen trips to Europe. All to entertain our troops."

RONNIE **DUNN**

JUNE 1, 1953 - COLEMAN, TEXAS

Ronnie joined Kix Brooks in 1990 to form the group Brooks & Dunn. They are the most award-winning duo in the industry.

Ronnie's dad loved country music and he passed the torch to his son. His dad was an oil field worker which meant that the family was always on the move. Ronnie attended thirteen schools in twelve years. While still in his teens, he started playing in bands. In the early 1970s, he moved back to within fifty miles of his birthplace and attended Abilene Christian College. While there he studied theology and psychology and played in local nightclubs. The college objected to this type of venue and Ronnie was given a choice to stop playing in honky-tonks or leave school. He chose to take his bass guitar and move to Tulsa. In Tulsa Ronnie recorded some songs in the mid-1980s with Churchill Records. His drummer entered Ronnie in the 1988 Marlboro National Country Talent Contest. He won and was given a recording session in Nashville.

In 1990 Ronnie moved to Nashville and met TIM DUBOIS, the head of Arista Records. Tim introduced Ronnie to KIX BROOKS and their partnership soon changed the playing field in country music. The combination created the most successful country music duo of the 1990s.

In 1991 their debut album, *Brand New Man,* sold more than five million copies. They had collaborated on two of the songs, "Brand New Man" and "My Next Broken Heart" which reached the top of the country charts. BROOKS AND DUNN have earned twenty Country Music Association Awards and have sold over thirty million records.

With his twenty-plus songwriting awards, Ronnie has twice been named Songwriter of the Year by Broadcast Music Incorporated. The song "Believe" earned him the Gospel Songwriter of the Year Award from the Gospel Music Association in 2006.

Ronnie and his wife Janine have three children: Whitney, Jesse, and Haley.

RALPH **EMERY**

MARCH 10, 1933 - MCEWEN, TENNESSEE

Ralph has been voted country radio's "Greatest Personality of the Century." He was inducted into the Country Music Hall of Fame® in 2007.

Walter Ralph Emery was reared by his grandparents until he was seven. In 1940 young Ralph moved to be with his mother in Nashville. With money saved from odd jobs at the local theater and Kroger's, Ralph enrolled in the Tennessee School of Broadcasting after high school and was taught by the legendary JOHN RICHBOURG, (aka John R.) the "Daddy of Rhythm and Blues." It was JOHN R. who recommended Ralph for the position as disc jockey at WTPR in Paris, Tennessee, in 1951. Two years later, Ralph got another break with national exposure as announcer on WSIX for *America's Town Meeting of the Air*. In 1957 Ralph got the career break of a lifetime. He applied and became the late-night host of *Opry Star Spotlight* on WSM radio. He had an open-door policy for country stars to drop in anytime.

In the early 1960s, Ralph went through some rough times after the end of his four-year marriage to SKEETER DAVIS. TEX RITTER was called in and co-hosted the show until 1972. That same year, WSM-TV launched the early morning *Ralph Emery Show*. From 1974 to 1980, country music began to take on more of the pop sound. Ralph was on the cutting edge as host of *Pop Goes the Country*. For ten years, beginning in 1983, Ralph hosted *Nashville Now*. The show was established by the newly-created TNN and could be seen across America.

In 2000 ASCAP president CONNIE BRADLEY wrote in the *Nashville Tennessean*, "Ralph Emery probably did as much for Nashville as anybody I know...his show...opened up country music to millions of people."

Ralph's book, *Memories: The Autobiography of Ralph Emery*, was a *New York Times* bestseller for twenty-five weeks in 1991. He returned to television to host *Ralph Emery LIVE* on RFD-TV in 2007. That same year Ralph was inducted into the Country Music Hall of Fame®.

DALE **EVANS**

OCTOBER 31, 1912 - UVALDE, TEXAS - FEBRUARY 7, 2001

Dale married Roy Rogers in 1947 after co-starring in movies with him at Republic Studios. Her book Angel Unaware *became a bestseller.*

Born Lucille Octavia Smith, Dale Evans had a tumultuous early life. She lived in Arkansas during her early teens and at fourteen eloped with her childhood friend, Thomas Fox. She had her first child at fifteen. At the same time she was trying to break into a singing career. In 1929 at seventeen, finding herself divorced or widowed, depending on the source, and a single mom, she got a job at a radio station in Memphis. Later that same year she married August Johns. The marriage lasted four years. She then married her accompanist and arranger, ROBERT DALE BUTTS in 1935 and soon after changed her name to Dale Evans.

In demand as a jazz and swing singer for the big bands in Chicago, Dale tried out for a part in the movie *Holiday Inn* but failed to make the cut. Her big break came when she signed a contract with Republic Pictures. The company was known for their B-movie Westerns.

Dale had met ROY ROGERS in 1941 when the two were entertaining the troops at Edwards Air Force Base. Three years later, they were paired in their first film together, *The Cowboy and the Senorita.* They were married in 1947. With their famous horses, Trigger and Buttermilk, they co-starred in thirty-five movies. Dale was also cast on *The Roy Rogers Show* which aired on television between 1951 and 1957. With Roy she co-wrote their theme song, "Happy Trails." Dale and Roy went on to record over four hundred songs together. This "Queen of the West" also authored more than twenty books. In *Angel Unaware* Dale tells the story of the life and death of their daughter, Robin Elizabeth, who was born with Down's Syndrome.

Dale and Roy were married for fifty-one years and upon her death in 2001, she was surrounded by her loving family. She ranks number thirty-four on CMT's 40 Greatest Women in Country Music.

SARA **EVANS**

Sara performed and competed at the 2006 Academy of Country Music Awards where she won her first award for "Top Female Vocalist."

Sara Lynn Evans was born in Booneville, Missouri, the third of seven children. She was reared across the Missouri River on a tobacco farm in New Franklin. Her family loved bluegrass music and by the time Sara was four her mother discovered that she had the talent to sing. Her brothers backed her up as they played the guitar and banjo. The family traveled all over Missouri with "The Sara Evans Show" painted on the side of their RV.

By sixteen Sara was singing every Saturday night at larger venues such as the Country Stampede near Columbia. In 1991 Sara moved to Nashville. She supported herself as a waitress at the Holiday Inn where she met her future husband, Craig Schelske, who also hailed from a musical family. Sara joined Craig and his two brothers in their family band when they returned to their home in Oregon. Sara and Craig were married in 1993 and returned to Nashville two years later. On October 12, 2006, they filed for a divorce.

It was the demo that Sara recorded of the song "I've Got a Tiger by the Tail" that got the attention of songwriter, HARLAN HOWARD. BUCK OWENS had recorded the song over thirty years before. Howard told her, "Girl, I have been looking for you for years to sing my music. You're great!" Sara signed with RCA, but her first album was not a commercial success. Her second album in 1998, *No Place That Far,* scored number one on the country charts. Sara was on her way. Her third album, *Born to Fly,* was released in 2000. It was her first to go platinum and had four hit singles. In 2004 *Born to Fly* was registered double platinum by the Recording Industry Association of America. With *Restless* in 2003 and *Real Fine Place* in 2005, fans can expect the hits to keep coming.

In 2006 Sara appeared on *Dancing with the Stars* with her partner TONY DOVOLANI. She was the first country singer to appear on the show.

DON EVERLY

FEBRUARY 1, 1937 - BROWNIE, KENTUCKY

Don and his brother Phil made up the Everly Brothers. They had their first hit with "Bye Bye Love" which reached number one on the country charts.

Isaac Donald Everly and his brother Phil are so connected in their musical careers, it is hard to separate one from the other. Don is two years older and was born in western Kentucky in the small community of Brownie. By contrast, Phil was born in Chicago.

Their parents, MARGARET and IKE EVERLY, had made a name for themselves in the 1940s, singing country melodies on the radio. By 1945 Don and Phil joined them on their live radio show in Iowa. The boys were introduced as "Little Donnie" and "Baby Boy Phil." By 1952 "The Everly Family Show" had moved to Indiana. A year later they moved to Knoxville and could be heard on WROL radio.

Nashville was their next stop to see what Don and Phil could do. Don told about their first big hit, "'Bye Bye Love' had been kicking around Nashville but nobody had done it, so we took it." After they recorded the classic song by BOUDLEAUX and FELICE BRYANT, "Bye Bye Love" stayed at number two on the pop charts for four weeks and also hit number one on the country charts. The Everlys had struck gold.

On May 11, 1957, a lifelong dream came true. The brothers stood backstage waiting to go on at the Ryman Auditorium. The crowd at the Grand Ole Opry loved their harmony and gave them a big ovation. "Wake Up Little Susie" and "All I Have to Do Is Dream" are two of their number one hits. Don wrote "Cathy's Clown" which became their biggest selling single and was their last number one hit.

In 1961 Don and Phil joined the marines and a year later Don, in his dress uniform, married Venetia Stevenson. Not long after he was released from the marines, Don collapsed on stage. Phil continued their tour alone. In 1983 they reunited their harmony for a concert in London at the Royal Albert Hall.

PHIL **EVERLY**

JANUARY 19, 1939 - CHICAGO, ILLINOIS

Phil, with his brother Don, created the close harmony of the Everly Brothers. Their top-selling country sound was an influence on rock and roll performers.

Although the EVERLY BROTHERS have their roots in Appalachian folk, bluegrass, and country music, they have had an influence on many rock groups. Their close harmony with Don singing the melody and Phil singing above him has been emulated by groups such as the BEATLES, the BYRDS, the HOLLIES, and even SIMON AND GARFUNKEL. PAUL MCCARTNEY mentioned the duo on his *On the Wings of a Nightingale* album.

The Everly family first had some success singing on the radio. When the brothers arrived in Nashville in the mid-1950s, Phil and Don received a six-month recording contract at Columbia with help from their old friend CHET ATKINS. Their first big hit "Bye Bye Love" was recorded in 1957 and soared to number one on the country charts.

After the Everly Brothers' career seemed to peak in the mid-1960s, Phil released his solo album, *Star Spangled Springer*, in 1973 with some success. He followed that up with *Phil's Diner,* but it didn't have the magic that fans had remembered from the famous duo. He also did some acting in the 1978 movie *Every Which Way But Loose* with CLINT EASTWOOD.

In 1985 the Everly Brothers were reunited after a decade of separation. They performed to a delighted audience in London at the Royal Albert Hall. That same year, Phil released his last solo album with Capitol. The brothers recorded three more albums in the late 1980s. Their final album was *Some Hearts*. In 2003 and 2004, Phil and Don were featured performers on the Simon and Garfunkel reunion tour. They also sang backup on PAUL SIMON'S *Graceland* album.

Rolling Stone ranked the Everlys at thirty-three on a list of the 100 Greatest Artists of All Time. The duo still perform together at state fairs and universities.

DONNA **FARGO**

NOVEMBER 10 - MOUNT AIRY, NORTH CAROLINA

Donna's composition of "Happiest Girl in the Whole U.S.A." was number one on country charts for nearly six months. The song also made the pop charts.

Growing up on a tobacco farm in Mount Airy, North Carolina, a community most people associated with the fictional town of *Mayberry*, Donna Fargo could only imagine where her journey would take her. She had two dreams in life: to become a teacher and a singer. Her dreams were fueled by her love of school and her love for music. Donna earned a degree at High Point College in her home state of North Carolina. After attending USC, she became a high school English teacher in Covina, California, and later the head of the English department.

In California, Donna met Stan Silver, who taught her to play the guitar, recorded her, and became her husband and manager/producer. In 1972 she recorded her own composition, "Happiest Girl in the Whole USA." Released by Dot Records, it turned out to be a mega hit, followed in that same year by the equally popular self-penned "Funny Face," which made Donna the first woman in country music history to have back-to-back million-selling singles.

In the 1970s, she became the fifth most successful female country singer. Although diagnosed with MS in 1978, she continued her career with several albums for Warner Brothers. Her performance at Carnegie Hall caught the attention of the Osmond family. They produced the television variety show, the *Donna Fargo Show*, during 1978 and 1979. Donna became one of few women ever to write and record a recitation, "That Was Yesterday" and see it hit number one on the pop charts. Donna also recorded a gospel album, *Brotherly Love*, in 1981.

Donna also writes books as well as greeting cards for Blue Mountain Arts. In 2008, "We Can Do Better in America," debuted on charts all over the country. She may just be the most underrated songwriter in the industry.

LESTER FLATT

JUNE 19, 1914 - (NEAR) SPARTA, TENNESSEE - MAY 11, 1979

In 1947 Lester Flatt, Earl Scruggs, Bill Monroe, Chubby Wise, and Howard Watts made up what was probably the best bluegrass band in history.

Lester Raymond Flatt was one of Nannie Mae and Isaac Flatt's nine children. Isaac taught young Lester to play the banjo, but he liked the guitar better and had mastered it by the time he has seven. He enjoyed playing for local functions at school and church.

Lester was still in his teens when he began working at the Sparta Silk Mill in Sparta, North Carolina. When the mill shut down in 1934, Lester and Gladys, his wife, moved to McMinnville, Tennessee, and began singing together. It wasn't long before they moved to near Roanoke, Virginia, to work at another mill. Lester's rheumatoid arthritis forced him to find another vocation. He joined CHARLES SCOTT'S HARMONIZERS and played on WDBJ radio. By 1943 Lester was playing the mandolin with CHARLIE MONROE'S KENTUCKY PARTNERS.

He preferred playing the guitar, but Charlie had already secured that position. Two years later, Charlie's brother, Bill offered Lester a position with his BLUE GRASS BOYS because Lester's voice fit in well. That same year, EARL SCRUGGS joined the band. In 1948 the FOGGY MOUNTAIN BOYS came into being and for the next twenty years the band that included FLATT, SCRUGGS, and MONROE made beautiful music.

In 1969 Flatt and Scruggs parted ways. Flatt chose most of the Foggy Mountain players and started the NASHVILLE GRASS. After Flatt's death in 1979, he was posthumously inducted into the Country Music Hall of Fame® as well as the International Bluegrass Music Hall of Honor.

Some of the songs that Lester composed are, "My Cabin in Carolina," "Come Back Darling," "Head Over Heels in Love with You," God Loves His Children," and "I'm Going to Make Heaven Home."

Lester Flatt and Earl Scruggs rank number twenty-four on CMT's 40 Greatest Men of Country Music.

RED FOLEY

JUNE 17, 1910 - BLUE LICK, KENTUCKY - SEPTEMBER 19, 1968

Red was a major country music star for more than two decades. "One by One" topped the charts in 1954.

Clyde "Red" Julian Foley was encouraged by his father to learn to play the harmonica and guitar as he soaked up songs and styles from all the local musicians. At seventeen Red took first place in a statewide talent competition.

While attending Georgetown College, Red was spotted by a talent scout from WLS in Chicago and chosen to sing on the *National Barn Dance* program. He went on to co-host *Avalon Time* with another redhead, RED SKELTON.

In 1941 Red signed a lifetime contract with Decca Records. His hit songs included "Old Shep," "Chattanoogie Shoe Shine Boy," "Sugarfoot Rag," and "Tennessee Saturday Night." In 1946 Foley replaced ROY ACUFF as the star of the *Prince Albert Show*, NBC's segment of the Grand Ole Opry. Red's mellow voice could handle all types of music and lacked the nasal quality heard in other country singers. Some compared him to BING CROSBY. As a popular gospel performer his recordings of "Steal Away," "Just a Closer Walk with Thee," and "Peace in the Valley" were all top sellers. *Peace in the Valley* became the first gospel album to sell a million copies.

Foley branched out into television, hosting the *Ozark Jubilee* program from 1955 to 1960. He joined FESS PARKER during the 1962-1963 season in the cast of *Mr. Smith Goes to Washington*, a TV series based on the movie.

Foley's daughter Shirley is married to pop and gospel singer PAT BOONE. Ten years after Foley's death, his granddaughter, DEBBIE BOONE, became successful in both pop and country music.

Red Foley has a star on the Hollywood Walk of Fame for his contributions to the music industry. He was elected in 1967 to the Country Music Hall of Fame®.

TENNESSEE ERNIE **FORD**

FEBRUARY 13, 1919 - BRISTOL, TENNESSEE - OCTOBER 7, 1991

Ernie scored an unexpected pop chart hit in 1955 with his rendition of Merle Travis' "Sixteen Tons."

Ernest Jennings Ford was born in a town that came to be known as one of the birthplaces of country music. In Bristol, Tennessee, he sang in the high school choir and learned to played the trombone. Ernie's first voice training was at Virginia Intermont College, and by 1939 he had moved to Ohio to study at the Cincinnati Conservatory of Music.

After serving in the U.S. Air Force during World War II, Ernie and his wife Betty moved to San Bernardino, California, where he landed a job as an announcer with KXLA radio in Pasadena. Television host, CLIFFIE STONE, liked Ernie's down-to-earth humor and invited him to become a regular member on the *Hometown Jamboree*. With Ernie's booming baritone voice, Capitol signed him in 1948. He stayed with the record company twenty-eight years and released eighty-three albums. Of the sixty million albums sold, forty million were of the gospel, hymn, or spiritual genre. Ernie's *Hymns* album, released in 1956, stayed on the *Billboard* Top Album Chart for 277 consecutive weeks. His album, *Great Gospel Songs,* with the help of the JORDANAIRES, won a Grammy in 1964 for Best Inspiration Recording. Ernie's recording of MERLE TRAVIS' coal-mining song, "Sixteen Tons," was the fastest selling single for Capitol Records.

The Ford Show, better known as the *Tennessee Ernie Ford Show*, ran from 1956 to 1961 and Ernie regularly appeared on *I Love Lucy* as "Cousin Ernie." He was the first country singer to perform at London's Palladium. Ernie has three stars on the Hollywood Walk of Fame for radio, records, and television. In 1984 PRESIDENT RONALD REAGAN presented Ernie with the Presidential Medal of Freedom, the highest honor a sitting president can bestow upon a civilian, and in 1990, Tennessee Ernie Ford was inducted into the Country Music Hall of Fame®.

JIMMY FORTUNE

MARCH 11, 1955 - WILLIAMSBURG, VIRGINIA

· ·

Jimmy harmonized with the Statler Brothers for twenty years. He wrote songs such as "Elizabeth" and "My Only Love."

With his wonderful tenor voice, Jimmy Fortune joined the STATLER BROTHERS on January 28, 1982. When LEW DEWITT heard Jimmy performing at a ski resort, he recommended Jimmy as his replacement. Lew suffered from the debilitating effects of Crohn's Disease.

As a songwriter, Jimmy quickly began to earn his keep by writing four number one hits for the Statlers: "Elizabeth," "My Only Love," "Too Much on My Heart," and "Forever." On *The Greatest Hits* album he co-wrote their last major hit, "More Than a Name on the Wall."

During Jimmy's twenty-one years of touring with the Statlers, he performed in all fifty states to crowds as large as 100,000. He sang for seven seasons on *The Statler Brothers Show* which debuted as the highest rated show on The Nashville Network. At a birthday celebration for ELIZABETH TAYLOR, Jimmy sang a song he wrote for the occasion, "Elizabeth." He also was with the Statlers to perform for two presidents, RONALD REAGAN and GEORGE H. W. BUSH.

When PHIL BALSLEY and DON and HAROLD REID retired the Statler Brothers on October 26, 2002, Jimmy had the opportunity to go on to a solo career. His first CD, released in 2003, was aptly named *When One Door Closes*. Jimmy went back to his gospel roots for his second project, *I Believe*. Released in 2005, this album featured such classics as "How Great Thou Art," "I'll Fly Away," "He Touched Me," and "The Lord's Prayer." In December 2006, he released his third album, "Feels Like Christmas."

Jimmy has relocated to Nashville and continues his writing. He was inducted, with the Statler Brothers, into the Gospel Music Hall of Fame in 2007 and the Country Music Hall of Fame® in 2008.

Janie **Fricke**

DECEMBER 19, 1947 - SOUTH WHITLEY, INDIANA

Janie has nine number one hits and was CMA's Female Vocalist of the Year in 1982 and 1983. "Don't Worry 'Bout Me Baby" was her first solo hit.

Known as the most successful jingle singer in the marketing industry, Janie began her career singing in a "little church up the road" in northern Indiana. Her father stopped long enough from farming his four hundred acres to teach her how to play the guitar. Janie's mother, the church's pianist, helped create a musical heritage for her future. After earning a degree in elementary education from Indiana University, she decided on a career in music. Janie first moved to Memphis and found work singing commercial jingles for a local radio station.

After moving to Nashville in 1975, Janie immediately became one of the most-requested session singers. Producer BILLY SHERRILL first saw her potential and teamed her with JOHNNY DUNCAN for two duets, "Joe and the Cowboy" and "Thinkin' of a Rendezvous." "What're You Doing Tonight," her first solo single, barely missed the Top Twenty. Janie scored a number one hit the next year on a collaboration with CHARLIE RICH, "On My Knees." The early 1980s were breakthrough years for Janie with two Top Five hits, "Down to My Last Broken Heart" and "I'll Need Someone to Hold (When I Cry)." Starting in 1982, she had an amazing six number one hits on the country charts including, "Don't Worry 'Bout Me Baby," "He's a Headache," "Tell Me a Lie," and "Your Heart's Not in It."

Janie has been selected by CMA and ACM as the Female Vocalist of the Year and as British-based Country Music Round Up's Most Popular International Female Solo Act. She has been nominated for two Grammy Awards and has earned thirty-six hits from her twenty-three albums.

Janie performed at Camp David by the request of PRESIDENT RONALD REAGAN. She appeared on her own TV special in 1983 and became a regular on *The Statler Brothers Show.* Whether Janie is singing a jingle for Cola-Cola or hymns of faith, she is always a crowd pleaser.

LEFTY FRIZZELL

In 1950, Lefty had his first number one hit, "If You've Got the Money, Honey, I've Got the Time." Fourteen years later "Saginaw, Michigan" climbed to number one.

William Orville Frizzell was called Sonny as a child. He was the eldest of eight children. By age fourteen, he was tagged with the name Lefty when he won a schoolyard fight. His father was an oiler from Texas, and the family moved to El Dorado, Arkansas, when Lefty was still a child.

Listening to the records of JIMMIE RODGERS was a big influence in attracting Lefty to country music. An uncle bought him a $2.00 guitar. Lefty was still in his teens when the family moved back to Texas where his music career got a big boost when he won a talent contest in Dallas. With his honky-tonk style, Lefty's popularity began to grow. During his teen years, he was featured regularly on the local radio station and he played in local nightclubs.

In 1950 Lefty recorded demos of several of his songs. The one that scored biggest was "If You've Got the Money, Honey, I've Got the Time." The back side, "I Love You a Thousand Ways" also climbed to number one. Soon after that he was invited to perform at the Grand Ole Opry. His primary band, the WESTERN CHEROKEES, was featured in his recording sessions and live performances. For several weeks, his "I Want to Be with You Always" and "Always Late (With Your Kisses)" were at number one. In 1964 "Saginaw, Michigan" was his last number one hit.

Lefty was a big influence on several singers, including MERLE HAGGARD, WILLIE NELSON, DWIGHT YOAKAM, and GEORGE JONES. In 1982 he was inducted into the Country Music Hall of Fame®. Lefty also is in the Rockabilly Hall of Fame and has a star on the Hollywood Walk of Fame. Lefty is ranked number thirty-one on CMT's 40 Greatest Men of Country Music in 2003.

Lefty was only forty-seven when he died in 1975. In his last interview he said, "When I sing, to me every word has a feeling about it."

LARRY **GATLIN**

MAY 2, 1948 - SEMINOLE, TEXAS

Best-known for singing "All the Gold in California" with the Gatlin Brothers, Larry also performed in The Will Rogers Follies *on Broadway.*

THE GATLIN BROTHERS were reared on country gospel music and were well-known for singing in church and on the radio at an early age. Larry, Steve, and Rudy recorded their first album on the Sword and Shield label owned by the WILLS FAMILY. While Larry was enrolled at the University of Houston in the late 1960s, he played wide receiver on the football team. He also began singing with the gospel group, the IMPERIALS, and performed in *Jimmy Dean's Las Vegas Revue.*

DOTTIE WEST recorded two of Larry's songs, "You're the Other Half of Me" and "Once You Were Mine" and helped him settle in Nashville where he sang backup for KRIS KRISTOFFERSON. In 1973 he signed with Monument Records. His debut album, *The Pilgrim,* produced his first Top Forty hit single, "Sweet Becky Walker." The following year, his album, *Rain Rainbow,* landed the single "Delta Dirt" in the Top Twenty on the country charts. "Broken Lady" earned Larry and his brothers their first Top Five hit from the album, *Larry Gatlin with Family & Friends,* in 1976. That same year the brothers joined the Grand Ole Opry. Two years later, Larry scored his first number one hit, "I Just Wish You Were Someone I Love."

By the end of the decade, Larry left Monument Records and started billing his group as the GATLIN BROTHERS BAND. They soon recorded their mega hit, "All the Gold in California." Larry and his brothers continued to score in the Top Ten on country charts with "Talkin' to the Moon" as their last Top Five hit.

In the 1990s, Larry starred in the Broadway hit, *The Will Rogers Follies,* and headlined a major theatrical production, *The Civil War.* In 1993 the brothers opened their own theater in Branson, Missouri. Larry's life story, *All the Gold in California,* was released by Thomas Nelson Publishers in 1998.

CRYSTAL GAYLE

JANUARY 9, 1951 - PAINTSVILLE, KENTUCKY

In 1977 Crystal had a mega hit with "Don't It Make My Brown Eyes Blue." She is a younger sister of Loretta Lynn.

A name change seemed necessary for one planning a career in country music, especially when one is born Brenda Gail Webb. That was the reasoning for this future superstar. Crystal's older sister, LORETTA LYNN suggested that she should avoid being confused with BRENDA LEE. Loretta had seen a sign for Krystal Hamburgers and by changing the "K" to "C" and giving a new spelling to her middle name...she became Crystal Gayle.

Although her older sister gave her career a big boost, Crystal intended to develop her own style. In 1970 she signed with Decca Records and released a debut single, written by Loretta. "I've Cried (The Blues Right Out of My Eyes)" peaked at number twenty-three on the country charts. While she also got exposure as a regular on JIM ED BROWN'S television show, *The Country Place,* Crystal became frustrated with some career choices that she made.

In 1974 she signed with United Artists where her producer, ALLEN REYNOLDS, wanted her to be more creative in her style. Her first country hits, "Wrong Road Again" and "I'll Get Over You," were the beginning of a series of seventeen number one hits. In 1977 Allen encouraged her to approach her next song as a jazz ballad, "Don't It Make My Brown Eyes Blue." This was the mega hit she needed to become an international superstar. The song not only ranked number one on the country charts, it climbed to number two on the pop charts. It also won Crystal a Grammy for Best Female Country Vocalist. It has been said that this one song opened the eyes of the world to Crystal Gayle.

Crystal lives in Nashville with her husband, Bill. They have two children and one grandson. Crystal is ranked number thirty-three in the 2002 CMT's countdown of the 40 Greatest Women of Country Music.

TEDDY GENTRY

JANUARY 22, 1952 - FORT PAYNE, ALABAMA

Teddy is best known as the bass guitar player, vocalist, and songwriter for the band ALABAMA. He and BERNARD PORTER have formed an entertainment consulting company.

Soon after Teddy Wayne Gentry was born, he and his mother went to live on his grandfather's sixty-acre cotton farm. His cousin, RANDY OWEN, was reared on a separate cotton farm on Lookout Mountain. Before high school they were playing the guitar and singing in church as a duo.

It wasn't long until another cousin, JEFF COOK, joined the duo. Teddy and his cousins continued with their day jobs and played in the evenings wherever someone would hire them. During their spare time, the three composed songs and practiced their harmony. Teddy always played by ear and has composed hundreds of songs including "How Do I Fall in Love," "My Home's in Alabama," and "Sad Lookin' Moon." With his cousin Randy, he co-wrote "When It Comes to Christmas," and "Hanging Up My Travelin' Shoes." Teddy remembers writing his first song at age ten. After ALABAMA retired in 2003, he decided to establish a venue for songwriting called Creative Cafe.

In 1980 each member of ALABAMA received his first check from RCA Records for $61,000. Teddy discussed with his wife Linda what they should do with this windfall. She suggested buying his "Papa's" farm. After the sale, the family was thinking of a proper name for the farm. First attempts were words that rhymed with Gentry. Their young son, Josh suggested Bent Tree. Later Teddy learned this bit of folklore: The Indians of Oklahoma would bend a tree to the ground and point to the direction the tribe would be moving. Teddy and his family now call their 140 acres "Bent Tree Farms" and have no plans to move.

In 1999 ALABAMA was honored by the RIAA as the "Country Group of the Century." Teddy was elected with ALABAMA to the Country Music Hall of Fame® in 2005.

TROY GENTRY

APRIL 5, 1967 - LEXINGTON, KENTUCKY

Troy makes half of the duo known as Montgomery Gentry. The two have scored twenty-one singles on the Billboard Hot Country Songs chart.

Troy Lee Gentry grew up listening to the lyrics of HANK WILLIAMS, the ALLMAN BROTHERS, and LYNYRD SKYNYRD. Their influential words that tell of real life stayed with him. After Troy won the Jim Beam National Contest in 1994, he became the opening act for PATTY LOVELESS. In his hometown of Lexington, Kentucky, Troy played in a band called YOUNG COUNTRY and along with EDDIE MONTGOMERY and his brother JOHN MICHAEL MONTGOMERY made up the group EARLY TYMZ. The band was successful in local clubs. Troy said, "We lived in the honky tonks...saw life happen, watched stuff going down that sometimes broke your heart..."

When John left the group for a solo career, Troy and Eddie began performing as MONTGOMERY GENTRY. They signed with Columbia Records in 1999 and released their debut album, *Tattoos and Scars.* The album was certified platinum by the end of that year.

Troy and Eddie could not be considered a "polished crew" but they tried to sing about real life. This real life theme has produced four more albums, *Carrying On* in 2001, *My Town* in 2002, *You Do Your Thing* in 2004, and *Some People Change* in 2006. In 2000 they beat out BROOKS AND DUNN for the CMA award "Duo of the Year." BROOKS AND DUNN held that title for the previous eight years.

In 2008 Troy partnered with the National Non-Profit Patient Advocate Foundation. His mother died of cancer in 2007. He had seen first-hand her battle with the disease and the battle to get healthcare coverage needed to survive. The organization provides direct case management services and healthcare information to millions.

Troy and his wife Angie have been selected to be Honorary Co-Chairs for the Make-A-Wish Foundation for Middle Tennessee in 2008.

DON GIBSON

APRIL 3, 1928 - SHELBY, NORTH CAROLINA - NOVEMBER 17, 2003

It was a great afternoon when Don wrote two classic songs, "Oh, Lonesome Me" and "I Can't Stop Loving You."

Donald Eugene Gibson always considered himself to be a songwriter who sings, rather than a singer who writes songs. At least three of his songs, "Sweet Dreams," "I Can't Stop Loving You," and "Oh, Lonesome Me," are thought to be some of the most important in country music history. Don was known as the "Sad Poet" because of the heartfelt lonely songs he wrote.

At the age of twenty, Don formed a band called SONS OF THE SOIL and they recorded their first album, "Automatic Mama." The group also became a regular on WOHS in Shelby, North Carolina. In 1952 Don was recording with Columbia Records and working at WNOX in Knoxville. Five years later, he recorded "Oh, Lonesome Me" on RCA with the help of CHET ATKINS in Nashville. They tried a different sound using guitars, drums, an upright bass fiddle, a piano, and backup singers. Without fiddles and steel guitars, they created what now is called the Nashville Sound. By 1958 Don had become a regular on the Grand Ole Opry. He left the Opry in 1964, but eleven years later he reinstated his membership.

In 1967 Don and his wife Bobbi moved to Nashville where Don devoted his time to songwriting. "I Can't Stop Loving You" has been recorded by more than 700 singers and sold more than thirty million records. In 1973 Don was inducted to the Nashville Songwriters Hall of Fame, and in 2001 he was elected to the Country Music Hall of Fame®.

This is what he said about his songwriting, "My songs are simple, and just about all of them are about love. I write about people, not things. People should listen to all types of music. They should be concerned with whether the song is any good, not with the type of music it is." Don passed away November 17, 2003, at Nashville Baptist Hospital.

VINCE GILL

In 2004 Vince received a Grammy Award for Best Vocal Performance. He married Christian/Pop singer, Amy Grant, in March of 2000.

Vincent Grant Gill was reared in a family of musicians. His mother played the harmonica; his dad was an attorney who also played in a country music band. Vince had mastered the guitar, banjo, mandolin, dobro, and fiddle before he entered high school. After graduation from Northwest Classen High in Oklahoma City, he moved to Louisville to play with the BLUEGRASS ALLIANCE. By 1983 Vince had seven years of experience singing lead on three albums. That was the year he moved to Nashville and signed with RCA Records. The next year he released *The Things That Matter* which included two Top Ten hits, "If It Weren't for You," and "Oklahoma Borderline."

In 1990 Vince earned his first Grammy Award and his first CMA Award for Single of the Year with his debut single "Oklahoma Swing." A year later, his album, *Pocket Full of Gold,* featuring four Top Ten hits, was certified platinum. Also in 1991, Vince joined forces with MARK O'CONNOR and the NEW NASHVILLE CATS to record *I Still Believe in You.* This album earned Vince his first CMA Vocal Event of the Year Award. The album also featured RICKY SKAGGS and STEVE WARINER.

Vince first hosted the CMA Awards in 1992 and continued the tradition for twelve years. It is believed that he set the record for consecutively hosting a televised award show. By 1999 Vince had become an in-demand duet singer. He has recorded with DOLLY PARTON, BARBRA STREISAND, PATTY LOVELESS, REBA MCENTIRE, and AMY GRANT.

Vince married Amy Grant in 2000. They had recorded "House of Love" in 1994. After their marriage, they recorded *Let's Make Sure We Kiss Goodbye.* Vince has sold over twenty-two million albums and has earned five CMA Male Vocalist of the Year Awards and eighteen Grammy Awards. He was inducted into the Country Music Hall of Fame® in 2007.

WILLIAM LEE **GOLDEN**

JANUARY 12, 1939 - BREWTON, ALABAMA

William joined the Oak Ridge Boys in 1965 and is credited with pushing the group to move in a more innovative direction in the late 1960s.

The show business career of William Golden began at the age of seven when he sang and played the guitar on his grandfather's weekly radio show. His talent for all of the arts came naturally in his family. His mother, Ruth, has published two books of poetry.

Today with his recognizable beard and baritone voice, William can be heard in three genres: gospel, pop, and country. He is also an accomplished artist. Many times he paints in his hotel room while waiting for the evening performance with the OAK RIDGE BOYS. While touring 165 days a year with the Oaks, he is thankful he can fulfill his passion for painting during the day and sing at night. He says, "Thank God for life and visions."

A friend of former PRESIDENT GEORGE H.W. BUSH and FIRST LADY BARBARA BUSH, William has been a guest at Walker's Point in Kennebunkport, Maine. A painting of his, "Walker's Point Vista," hangs at the compound.

William has earned the respect of Native Americans and was named "Celebrity of the Year" by the Indian Exposition of Anadarko, Oklahoma, which is made up of fifteen tribes. He says, "I have a deep respect for our Native American Indians and their culture. My heart has deep feelings for their contribution to our land and goes out to them for their suffering during the time of European colonization."

In 1965 at the time William joined the Oak Ridge Boys, they were considered a southern gospel group. He was replaced by a former gospel singer STEVE SANDERS in 1987 and after Sanders left in 1995, William rejoined the group.

William and his wife Brenda, live in Hendersonville, Tennessee, in a 1786 Federal-style structure they call Golden Era Plantation.

JOSH **GRACIN**

OCTOBER 18, 1980 - WESTLAND, MICHIGAN

Josh finished in fourth place on the second season of American Idol. His debut album received a gold certification in 2004.

Joshua Mario Gracin had his singing debut during his church's Easter pageant. Josh had always loved listening to vintage rock on a radio station that changed its format to country. He began to enjoy the music of GEORGE STRAIT and RANDY TRAVIS. In the eighth grade, he choose a GARTH BROOKS song, "Standing Outside the Fire," for a talent competition and received an overwhelming ovation.

Josh enlisted in the U. S. Marine Corps after graduating from John Glenn High School and briefly attending Western Michigan University. He married Ann Marie when basic training was finished. They have two daughters, Briana Marie, Gabriella Ann, and a son, Landon Joshua.

In 2003 for the second season of *American Idol*, Josh auditioned halfway through his four-year commitment to the marines. When he finished in fourth place overall, he did not participate in the American Idol Concert Tour because of active duty in the USMC. One of the songs he chose for the contest was RASCAL FLATTS' "I'm Moving On." JAY DEMARCUS, bass player for Rascal Flatts, was so impressed with Josh's talent that he called Josh and told him to call their co-producer, MARTY WILLIAMS. Josh eventually signed with Disney's Lyric Street Records.

On June 15, 2004, his debut album, *Josh Gracin,* sold over 750,000 copies and the first three singles reached the Top Five on the *Billboard* Hot Country Charts. "Nothin' to Lose" went to number one.

Josh says about his music, "There's nothing I love more than getting a crowd on its feet and getting them to sing along and rock with me to a great song. I also wanted songs of substance that really explain who I am and what I stand for."

This Michigan native, with his powerful stage presence and love for authentic country music, has won the hearts of millions.

JACK **GREENE**

JANUARY 7, 1930 - MARYVILLE, TENNESSEE

Nicknamed "Jolly Green Giant," Jack is best known for his 1966 hit, "There Goes My Everything."

Jack moved from his hometown of Maryville, Tennessee, to Atlanta when he turned twenty and started his own band called the PEACH TREE BOYS. By 1959 he had moved to Nashville and formed another band, the TENNESSEE MOUNTAIN BOYS. Two years later, ERNEST TUBB was looking for a drummer for his backup band, the TEXAS TROUBADORS. Jack got the job because of his multiple talents on drums and guitar, as well as his vocal skills.

By 1964 Jack's debut solo album with "The Last Letter" got the attention of Decca Records. A year later, he recorded "Don't You Ever Get Tired (of Hurtin' Me)" which was released at the same time as RAY PRICE'S version. Jack's version did not make the charts, but Ernest Tubb kept encouraging him to pursue his solo career. In 1966 Jack made the Top 40 chart with "Ever Since My Baby Went Away." Later that year he stayed at the number one slot on the country charts for seven weeks with "There Goes My Everything." This song was also a crossover hit on the pop charts.

In 1967 Jack had another number one hit with "There Goes My Baby" which stayed at number one for five weeks. His successes kept coming with "All the Time" and "What Locks the Door." Jack became a member of the Grand Ole Opry that same year. He has collected nine number one hits and has received Male Vocalist of the Year, Single of the Year, and Album of the Year from the Country Music Association.

By 1970 Jack had toured with JEANNIE SEELY and with her recorded "Wish I Didn't Have to Miss You" which soared to number two on the country charts. Ten years later, Jack had a brief comeback with "Yours for the Taking" which made it to the Top 30 on the country charts.

The "Jolly Green Giant" with his mellow voice was selected in 1967 as the first country artist to ride in Macy's Thanksgiving Day Parade.

LEE **GREENWOOD**

OCTOBER 27, 1942 - SOUTHGATE, CALIFORNIA

In 1984 Lee wrote and recorded his signature song, "God Bless the U.S.A." It earned him ACM's Male Vocalist of the Year and CMA's Song of the Year.

By the time young Melvin Lee Greenwood was fourteen, he had mastered most of the instruments in the Junior High orchestra. A seasoned performer by the time he was to graduate from high school, Lee skipped the ceremony to fulfil his obligation to perform an engagement at the Golden Hotel (now Harrahs) in Reno, Nevada.

Lee had experience playing with various country and dixieland bands, but it was playing the saxophone for DEL REEVES that taught him what it was like to be a showman. Lee formed his own band, APOLLO, in 1962 and moved to Las Vegas. He changed the name of the band five years later to the LEE GREENWOOD AFFAIR and moved to Los Angeles. Through a series of missed opportunities, he was singing in lounges back in Reno in 1978. Then Lee met MEL TILLIS' bandleader, LARRY MCFADEN, who later became Lee's manager. He encouraged Lee to concentrate on his writing to reflect country-oriented lyrics. In 1981 MCA Records took a chance with Lee. His first release was *Inside and Out*. It was not until *Somebody's Gonna Love You* that the title cut climbed to number one on the country charts in 1983.

BARBARA MANDRELL paired with Lee and the hits kept coming. In the summer of 1984, Lee's signature song, "God Bless the U.S.A." was released. Lee said, "One of the reasons I wrote the lyric 'I'm proud to be an American,' is I really wanted to instill the pride back in America." The song earned Lee the CMA Award for Song of the Year and Male Vocalist of the Year, as well as a Grammy for Best Country Vocal Performance. During the Gulf War in 1991 and after September 11, 2001, the song had another surge in sales.

Lee married KIMBERLY PAYNE, a former Miss Tennessee, in 1992 and they have two sons, Dalton and Parker. In 1996 he opened his theater in the Smokies but as of 2001 he has resumed touring nationally.

ANDY GRIFFITH

JUNE 1, 1926 - MOUNT AIRY, NORTH CAROLINA

In his television shows, Andy has presented country music to millions. He recorded a video, Waiting for a Woman, *with Brad Paisley.*

The man who brought tranquillity to a hectic world once considered a career in music, as an opera singer. Andy Griffith grew up in Mount Airy, North Carolina, known to most of us as Mayberry, where in high school he demonstrated many talents in the Rockford Street School Auditorium where he sang with a group called the DARLINGS. He also thought seriously of becoming a Moravian minister, enrolling in 1944 at the University of North Carolina as a pre-divinity student. By graduation, he had changed his direction to drama and musical theater.

After college, Andy taught high school music for three years. He married BARBARA EDWARDS and the two set out on a career in entertainment. Their routine mixed singing and dancing with Andy's monologues. In 1953 his recitation, "What It Was, Was Football!," became one of the most popular comedy routines of all time. Moving to New York, Andy made his television debut on the *Ed Sullivan Show* and landed a role in *No Time for Sergeants* on Broadway. With favorable reviews, Andy was nominated for a Tony Award. He reprised the role on film three years later. In 1957 he starred in the movie, *A Face in the Crowd.* 1987 Country Music Hall of Famer ROD BRASFIELD played Andy's sidekick.

Andy's role in *Make Room for Daddy* created a spin-off for his own sitcom, *The Andy Griffith Show.* Andy featured country or bluegrass music at the drop of a hat. As a result, many homes were exposed to country music almost ten years before *Hee Haw* made it to television. When NBC launched the *Matlock* series, Andy was seen playing his ukulele and guitar. The show, which featured RANDY TRAVIS on two episodes, gave Andy a chance to demonstrate his love for country music. In 2005 Andy released an album, *The Best of Andy Griffith, Pickin' and Grinnin'.*

Andy was awarded the Presidential Medal of Freedom in 2005.

MERLE **HAGGARD**

Merle's 1969 pop hit, "Okie from Muskogee," first believed to be a political statement, was actually written as a humorous character portrait.

When Merle Haggard was born to James and Flossie Haggard, his parents had already moved to California from Oklahoma during the Great Depression. Before his marriage, James had played in honky-tonk bars, a job that Flossie put an end to. James died from a brain tumor when Merle was nine. Merle became rebellious and spent time in juvenile centers to no avail.

When Merle was twelve, his brother gave him a guitar. Merle taught himself to play by listening to records found around his home.

Merle served time in prison in the late 1950s. Conversations with a fellow inmate and time spent in isolation helped him choose to turn his life around. While still incarcerated, he took high school equivalency classes and played in the prison band.

Once out of prison and playing in local bars at night, Merle caught the attention of Charles "FUZZY" OWEN, owner of Talley Records. Charles and his cousin LEWIS TALLEY were helpful at the beginning of Merle's music career. Other influences were Bakersfield artists, TOMMY COLLINS and WYNN STEWART. Merle admired Stewart's vocal style. It was an admiration that helped Merle with his own phrasing.

Maybe the most important songwriter and performer to come out of the 1960s, Merle has recorded more than six hundred songs. Many were self-penned. As one of the foremost persons of Bakersfield country, he pushed the limits as far as possible. He admired BOB WILLS and his music has reflected Wills' style, drawing from all forms of American music—country, blues, folk, and jazz—blending it into something of his own. His music remains some of the most interesting and creative in his field. Merle was inducted into the Country Music Hall of Fame® in 1994.

Still singing, Merle released *The Bluegrass Sessions* in 2007.

Tom T. Hall

MAY 25, 1936 - OLIVE HILL, KENTUCKY

As a songwriter, Tom's first big hit was "Harper Valley P.T.A." The song was recorded by Jeannie C. Riley and sold six million copies.

Tom T. Hall is the son of a brick-laying minister. His father gave him a guitar when he was eight years old. Since Tom had already begun to write poetry, it was easy to turn poems into songs. At the same time Tom was learning music and the art of performance from a nearby neighbor, LONNIE EASTERLY.

When Tom was eleven, his mother died. Four years later, his father had a hunting accident that prevented him from working. Tom left school and began supporting himself and his father by working in a local garment factory. During this time, Tom formed his first band, the KENTUCKY TRAVELERS. The group performed bluegrass and played on a radio station in Morehead, Kentucky. Tom wrote a jingle for the station's sponsor, the Polar Bear Flour Company. When the band broke up, Tom became a DJ at the station. In 1957 Tom joined the army and while stationed in Germany performed in local NCO clubs on the Armed Forces Radio Network. He usually sang original music with a comedic twist.

After returning to the States, Tom enrolled at Roanoke College to study journalism. He supported himself as a DJ at a radio station in Salem, Virginia. A Nashville songwriter visited the station, heard Hall's songs, and sent them to JIMMY KEY at New Key Publishing. Key signed Tom to write songs for the company. Back-to-back hits convinced Tom to move to Nashville. In 1968 JEANNIE C. RILEY had a major hit with Tom's "Harper Valley P.T.A." The song was at the top of the charts for three weeks and won both a Grammy and a CMA Award. This highlighted Tom's career as a singer. Other successes have included "Ballad of Forty Dollars," "Shoeshine Man," and "Salute to a Switchblade." "The Year That Clayton Delaney Died," his biggest hit, came in 1971. It was based on the life of his neighbor and childhood mentor, Lonnie Easterly.

EMMYLOU HARRIS

APRIL 2, 1947 - BIRMINGHAM, ALABAMA

Emmylou embraced her roots with her Grammy Award album, Red Dirt Girl. *She ranks number five in the 40 Greatest Women of Country Music.*

Although Emmylou was born in the Heart of Dixie, she spent her childhood in North Carolina and in the suburbs of Washington, D. C. Graduating at the top of her high school class, she studied music with a scholarship in drama at the University of North Carolina. Learning to play the guitar and writing songs became her passion. BOB DYLAN and JOAN BAEZ were big influences. Emmylou decided to leave college and move to Greenwich Village. While in New York, she worked as a waitress and performed in coffeehouses. Emmylou soon met and married another songwriter, TOM SLOCUM. They moved to Nashville but the marriage was soon over, leaving her to rear their child, Hallie.

During her time in New York, Emmylou met GRAM PARSONS and in 1973 she began touring with his band, THE FLYING BURRITO BROTHERS. That same year, Emmylou recorded the album, *Grievous Angel.* After Parsons' tragic death from an overdose of drugs and alcohol, she wrote "Boulder to Birmingham" about Parsons. In 1975 Emmylou recorded *Pieces of the Sky,* a debut album which launched her career. She received her first Grammy in 1976 for the single, "Elite Hotel" and three years later won her second award for "Blue Kentucky Girl." In 2000 she collected a Grammy for "Red Dirt Girl." Emmylou has won a total of twelve Grammys. LINDA RONSTADT admired Emmylou's talent and invited her to move to Los Angeles where she was able to get work on Sunset Strip. She credits Linda as the force behind her record contract.

Emmylou has been an activist involved in preserving institutions such as the Country Music Foundation and the Grand Ole Opry. As a gifted songwriter with a soothing voice, she has reached audiences in pop, folk, alternative, and country music. *Billboard* magazine describes her as a "truly venturesome, genre-transcending pathfinder."

HAWKSHAW **HAWKINS**

DECEMBER 22, 1921 - HUNTINGTON, WEST VIRGINIA - MARCH 5, 1963

Hawkshaw traded five trapped rabbits for his first guitar. "The Sunny Side of the Mountain" was his signature song.

With his tall six feet, six inch frame and deep bass voice, Harold Franklin Hawkins became a popular member of the Grand Ole Opry. Nicknamed Hawkshaw, he began his musical career at the age of fifteen after winning a talent contest and landing a singing job on the local radio station. His next stop was WCHS in Charleston, West Virginia. At the outbreak of WWII, Hawkshaw joined the military and sang on the local army radio station in the Philippines.

Hawkshaw signed with King Records after his discharge and became a regular on WWVA's *Wheeling Jamboree* from 1946 to 1954. "The Sunny Side of the Mountain" became Hawkshaw's signature song. Beginning in 1948, he recorded five hit singles, "Pan America," "Dog House Boogie," "I Love You a Thousand Ways," "I'm Waiting Just for You," and "Slow Poke," all of which made the Top Ten on country charts.

Hawkshaw was invited to become a member of the Grand Ole Opry in 1955. When he signed with Columbia Records in 1959 he released "Soldier's Joy" which landed in the Top Twenty.

In 1960 Hawkshaw married country singer, JEAN SHEPARD, and they began breeding horses on their farm near Nashville. Three years later, he rejoined King Records and released his comeback number one single, "Lonesome 7-7203," written by ERNEST TUBB'S son, JUSTIN TUBB.

Hawkshaw and Jean had two sons. Their first son, Don Robin, was named for two close friends, DON GIBSON and MARTY ROBBINS. Harold Franklin Hawkins II never saw his father, since Hawkshaw was a passenger on the ill-fated flight that also sent PATSY CLINE, COWBOY COPAS, and pilot, RANDY HUGHES to their deaths on March 5, 1963. Hawkshaw's recording of "Lonesome 7-7203" became a number one hit after his death.

MARK **HERNDON**

MAY 11, 1955 - SPRINGFIELD, MASSACHUSETTS

Mark played the drums for ALABAMA, one of the most popular country bands in history. He joined the group 1979.

Growing up in a military family, Mark Joel Herndon traveled all over the country before his father, a marine pilot, settled in South Carolina. As it turned out there were three cousins from the state of Alabama honing their craft in the same area. In Myrtle Beach, Mark played the drums in clubs. His eclectic taste in music ranges from BOB SEEGER to TCHAIKOVSKY to HANK WILLIAMS JR. After the cousins had witnessed what Mark could do on a set of drums, they invited him to join their group. RANDY OWEN, TEDDY GENTRY, and JEFF COOK were playing under the name WILDCOUNTRY but changed their name to honor their home state of Alabama.

After Mark joined ALABAMA in 1979, he reflected back by saying, "We were among the first country acts to introduce what was considered at the time to be [a] rock-n-roll production on our tours. We employed a lot of ideas, set designs and video innovations into our shows. I believe ALABAMA provided a new dimension to the format. I'm proud to have been a part of what we were doing that helped attract younger audiences to our concerts without alienating our older fans."

When ALABAMA signed with RCA in 1981, no one imagined how big this band would become. In 1989 the Academy of Country Music named the group "Artist of the Decade" while the Recording Industry Association of America named them "Country Group of the Century" in 1999. With ALABAMA, Mark was inducted into the Country Music Hall of Fame®. The group retired from touring in 2004 but has since released two albums, *Songs of Inspiration* and *Songs of Inspiration II.*

These days, as a licensed pilot, Mark enjoys flying or riding his motorcycle. His message to his fans is "Thank you for the letters, the love, and all the support!"

FAITH **HILL**

SEPTEMBER 21, 1967 - JACKSON, MISSISSIPPI

Faith's "Soul2Soul II Tour" with husband Tim McGraw became the highest-grossing country tour of all time.

Audrey Faith was adopted by Edna and Ted Perry when she was only a week old and was reared in Star, Mississippi. She was singing in church and at family functions by the age of three. At seventeen she had formed her own band and was singing at rodeos, fairs, and churches. Faith enrolled at Hinds Community College but soon realized the need to pursue her musical career. At nineteen she packed her bags for Nashville. Faith's first job was selling T-shirts at Fan Fair, an annual music festival in Nashville. Next she was hired in the office of songwriter, GARY MORRIS. With encouragement from Gary to continue her dream of a career in music, Faith cut a demo. By 1988 she had met DAN HILL, a music executive, and married him. After a divorce six years later, Faith met another songwriter, GARY BURR, and was invited to become his backup singer. When a representative from Warner Brothers Records heard her singing with Gary at the Bluebird Cafe, the company gave her a contract.

In 1993 Faith's debut album, *Take Me As I Am,* was released and made country music history. A single from that album, "Wild One," stayed at number one on *Billboard's* country charts for four weeks. This was the first time since 1964 when CONNIE SMITH's "Once a Day" had accomplished this feat for a debut single. Faith's album eventually was certified triple-platinum. "This Kiss" from the *Faith* album was the cross-over hit that established her as a star. Other number one albums followed, *Breathe* in 1999 and *Cry* in 2002.

Faith married TIM MCGRAW on October 6, 1996. Ten years later, their Soul2SoulII Tour sold more than a million tickets. Their duet, "Like We Never Loved at All" scored another major hit.

The lady from Star, Mississippi, was destined to become a superstar.

JOHNNY **HORTON**

APRIL 30, 1925 - LOS ANGELES, CALIFORNIA - NOVEMBER 5, 1960

Three of Johnny's recordings topped the charts in both country and pop, "North to Alaska," "Sink the Bismarck," and "The Battle of New Orleans."

John Gale Horton became known as the "Singing Fisherman." After he graduated from high school in 1944, his plan was to become a minister. It was not long before Johnny left seminary and moved to Alaska in 1949 to become a fisherman. Johnny had been taught by his mother to play the guitar when he was eleven and while in Alaska he began writing songs. A year later, he decided to move back to his roots in east Texas. Johnny was hired to sing on KXLA in Pasadena, Texas. After winning a talent contest hosted by JIM REEVES, Johnny began performing under the name of the SINGING FISHERMAN on the *Louisiana Hayride* in Shreveport, Louisiana.

Johnny was mentored by HANK WILLIAMS while they were part of the cast of *Louisiana Hayride*. After Hank died December 31, 1952, Johnny became a close friend to Hank's wife, Billie Jean. They were married in September 1953 and had two daughters, Nina and Melody.

It wasn't until 1955, when Johnny secured a record contract with Columbia Records, that his career got on track. His first single, "Honky Tonk Man" was released in 1956 and the song became a honky-tonk classic. Although Johnny's "I'm a One-Woman Man" and "The Woman I Need" made it into the Top Ten, the rockabilly genre was beginning to wane in popularity. In the fall of 1958, Johnny's career got a big boost with his recording of "When It's Springtime in Alaska (It's Forty Below)."

The next major releases were considered Johnny's "saga songs," "The Battle of New Orleans" and "Sink the Bismarck." Not long after his number one hit, "North to Alaska," was released in the fall of 1960, Johnny Horton was killed in a car crash. His music influenced other singers such as GEORGE JONES, MARTY STUART, and DWIGHT YOAKAM and endured into the 1990s and beyond.

Ferlin **Husky**

DECEMBER 3, 1925 - (NEAR) FLAT RIVER, MISSOURI

Ferlin's biggest hit was in 1959 with "Country Music Is Here to Stay" The song was number two for three weeks.

Born and raised on a Missouri farm, Ferlin Husky learned to love music and play a guitar when he was but a child.

Ferlin enlisted in the Merchant Marines during World War II. Aboard his ship he sometimes entertained the men. After the war, Ferlin became a DJ, first in Missouri and later in California where he used the name TERRY PRESTON. He also sang in honky-tonks using the Preston name. When TENNESSEE ERNIE FORD'S manager, CLIFFIE STONE heard him, he helped Ferlin gain a record contract at Capitol Records.

At that time, he returned to using Ferlin Husky when he was performing. Although Ferlin's first records were ignored, when he sang on JEAN SHEPHARD'S recording of "A Dear John Letter," it became a hit. The duo had a second hit later the same year with "Forgive Me John." Ferlin's first solo hit came in 1955 when "I Feel Better All Over" and its flip side, "Little Tom" made it to the country Top Ten. Ferlin then developed a comic alter ego known as SIMON CRUM. Ferlin signed Crum to his own contract with Capitol and in 1958 Crum had a number two hit with "Country Music Is Here to Stay." Ferlin had several hits in the late 1950s, with his high point coming in 1957 when "Gone" stayed ten weeks at number one. In 1960 Ferlin had his biggest hit with the gospel song, "Wings of a Dove." The song was number one for ten weeks and reached number twelve on pop charts.

Ferlin's career in movies included *Mr. Rock and Roll*, *Country Music Holiday*, *Las Vegas Hillbillies*, and *Hillbillies in a Haunted House*.

Ferlin opened his Wings of a Dove Museum in 1984 in Twitty City. The museum moved to Myrtle Beach after CONWAY TWITTY died where it remained until Hurricane Hugo came through the area.

ALAN JACKSON

OCTOBER 17, 1958 - NEWNAN, GEORGIA

Influenced by the new traditional country of the 1980s, Alan became a popular country singer of the 1990s.

Alan Eugene Jackson grew up in a blue-collar family with four older sisters. Early on, he mainly listened to gospel music before a friend introduced him to the music of HANK WILLIAMS JR. His folks, Ruth and Eugene, purchased a fifty-dollar guitar for Alan when he was fifteen. He got a taste of show business at seventeen with his first public appearance in a high school production of *Oklahoma*. Soon after that, he dropped out of school and started his own band, DIXIE STEEL.

Alan met his future wife, Denise, at Dairy Queen. They were married in 1979 and have three daughters, Mattie, Alexandra, and Dani. Alan and Denise moved to Nashville in 1985. Denise was hired as a flight attendant. After meeting GLEN CAMPBELL in the airport, Denise told him about her husband and gave Glen a tape of Alan's songs. Glen encouraged her to have Alan contact his publishing company and it wasn't long before Alan was hired as a staff writer.

Alan was the first singer signed by the country division of Arista Records, and in 1989 they released his first album, *Here in the Real World*. This proved to be the first of many number one hits for Alan Jackson. Two years later, he had three number one hits with "I'd Love You All Over Again," "Don't Rock the Jukebox," and "Someday." In 1992 Alan and RANDY TRAVIS teamed up with three charted songs, "Forever Together," "Better Class of Losers," and "I'd Surrender All."

With Alan's song, "Murder on Music Row," he has sparked a debate to return to a more traditional style of country music. Alan is staying on the cutting edge of current events with his song, "Where Were You (When the World Stopped Turning)," that was released after September 11, 2001. Since 1989 this superstar has sold over forty million albums and has had thirty number one singles.

STONEWALL **JACKSON**

NOVEMBER 6, 1932 - EMERSON, NORTH CAROLINA

Stonewall's "Waterloo" had five weeks atop the country charts and was number four on pop charts. In 1963 he hit number one with "B.J. the D.J."

According to a Jackson family legend, Stonewall Jackson is related to the Confederate general, Thomas "Stonewall" Jackson, for whom he was named. Although he was born near the state line between North Carolina and South Carolina, Stonewall spent his youth on a farm in Georgia. His country boy roots were the traditional themes that he chose to write about and record. He traded his bike for his first guitar when he was ten and began writing songs. Stonewall became a prolific writer. Many of the songs he recorded were his songs or those he co-wrote, such as "Can't Go on Living This Way," "The Sadness in a Song," "You Haven't Heard," and "I Can't Dry Your Tears."

Stonewall Jackson began his singing career in the mid-1950s and in 1956 moved to Nashville. He dropped off a demo tape at Acuff-Rose Music Publishing Company. WESLEY ROSE liked what he heard and set up an audition for Stonewall at the Grand Ole Opry. At his first Opry appearance, backed up by ERNEST TUBB'S TEXAS TROUBADOURS, Stonewall was an instant hit with the audience. A year later, he signed a record contract with Columbia and began touring with Ernest Tubb. His first recording in 1958 was "Don't Be Angry." The next year, he recorded GEORGE JONES' "Life to Go."

The song that really put Stonewall on the map was "Waterloo." The line that country music fans were singing in 1959 was "Everybody has to meet his Waterloo." "Waterloo" stayed at number one on the country charts for five weeks and climbed to number four on the Top Forty pop charts.

Stonewall was the first musician to join the Grand Ole Opry without a record contract and the first to record a live album from the Opry. His last number one hit was his 1963 recording of "B.J. the D.J."

Sonny **James**

MAY 1, 1929 - HACKLEBURG, ALABAMA

Dubbed the "Southern Gentleman," in 1957 Sonny recorded "Young Love," a 45 rpm single for which he would forever be remembered.

Born James Loden into a family who loved hard work and country music, Sonny began performing at the age of four. His parents, Archie and Della, operated a three hundred acre farm in northern Alabama, raising cotton, corn, and hay.

In 1933 the family's music impressed the manager of WMSD in Muscle Shoals, Alabama, and the family began regularly filling a Saturday slot. Sonny became proficient on the guitar and sang with his nine-year-old sister, Thelma. The family landed a two week gig at one of the largest radio stations in Alabama after winning the Mid-South Champion Band Contest. KATE SMITH picked their group as the winner and Sonny remembers, "She took kind of a liking to us. She had me on her lap, gave me a silver dollar and said that some day I would have a bright future in the entertainment field."

With tenants taking care of the family farm, SONNY BOY AND THE LODEN FAMILY took to the road, appearing in theaters, auditoriums, and schoolhouses around the southern states and on the *Louisiana Hayride* in Shreveport, Louisiana.

In 1950 at twenty-one, Sonny joined the National Guard. He says, "Our company and a unit from Pennsylvania, I believe, were the first National Guard Troops in Korea." Sonny began writing songs and by the time he returned he had filled a notebook. His old friend, CHET ATKINS in Nashville, introduced him to Capitol Records producer, KEN NELSON. Ken liked Sonny's sound and suggested a name change to Sonny James. Sonny's first recording session was on June 11, 1952.

From 1960 until 1979, Sonny spent a total of fifty-seven weeks in the number one position on country charts, more than any other country artist. Recorded in 1956, "Young Love" became his signature hit song.

WAYLON JENNINGS

JUNE 15, 1937 - LITTLEFIELD, TEXAS - FEBRUARY 13, 2002

Waylon became the first country singer to sell a million records. His career spanned six decades as a Grammy winner, songwriter, and actor.

Known as one of the founding members of the "outlaw country movement" in the 1970s, Waylon preferred the hardcore honky-tonk genre. He refused to use studio musicians who had a pop sound which was becoming the norm in Nashville during the 1960s and 1970s.

Waylon Arnold Jennings taught himself to play the guitar by the time he was eight. At age twelve, he landed a job as a DJ and soon formed his own band. By the time he was fourteen, he had quit school. Eventually he moved to Lubbock, Texas, in 1954. While working at a local radio station, Waylon was befriended by BUDDY HOLLY. He became the temporary bass player for the CRICKETS on Buddy's final tour. Ironically Waylon gave up his seat for the BIG BOPPER (J. P. Richardson) on the plane that crashed, killing all on board. This tragedy was devastating for Waylon. It was months before he could get his career back on track.

Waylon moved to Phoenix in 1960 and formed a rockabilly band called the WAYLORS. The group signed with an independent label in 1961. In 1963 he moved to Los Angeles to sign with A&M Records. It wasn't until Waylon moved to Nashville in 1965 and signed with RCA that his career started to pick up some momentum. After renegotiating his contract with RCA in 1972 and collaborating with WILLIE NELSON, Waylon released *Honky Tonk Heroes*. Two years later, he had two number one hits, "This Time" and "I'm a Ramblin' Man." His *Wanted! The Outlaws* album became the first country record to be certified platinum. "Mammas Don't Let Your Babies Grow Up to Be Cowboys" earned Waylon and Willie a Grammy in 1978.

Waylon has sold more than forty million records world-wide, including sixteen number one songs. Waylon was elected to the Country Music Hall of Fame® in 2000.

GEORGE JONES

George was honored in 2007 by the Grammy Hall of Fame for his 1980 hit "He Stopped Loving Her Today."

George Glenn Jones was the eighth child in a poor family. His beloved and patient mother introduced him to country music and by the time George was twelve he was singing and playing the guitar. He would sing for tips on the streets near his hometown. George landed a job at the radio station KTXJ in Jasper, Texas, when he was fifteen. While singing at the radio station, George briefly met his hero, HANK WILLIAMS.

When his first marriage failed, George joined the USMC and was shipped to Korea. By 1954 while trying to get his career back on track, George recorded his first album, *No Money in This Deal*. It wasn't until the next year when he released "Why Baby Why" that the album reached number four on the *Billboard* country charts. In 1959 George changed his record label to Mercury and recorded his first number one hit, "White Lightning," under the name THUMPER JONES. He had two more hits with "Tender Years" and "She Still Cares." When George married TAMMY WYNETTE in 1969, he switched to her record label, Epic Records. This began a twenty year association with his producer, BILLY SHERRILL.

"He Stopped Loving Her Today" has been called the greatest country song ever recorded. In 1980 the song won George a Grammy for Best Male Country Vocal Performance, while the CMA awarded him Male Vocalist of the Year. The song also won Song of the Year and Single of the Year from the CMA. In 2005 George's album, *Hits I Missed...And One I Didn't*, ranked as one of CMT's Top Ten Albums of the Year.

With 167, George has had more songs on country charts than any other artist. Of those, 143 have been in the Top Forty. This Country Music Hall of Famer was ranked number three on the 40 Greatest Men of Country Music. According to FRANK SINATRA, George Jones is "the second best white male singer."

GRANDPA **JONES**

OCTOBER 20, 1913 - NIAGARA, KENTUCKY - FEBRUARY 19, 1998

"Grandpa" Jones was a popular cast member of the long-running television show, Hee Haw, *and appeared at the Opry for over fifty years.*

The career of Lewis Marshall Jones goes back to the 1920s. His flamboyant singing and old-style banjo playing attracted national attention in the 1940s. Born in Niagara, Kentucky, he grew up in factory towns in Kentucky and Ohio and not in the mountains or countryside as his music would imply. His fiddle-playing father and ballad-singing mother were early influences, as were gospel music and JIMMIE RODGERS whom he heard on the *National Barn Dance* from Chicago. It was Rodgers who led Jones to try yodeling. His brother Aubrey bought him a guitar for seventy-five cents which Jones learned to play well enough to join a band to play for local dances. In high school, Jones won a talent contest. The prize, fifty dollars, he used to buy a Gibson guitar.

After performing on Cleveland radio in a duo with JOE TROYEN, the two moved to Boston and worked with another Kentucky native. It was BRADLEY KINCADE who first called Jones "Grandpa" because he sounded much older than his then twenty-two years. Wire-rimmed glasses, a smashed hat, and fake mustache completed his unique character.

George's first published song in 1937, "An Answer to the Maple on the Hill," was followed by many others. During his road days from Fairmont and Charleston to Wheeling, he met and learned to play the banjo from COUSIN EMMY, a fellow entertainer. After a stint in Germany in World War II, he returned to Cincinnati and in 1946 married his beloved Ramona. In 1947 they moved to Nashville when he was invited to join the Grand Ole Opry. In 1968 CBS included him in the cast of their new country music and comedy show, *Hee Haw.*

George was elected to the Country Music Hall of Fame® in 1978. His autobiography, *Everybody's Grandpa: Fifty Years Behind the Mike,* was published in 1984 with the assistance of CHARLES K. WOLFE.

Naomi **Judd**

JANUARY 11, 1946 - ASHLAND, KENTUCKY

With daughter, Wynonna, Naomi formed the highly successful duo, the Judds. Her second daughter, Ashley Judd, is a film and stage actress.

Naomi was born Diana Ellen to Charles and Pauline Judd in Ashland, Kentucky. It was 1946. Her father owned a gas station; her mother was a riverboat cook. Naomi is known in the music business as "Cinderella" because of her rags to riches story. When her girls were small, Naomi worked as a nurse in the local infirmary. After work and school, the three amused themselves by singing, anything from bluegrass to showbiz tunes. When daughter WYNONNA had thoughts of going professional, Naomi encouraged her and moved the family to Nashville in 1979.

After tending a hospitalized relative of RCA's label producer, BRENT MAHER, Naomi gained an audition. The studio was not disappointed with their first mini-album containing "John Deere Tractor." In 1984 the JUDDS had their first of fourteen number one hits, "Mama He's Crazy." The small town country girl was on her way. With daughter Wynonna, Naomi created the highly successful duo, the Judds. Among numerous awards, "Love Can Build a Bridge," a song Naomi composed, won a Grammy for Country Song of the Year.

After an eight-year reign as superstars, Naomi was diagnosed in 1990 with a life-threatening liver disease. The Judds' farewell tour was the industry's top grossing tour in 1991. Music critic GERRY WOOD referred to Naomi as "the most fan-oriented superstar in country music history."

Naomi's ability to face the worst tests of life and retain her down-to-earth outlook has made her one of entertainment's "most admired women and has endeared her to fans as the 'star next door.'" Today, as an inspirational and motivational speaker, Naomi combines her faith, values, knowledge of medicine, humor, and common sense into a message that is powerful and hard to forget.

WYNONNA **JUDD**

MAY 30, 1964 - ASHLAND, KENTUCKY

Wynonna's self-titled solo debut album in 1991 produced three straight number one singles and was certified platinum.

One half of the famous duo, the JUDDS, Wynonna was given the name Christina Claire Ciminella at birth. She later changed her name based on the lyrics "Don't forget Winona" from the song "Get Your Kicks on Route 66." Her mother, NAOMI, was still in high school when she was born. Her biological father, Charles Jordan, was never part of her life. Naomi married Michael Ciminella and the family moved to Los Angeles. The marriage ended eight years later, and by 1976, Naomi and twelve-year-old Wynonna were back in Kentucky living with Naomi's mother, Pauline Judd. With a sparse setting in this mountain home, mother and daughter began listening to country music on the radio, playing the guitar, and harmonizing.

Wynonna's talent was evident while she was in high school and by 1979 the family moved to Nashville. Their singing in close harmony made the difference when the Judds secured a record contract with RCA in 1983. For the rest of the decade, Wynonna and Naomi became the biggest-selling duo in country music history. They announced their farewell tour in 1991 when Naomi was diagnosed with hepatitis C. Although Wynonna had some ambivalence as to a solo career, she signed a record contract with MCA. Her debut album, *Wynonna,* produced three singles, "She Is His Only Need," "I Saw the Light," and "No One Else on Earth," that topped the country charts and soared to the Top Five on the pop charts.

In 1996 she released her third album, *Revelation,* and the single "To Be Loved by You" was certified platinum. The next year, she released a fourth album, *The Other Side,* which was rock-influenced. Wynonna reunited with her mother in a New Year's Eve concert to welcome in the new century. *What the World Needs Now Is Love* was released in 2003 and brought her back to her roots with the country sound that her fans love.

TOBY KEITH

In 1994 Toby's debut single, "Should've Been a Cowboy" went to number one on the Billboard *country single charts.*

Toby Keith Covel's interest in music came from meeting the performers at his grandmother's supper club, but it wasn't until he was twenty that he considered music as a career. In 1981 Toby and his band EASY MONEY began playing in local bars. To make ends meet he worked as a derrick hand. He sometimes left a gig when he got a page to come to work at the oil field. Toby also played football for the semi-pro Oklahoma City Drillers.

Toby dropped his last name of "Covel" and caught a break when one-time ALABAMA producer HAROLD SHEDD was given a demo tape. Harold signed Toby to a contract with Mercury Records. His debut single, "Should've Been a Cowboy," soared to number one on the *Billboard* country charts in 1993. The next year, Toby's second album, *Boomtown,* produced another number one hit, "Who's That Man." "You Ain't Much Fun" ranked in the Top Five on the country charts. In 1999 Toby switched recording labels to DreamWorks and JAMES STROUD produced the album, *How Do You Like Me Now?!* The title cut stayed at number one on the country charts for five weeks. The Academy of Country Music awarded Toby Vocalist of the Year and Album of the Year in 2000. The next year, he received Male Vocalist of the Year from the CMA.

Six months before 9/11, Toby's father, H. K. Covel was killed in a traffic accident. After that fateful day, Toby wrote and recorded on his *Unleashed* album, "Courtesy of the Red, White, and Blue." The song honored his father's patriotism. By the July 4th weekend in 2002, the song peaked at number one on country and pop charts. That same year, Toby joined WILLIE NELSON on the song "Who's Your Daddy?," another number one hit. Mercury released a collection of Toby's biggest selling albums in 2005, and in 2006 he started his own record label, Show Dog Nashville. *Shock'n Y'All* produced two hits, "White Trash" and "Money."

DOUG KERSHAW

JANUARY 24, 1936 - TIEL RIDGE, LOUISIANA

Doug's song, "Louisiana Man," not only sold a million copies but became a symbol for Cajun music.

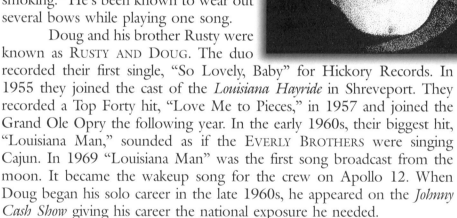

Known as the "Ragin Cajun," Douglas James Kershaw was born in Cameron Parish, Louisiana. One of the twenty-eight instruments he mastered at an early age was the fiddle. Doug is possibly one of the fastest fiddlers around. He plays so fast it's said that "clouds of rosin soar from his horse hair bow, giving the impression that it is smoking." He's been known to wear out several bows while playing one song.

Doug and his brother Rusty were known as RUSTY AND DOUG. The duo recorded their first single, "So Lovely, Baby" for Hickory Records. In 1955 they joined the cast of the *Louisiana Hayride* in Shreveport. They recorded a Top Forty hit, "Love Me to Pieces," in 1957 and joined the Grand Ole Opry the following year. In the early 1960s, their biggest hit, "Louisiana Man," sounded as if the EVERLY BROTHERS were singing Cajun. In 1969 "Louisiana Man" was the first song broadcast from the moon. It became the wakeup song for the crew on Apollo 12. When Doug began his solo career in the late 1960s, he appeared on the *Johnny Cash Show* giving his career the national exposure he needed.

In 1975 Doug married his wife Pam at Houston's Astro Dome before a game and then gave a concert after the game. They have five musical sons, Douglas, Victor, Zachary, Tyler, and Elijah. Tyler often plays the drums for the band. Doug and Pam also have two grandchildren.

Although Doug had hits with his autobiographical song, "Louisiana Man," and novelty song, "Diggy Diggy Lo" it wasn't until 1981 that he had a rebound with his biggest selling hit, "Hello Woman." Seven years later, Doug recorded "Cajun Baby" with HANK WILLIAMS JR. The song made it into the Top Fifty on the country charts.

Whether it's the *Louisiana Hayride*, the Opry, the Astro Dome, or at his restaurant in Colorado, Doug's fans love his energetic show.

BUDDY **KILLEN**

NOVEMBER 13, 1932 - FLORENCE, ALABAMA - NOVEMBER 1, 2006

Buddy began his music career playing bass at the Grand Ole Opry. He later became the sole owner of Tree Publishers in Nashville.

From a meager beginning with a weekly salary of thirty-five dollars in 1953 at Tree Publishing, Buddy became sole owner in 1980. In that year, the founder, JACK STAPP, passed away at the age of sixty-seven. Jack had made an agreement with Buddy which now allowed him to purchase the company. Buddy now owned the largest music publishing company in Nashville and the largest publisher of country music in the world. He sold the business to Sony in 1989 for over thirty million dollars.

Working out of his home in the early days, Buddy would hang out with songwriters in the country music industry. A charismatic figure, Buddy was successful at getting singers to record songs from the Tree catalog. His first big break came in January 1956, when ELVIS PRESLEY signed with RCA. With CHET ATKINS as producer, Elvis recorded "Heartbreak Hotel" at the Methodist Publishing Studios. The song, written by MAE BOREN AXTON, had been published by Tree. The record soon went platinum and the careers of Elvis and Buddy started to soar.

The next year, Tree's co-owner, LOU COWAN, moved on to become head of CBS Television and Jack had a new partner in HARRY FLEISHMAN. Jack gave Buddy thirty percent of the company and made him vice president. The midas touch struck again with ROGER MILLER'S "Dang Me" and "Chug-A-Lug." "Green Green Grass of Home" and "D-I-V-O-R-C-E" were other hits by a Tree staff writer, CURLY PUTMAN.

By 1968 Tree Publishing had gone global with thirteen overseas offices. They purchased the songs of WILLIE NELSON from Pamper Music, including "Crazy" and "Make the World Go Away" for 1.6 million. Tree became country music's number one publisher in 1972.

Buddy Killen was a member of the Songwriter's Hall of Fame and the Alabama Music Hall of Fame.

PEE WEE **KING**

FEBRUARY 18, 1914 - MILWAUKEE, WISCONSIN - MARCH 7, 2000

Pee Wee co-wrote the American classic, "Tennessee Waltz," and his recording of "Slow Poke" was Billboard's *number one hit in 1951.*

There were two reasons why GENE AUTRY gave Pee Wee his nickname. First, there were three other Franks (Pee Wee's given name) in the band that backed Gene up. And then there was Pee Wee's height of five and a half feet.

Julius Frank Anthony Kuczynski was the son of a polka bandleader and made his professional radio debut playing the accordion at the age of fourteen. He changed his name to Frank King as a tribute to WAYNE KING, who was known as "America's Waltz King." While Pee Wee and his band were a regular act on Milwaukee's *Badger State Barn Dance* radio show, they were discovered by the "Singing Cowboy" Gene Autry. In 1937 REDD STEWART joined Pee Wee's band, the GOLDEN WEST COWBOYS. Redd later became Pee Wee's partner in writing lyrics to a number their band played. They called it the "No Name Waltz." After hearing BILL MONROE'S "Kentucky Waltz," the two decided that Tennessee needed a waltz and the "Tennessee Waltz" came into being.

Starting in 1937, Pee Wee would bring an unorthodox sound and mode of dress to the Grand Ole Opry. He introduced polka and waltz rhythms and by the early 1940s was accompanied with amplified electric guitar. By the end of the decade, drums were added. Pee Wee's flamboyant suits soon became the norm for many performers at the Opry. After ten years on the Opry, Pee Wee moved to Louisville, Kentucky.

Pee Wee's version of the "Tennessee Waltz" ranked number three on the country charts in 1947. Three years later, PATTI PAGE sent the song to first place on pop and country charts. "Slow Poke" was another huge hit for Pee Wee, staying at number one for three months. Other songs by Pee Wee include "Silver and Gold," "Bonaparte's Retreat," and "You Belong to Me."

In the mid-1950s to the early 1960s, Pee Wee reunited the Golden West Cowboys. He was elected to Country Music Hall of Fame® in 1974.

ALISON **KRAUSS**

JULY 23, 1971 - DECATUR, ILLINOIS

Alison has won twenty-one Grammy Awards — more than any other female singer and the seventh-most among all artists.

Country and bluegrass singer, Alison Krauss, was encouraged by her parents to learn to play the violin at an early age. It was an easy step to the fiddle, fiddle contests, and bluegrass festivals. Early recognition as an instrumentalist led to singing which drew even more attention. Alison was winning contests at age ten, recorded for the first time on her brother's album at fourteen, and signed with Rounder Records in 1985. Alison was then invited to join the band UNION STATION with whom she still performs. Her first solo album followed at age sixteen.

Since that time, Alison has released more than ten albums and played on many soundtracks, including the Grammy-winning, *O Brother, Where Art Thou?* Thanks to Alison, bluegrass music has enjoyed increased popularity. The Society for the Preservation of Bluegrass in America named her the Most Promising Fiddler in the Midwest.

Not only is Alison an accomplished musician, she also has gained expertise as a producer, arranger, and song finder. Besides producing her own albums, she has also produced recordings for the COX FAMILY, NICKEL CREEK, and a single for REBA MCENTIRE. Movie and TV soundtracks that ALISON KRAUSS AND UNION STATION have contributed to are *Divine Secrets of the Ya-Ya Sisterhood, Where the Red Fern Grows, Mona Lisa Smile, Crossing Jordan, Buffy the Vampire Slayer,* and *Midnight in the Garden of Good and Evil.* Alison and rock musician STING combined their talents on "You Will Be My Ain True Love" for the movie *Cold Mountain.* The song was nominated for an Oscar. Alison Krauss and Union Station won three Grammys for *Lonely Runs Both Ways.* After winning two CMA Awards with BRAD PAISLEY, she produced his album, *Like Red on a Rose.* Alison and LED ZEPPELIN'S ROBERT PLANT surpised both bluegrass and rock fans with their successful platinum *Raising Sand.*

KRIS **KRISTOFFERSON**

JUNE 22, 1936 - BROWNSVILLE, TEXAS

Over 450 musicians have recorded Kris' songs such as "Help Me Make It Through the Night," "Me and Bobby McGee," and "For the Good Times."

This Oxford educated, helicopter pilot, captain in the U.S. Army, Golden Glove boxer doesn't fit the mold as one of best songwriters in Nashville. In 1965 Kris gave up his army commission to take a janitor's job at Columbia Recording Studios with hopes of getting his songs heard. Kris also was employed by a petroleum company in Louisiana as a commercial helicopter pilot. He wrote "Help Me Make It Through the Night" and "Me and Bobby McGee" while sitting on an oil platform. ROGER MILLER'S version of "Me and Bobby McGee" climbed to number twelve on the country charts while JANIS JOPLIN'S hit number one on pop charts.

The story goes that Kris set his helicopter down on Johnny Cash's lawn to get Johnny's attention. Kris presented Johnny with some of his tapes. Not long after that, Johnny recorded "Sunday Morning Coming Down." In 1970 it won Song of the Year from the CMA.

Kris grew up in a military family where moving around the country was the norm. His father, a U.S. Air Force general, finally settled in California where Kris graduated from San Mateo High School. He attend Pomona College before earning a Rhodes Scholarship to study literature at Oxford University.

After achieving his songwriting dream, Kris recorded his first album which had little success until it was re-released as *Me and Bobby McGee*. His second album, *The Silver Tongued Devil and I,* established Kris as a recording artist. Kris and his then wife, RITA COOLIDGE, were awarded two Grammys for "From the Bottle to the Bottom" in 1973. In the mid-1980s, Kris joined forces with JOHNNY CASH, WILLIE NELSON, and WAYLON JENNINGS to create the supergroup, the HIGHWAYMEN. As an actor, Kris has appeared in over forty films including *A Star Is Born, Convoy, Heaven's Gate, Lone Star,* and *Alice Doesn't Live Here Anymore.*

MIRANDA **LAMBERT**

NOVEMBER 10, 1983 - LONGVIEW, TEXAS

Miranda's first album, "Kerosene" debuted at number one on the country charts in 2005 and has since gone platinum.

At first glance, one might be fooled when seeing this young, blue-eyed, and dimpled performer. Miranda Lambert has proven to be one of the best country singers of the new millennium. Her hard-driven lyrics paint a picture conjuring up emotions that have touched her fans. Her father, Rick, has co-written some of her songs. On a rainy night in Texas, they composed the sad song, "Greyhound Bound for Nowhere." Miranda would write a line and her father would write a line. Miranda says, "I don't want my music to be taken as something you just hum along with...no matter what I'm singing, I want to say something that makes people think."

When her father bought her a guitar at fourteen, she had no interest in learning to play. Miranda says "I didn't really have an interest...I did the teenage high school thing. I was in choir and all that, but when I was sixteen I really got into that [music]." Miranda appeared on the *Johnny High Country Music Review* and after attending a music-business seminar in Nashville, decided to learn to play the guitar. Her father taught her three chords and Miranda then wrote her first song. Her best break came from entering *Nashville Star*, country music's version of *American Idol*. She placed third out of 8,000 hopefuls. After that win, Miranda signed with Columbia Records in 2003. On her debut album, *Kerosene*, Miranda co-wrote eleven of the twelve songs. The album was number one on the *Billboard* charts early in 2005 and was eventually certified platinum. Miranda won a nomination for Best Female Country Vocal Performance for the single "Kerosene" in 2007. She wrote eight of the eleven songs on her second album, *Crazy Ex-Girlfriend*, released in 2007, including "Famous in a Small Town." Miranda knows first hand about small towns. Her hometown of Lindale, Texas, population 2,500, can be proud of their local celebrity.

108

K.D. LANG

k.d. was chosen by Roy Orbison to sing "Crying" with him. The recording was awarded a Grammy for Best Country Collaboration with Vocals in 1988.

Kathryn Dawn Lang grew up on the Canadian prairies. While she attended Red Deer College in Alberta, Canada, k.d. became a fan of country music after starring in a college theatrical tribute to PATSY CLINE. k.d. was fascinated by the life and music of Patsy and she became the inspiration for k.d.'s pursuit of a career in music. With help from co-songwriter, BEN MINK, k.d. formed the band RECLINES in 1983 and they cut their first album, *Friday Dance Promenade*. Their second album, *A Truly Western Experience*, was released the next year with favorable reviews in Canada. After k.d. had recorded several other albums, she earned a 1985 Canadian Juno Award for the Most Promising Female Vocalist.

In 1986 k.d. signed with her first major record label, Sire. DAVE EDMUNDS became her producer and k.d.'s debut album, *Angel with a Lariat* was a mixture of 1950s ballads, honky-tonk, and rockabilly. Although the album had good reviews, Nashville was still critical. It was the song, "Crying," recorded with ROY ORBISON, that gave k.d. her first appearance on the country charts. k.d. paid tribute to Patsy Cline with her second Sire album, *Shadowland*, followed in 1989 by *Absolute Torch and Twang* which earned her a Grammy.

k.d. toured with TONY BENNETT in 2001 after they recorded Tony's *Playin' with My Friends: Bennett Sings the Blues*. By 2004 her contract with Sire records had ended and k.d. signed with Nonesuch Records which is distributed through Warner Brothers. She recorded tunes from her favorite Canadian songwriters on her next album, *Hymns of the 49th Parallel*. "Helpless" by NEIL YOUNG and "A Case of You" by JONI MITCHELL were included on this album.

k.d. lang was ranked number twenty-six on CMT's Greatest Women in Country Music in 2002.

TRACY LAWRENCE

JANUARY 27, 1968 - ATLANTA, TEXAS

In 1991 his first album, Sticks and Stones, *sent Tracy to the top of the charts with three number one hits, including the title track.*

Tracy Lawrence was born in Atlanta, Texas, but grew up in the tiny town of Foreman, Arkansas. His rich country background included Southern rockers such as ZZ TOP and LYNYRD SKYNYRD, as well as the more traditional GEORGE STRAIT and MERLE HAGGARD. When he was just old enough to drive, Tracy began performing in area bars, honky-tonks, and at jamborees. Tracy remembers that it was a tough period but he learned some valuable lessons about the entertainment world.

After he arrived in Nashville, it was only a few months before he landed a record contract. His first album, *Sticks and Stones* in 1991, sent him to the top of the charts with three number one hits (including the title song) as well as a Top Ten hit. *Sticks and Stones* went platinum and set a pattern for his career. Terry has had two platinum records, two double-platinum records, and in 1993 was named Top New Vocalist by the Academy of Country Music.

Tracy next began to develop his writing skills and was affirmed when his "If the World Had a Front Porch" went to number one in 1994. From then on, he included songs he had written on his recordings. Tracy has established a lasting place for himself by delivering solid country music that embraces real life and small-town values. He has the ability to choose songs that combine drama, emotion, and philosophy from both everyday events and the nostalgic.

Early on, Tracy opened his own music publishing company to produce his own and other artists' projects. In 2006 he started his own record label, Rocky Comfort Records, as a partnership with his brother and manager, LANEY LAWRENCE. A remixed version of Tracy's current single, "Find Out Who Your Friends Are," with TIM MCGRAW and KENNY CHESNEY won a CMA Award for Musical Event of the Year in 2007.

Brenda **Lee**

Brenda had more charted hits in the 1960s than any other woman. Only Elvis Presley, Ray Charles, and the Beatles outpaced her.

At the age of five, Brenda Mae Tarpley won first place at the annual talent contest in the Conyer, Georgia, grade school. This opened the door to singing on the radio. Brenda appeared for a year on Atlanta's popular radio show, *Starmaker Revue*. Other doors opened for Brenda. Each Saturday, she sang with a local personality, BOOTS WOODALL and the TV WRANGLERS. By 1955 the family had moved to Augusta, Georgia, and Brenda started appearing on WJAT-TV's *Peach Blossom Special*. It was the show's producer, SAMMY BARTON who suggested that she change her last name to Lee.

An appearance on *Red Foley's Ozark Jubilee* gave Brenda her biggest break. RED FOLEY said, "I still get cold chills thinking about the first time I heard that voice." On March 31, 1956, she sang "Jambalaya" on her first network television appearance from Springfield, Missouri. Four months later, at the age of eleven, Brenda signed a record contract with Decca Records. Her first single was HANK WILLIAMS' classic, "Jambalaya." By 1957 her family had moved to Nashville and in December of that year she first appeared on the Grand Ole Opry. Brenda said that one of her fondest memories was appearing on the show with ELVIS PRESLEY. On October 19, 1958, she released "Rockin' Around the Christmas Tree" which failed to make the charts until it was re-released in 1960. It now appears in several lists of all-time favorite Christmas songs. "Sweet Nothin's" was her first single to make the Top Ten in 1959.

Six months before Brenda's sixteenth birthday, she recorded her first number one hit, "I'm Sorry." This gold record stayed in the Top 100 for over six months and by the end of 1960, Brenda Lee had become an international recording star. With over one hundred million records sold, she holds the record for selling the most records by a female country artist.

Gary **LeVox**

JULY 10, 1970 - COLUMBUS, OHIO

Born Gary Wayne Vernon Jr., he is the lead vocalist in Rascal Flatts. Gary and his second cousin, Jay DeMarcus, co-founded the group.

Gary LeVox's second cousin, JAY DEMARCUS, remembers "sitting around the living room on Friday and Saturday nights and everybody coming around to the house and picking up whatever instrument was laying around and playing music all night long." Because their mothers are cousins and as close as sisters, Gary has many of the same memories. Gary says, "We spent a lot of weekends at Jay's house as kids, doing kid stuff and making music." Jay was the first to make the move to Nashville in 1992. It took Jay until 1997 to convince Gary to join him. The cousins began writing and singing together whenever they had the chance. Gary and Jay were playing gigs in Nashville's Printers Alley and Jay got a job in CHELY WRIGHT'S band. It was there that Jay met JOE DON ROONEY. One night when Gary and Jay needed a guitarist, the cousins asked Joe Don to play with them. The result was pure magic. The guys recorded some rough demos that made their way to producer DANN HUFF. Huff was so excited by what he heard that he called Lyric Street Records and said, "You have to hear this group." When Lyric Street heard the demos four days later, they were ready to sign the new group, known as RASCAL FLATTS.

It would be hard to say which single element makes the music of Rascal Flatts so incredible. Joe Don says, "We just really jelled because of our influences: pop, R&B, country, gospel, [and] bluegrass roots." Gary points out that the group has "always liked to try to be different...when someone listens to Rascal Flatts, they're going to hear a lot of harmony, a lot of funkiness because we love to groove. It's so encouraging for us to see country music going more [in] that direction."

In 2008 Rascal Flatts won their sixth CMA Award for Vocal Group of the Year.

GORDON **LIGHTFOOT**

NOVEMBER 17, 1938 - ORILLIA, ONTARIO, CANADA

The lyrics for Gordon's "The Wreck of the Edmund Fitzgerald" came mostly from an article he read in Newsweek.

Gordon Meredith Lightfoot, Canada's most popular male vocalist in the 1970s, is known for writing "Early Morning Rain" which was recorded by ELVIS PRESLEY, JUDY COLLINS, and folk singers, PETER, PAUL, AND MARY.

Gordon's parents realized and encouraged his musical interest. He sang in the choir of St. Paul's Church and credits his choirmaster, RAY WILLIAMS, for giving him confidence and teaching him to sing with emotion. Gordon was heard on local radio at an early age and performed locally in operettas and oratorios. At age twelve, he sang for the first time in Toronto's Massey Hall, winning a competition for boys with unchanged voices. In his teens, Gordon took piano lessons and taught himself to play drums and percussion. While in high school, he was seen in plays, operettas, and barbershop quartets, as well as in a dance band. Gordon also participated in sports, setting records in shot put and pole vault.

After high school, Gordon spent two years at Hollywood's Westlake College of Music where he discovered the folk music of PETE SEEGER AND THE WEAVERS. Back in Canada in the late 1950s, he performed for three years with the SWINGING EIGHT. The group was featured on CBS TV's *Country Hoedown*. By 1970 Gordon had become a major recording star in the United States with his hit song, "If You Could Read My Mind." His follow-up number one hit, "Sundown," came in 1974. An unexpected mega hit came two years later when he wrote and recorded "The Wreck of the Edmund Fitzgerald."

Gordon's signature sound comes from his distinctive baritone voice and acoustic guitar. His career has spanned over forty years with more than two hundred records. He has been nominated for five Grammy Awards and was inducted into the Canadian Country Music Hall of Fame.

HANK **LOCKLIN**

FEBRUARY 15, 1918 - MCLELLAN, FLORIDA

Hank's signature song, "Please Help Me I'm Falling" ranks number two on Billboard's list of the most popular country songs of the first 100 years.

It took an accidental injury to his leg and a long recovery period to give Lawrence Hankins Locklin time to develop his skill of playing the guitar. Hank began to take country music seriously in his mid-teens. After winning first prize in a talent contest in high school, he landed a spot playing on a local radio show. Hank was ineligible for military service during WWII, because of his leg injury. He played with various bands and began writing and singing in the style of ERNEST TUBB.

In the mid-1940s, Hank began to develop his own style and joined the dance band of JIMMY SWAN. By 1947 he had formed his own band. The group was hired on the morning show at KLEE in Houston in 1948, and in 1949, Hank signed a contract with Four Star Records.

The timing was right to record his own compositions, "Send Me the Pillow You Dream On," "Same Sweet Girl," "The Last Look at Mother," "Born to Ramble," "Let Me Be the One," and "Knocking at the Door." In 1955 at the end of his contract with Four Star, Hank signed with RCA. "Geisha Girl" was recorded two years later and stayed on the *Billboard* country charts for over six months. In 1960 Hank had a mega hit with HAL BLAIR'S and DONALD ROBERTSON'S, "Please Help Me, I'm Falling." The recording stayed at number one on the *Billboard* country charts for thirty-six weeks and climbed to number eight on the *Billboard* pop charts. Hank's recording was nominated for a Grammy in 1960 and won the Cash Box Award for Best Country Song.

Hank has said, "The Lord gave me a good voice and I can still sing. I am blessed. I wrote a song that became a huge hit and CHET ATKINS gave me another big song (Please Help Me) to record. I've recorded with the best musicians in the business and have called many of country music's biggest stars my friends."

Charlie **Louvin**

JULY 7, 1927 - HENAGER, ALABAMA

Charlie and his brother Ira released numerous singles, among them, "Little Reasons," and had over twenty recordings on the country music charts.

Born on Sand Mountain in northeast Alabama, Charles Elzer Loudermilk and his brother IRA became one of the most important influences on country music in the 1940s and 1950s. With their smooth close harmony, they had listened to the DELMORE BROTHERS, another Alabama duo, for inspiration. After working days as field hands on the family farm, they would spend the evening listening to the Victrola. In 1940 Charlie was only twelve when the brothers first got paid for singing. Not long after that they won first prize in a talent contest to perform on Chattanooga's WDEF. They teamed up with other groups before landing steady jobs on stations in Knoxville and Memphis. Charlie left briefly to serve in WWII and later in the Korean War.

The Louvins signed a publishing contract with Acuff-Rose in 1948. Charlie said, "Our compositions are about things that we know and have experienced—they are authentic—which is the main reason for their success."

In 1955 they shifted from strictly gospel music to secular with "When I Stop Dreaming." ELVIS PRESLEY toured with them as an opening act early in 1955. That same year they became members of the Grand Ole Opry. For the next seven years, they had twelve hits on the *Billboard* charts including, "I Don't Believe You've Met My Baby," "You're Running Wild," "Cash on the Barrelhead," and "Knoxville Girl." In 1964 Charlie's solo career had success with "I Don't Love You Anymore."

In 2003 Charlie toured with the groups CHEAP TRICK and CAKE. JAMES TAYLOR, MERLE HAGGARD, DOLLY PARTON and JOHNNY CASH collaborated on a Louvin tribute album that won two Grammy Awards. In 2001 the LOUVIN BROTHERS were inducted into the Country Music Hall of Fame®. Charlie embarked on a national tour in 2007 and celebrated his eightieth birthday in 2003 on July 7.

IRA LOUVIN

APRIL 21, 1924 - SECTION, ALABAMA - JUNE 20, 1965

Ira, born Ira Lonnie Loudermilk, and his brother, Charlie, sang together in close harmony tradition as the Louvin Brothers.

Ira Lonnie Loudermilk and his younger brother Charlie had a distinctive sound known as "shape note singing" learned from singing gospel songs in church. It wasn't until the mid-1950s that they made the shift to include secular material. The DELMORE BROTHERS' close harmony was a big influence on their style. Twenty-five years later, the EVERLY BROTHERS were attracted to the same blended voices.

Ira and Charlie were encouraged by their parents to pursue a musical career. With Ira on the mandolin, singing tenor, and Charlie on the guitar, they got their first break on WDEF in Chattanooga. On Knoxville's WROL in 1947, they became known as the LOUVIN BROTHERS. The next year, they signed a publishing contract with Acuff-Rose. It was FRED ROSE who helped the brothers secure a contract with Capitol Records. Their first release was "Love Thy Neighbor."

Once they had temporarily left their gospel roots, the brothers began writing and recording secular music with commercial success in 1955. Although rock 'n' roll hurt their sales, they reached the Top Ten on the country charts with "My Baby's Gone" in 1958. A year later, they had a moderate hit with their traditional ballad, "Knoxville Girl." In the early 1960s, they recorded tribute albums to the Delmore Brothers and ROY ACUFF and returned to their gospel heritage with "Satan Is Real."

In 1963 the brothers decided to go their separate ways. Ira began a solo career with Capitol Records and sang with his wife, ANNE YOUNG. After a concert in Kansas City, both were killed in an automobile accident in Williamsburg, Missouri, on June 20, 1965. "Yodel, Sweet Molly" was released after Ira's death and was a moderate hit.

Ira Louvin was inducted posthumously into the Country Music Hall of Fame® in October 2001.

116

PATTY **LOVELESS**

JANUARY 4, 1957 - PIKEVILLE, KENTUCKY

In 1994 Patty won the Country Music Association's Album of the Year Award for "When Fallen Angels Fly."

This "big-voiced child" grew up to be one the most celebrated female country singers. Patricia (Patty) Ramey was born in Kentucky coal mining country. She loved listening to the Grand Ole Opry in the family kitchen. Patty had a brief glimpse of a musical career when her father took her to a live concert featuring LESTER FLATT and EARL SCRUGGS. When she was fourteen, Patty and her brother Roger traveled to Nashville and by chance met PORTER WAGONER. After following Porter's advice to graduate from high school, Patty landed a job with the WILBURN BROTHERS' publishing company, Sure-Fire Music.

In 1976 Patty married the Wilburns' drummer, TERRY LOVELACE. When the marriage failed nine years later, Patty moved back to Nashville and changed her last name to Loveless. She secured a record contract with TONY BROWN at MCA Records. Patty's first Top Ten hit was with an old GEORGE JONES hit, "If My Heart Had Windows." In 1988 Patty was inducted into the Grand Ole Opry and the next year she married her producer, EMORY GORDY JR. In 1992 Patty signed with Epic Records and recorded her first number one hit, "Blame It on Your Heart." She was awarded the CMA Album of the Year in 1995 for *When Fallen Angels Fly*. Other number one hits followed, "You Can Feel Bad" and "Lonely Too Long" from her *Trouble with the Truth* album in 1996. That was a great year for Patty; she won CMA's Female Vocalist of the Year and the Academy of Country Music's Top Female Vocalist.

With her husband, Emory, and JUSTIN NIEBANK as producers, Patty's albums, *On the Way*, *When Fallen Angels Fly*, and *Mountain Soul* have given fans some of her most inventive stellar performances. Patty says, "If I can just be a little part of touching lives through music, that's wonderful. It's something I've always wanted to do."

117

LYLE **LOVETT**

NOVEMBER 1, 1957 - KLEIN (SUBURB OF HOUSTON), TEXAS

Lyle has won four Grammy Awards, including Best Country Album in 1996 for "The Road to Ensenada."

Lyle Pearce Lovett's first public performance was in a school talent show where he sang "Long Tall Texan." He recalled this event when addressing the U.S. Senate on November 13, 2007. He was pleading the case that "the musicians and singers who perform the song are also creators and deserve to be compensated as well."

In the late 1970s, while Lyle was studying German and journalism at Texas A&M, that he began composing songs. It was after he returned from Germany, where he had been a graduate student, that Lyle seriously considered music as a career. Besides his interest in music, he has also tried his hand at acting, appearing in twelve movies and on television sitcoms.

Lyle began playing in clubs and recorded a demo that eventually got into the hands TONY BROWN of MCA Records. In 1986 Lyle signed a contract with MCA. His debut album, *Lyle Lovett,* included "Cowboy Man," "God's Will," "Why I Don't Know," "Farther Down the Line," and "Give Me Back My Heart." Lyle's music was getting noticed on the country charts but his eclectic arrangements ranged from country to big-band swing to pop. His second album, *Pontiac,* received excellent reviews.

Lyle was gathering a broader market which included a pop audience. His third album, *Lyle Lovett and His Large Band,* reinforced his direction to the big-band sound by adding a cellist, piano, horns, and a backup singer. Although Lyle was beginning to strike gold with record sales, his appeal to country fans started to wane. When Lyle released *The Road to Ensenada* in 1996, it was the first album to capture back the country audience since *Pontiac* was released nine years earlier.

Once married to JULIA ROBERTS, Lyle Lovett has always been more than the singer/composer with the tousled hair who created a style of music that has captured the interest of music lovers of all genres.

LORETTA **LYNN**

Loretta, with sixteen number one and a total of seventy hits as a solo artist, has been called the "Queen of Country Music."

The coal miner's daughter from Butcher Holler captured the nation with her music in the early 1960s. Loretta was the second child of Clara and Ted Webb's eight children. As she states in her best-selling autobiography and number one hit song, "I never thought of leavin' Butcher Holler." That was before she met OLIVER "DOO" LYNN. The couple were married when Loretta was barely fourteen and moved to Custer, Washington, where they reared their four children. With Doo's encouragement and the influence of KITTY WELLS, Loretta began playing the guitar and singing in local clubs in 1961. BUCK OWENS was hosting a televised talent show in Tacoma, Washington, where NORM BURLEY heard Loretta sing. Norm formed Zero Records just to record Loretta's first single, "I'm a Honky Tonk Girl." As in the movie, the family toured cross-country, spotting radio station towers where they would stop and push her Zero release. By the time they arrived in Nashville, Loretta was on her way to becoming a country recording star.

Loretta toured with the WILBURN BROTHERS and was encouraged to move to Nashville in the late 1960s. PATSY CLINE'S producer, OWEN BRADLEY, worked with Loretta when she signed with Decca Records. Her first single with Decca, "Success," climbed to number six on the country charts. In 1966 Loretta wrote and recorded her number two hit "You Ain't Woman Enough (to Take My Man)." A year later, she had her first number one hit, "Don't Come Home A' Drinkin' (with Lovin' on Your Mind)." "Fist City" also reached number one but it was her 1970 mega hit, "Coal Miner's Daughter," that made her a superstar.

Loretta placed number three on the CMT Greatest Women of Country Music and was inducted into the Country Music Hall of Fame®. She was honored as the "Artist of the Decade" for the 1970s by ACM.

MARTIE MAGUIRE

OCTOBER 12, 1969 - YORK, PENNSYLVANIA

A multi-instrumentalist, singer, and songwriter, Martie Maguire is a founding member of the Grammy Award winning Dixie Chicks.

Martha "Martie" Eleanor Erwin and her younger sister Emily remember practicing their music everyday and being timed with an egg timer. Playing classical violin at five, Martie progressed to master four other instruments, viola, guitar, mandolin, and bass. By the time she was twelve, Martie was leaning toward bluegrass music. With four friends from her high school in Addison, Texas, she formed BLUE NIGHT EXPRESS.

While Martie was attending Southwestern University, she played in the orchestra and placed third in the National Fiddle Championship. Martie and her sister Emily began touring with ROBIN LYNN MACY and LAURA LYNCH in 1989. The name they chose for their band came from a song written by LOWELL GEORGE, "Dixie Chicken." Martie's first recording with the DIXIE CHICKS was "Thank Heavens for Dale Evans" in 1990. The group performed as an opening act for GARTH BROOKS, REBA MCENTIRE, and GEORGE STRAIT.

After their second album, *Little Ol' Cowgirl,* was released in 1992, Robin left the group. The next album, *Shouldn't a Told You That* was released in 1993 and soon after that Laura left the group. With NATALIE MAINES joining the Dixie Chicks to fill the vacant position, the group signed with Sony's Monument Records. They released the single, "I Can't Love You Better" which climbed to the Top Ten on the country charts in 1997. Their next album, *Wide Open Spaces,* earned the group a Grammy for Best Country Album in 1998 and sold over twelve million copies. The album also produced a number one single, "There's Your Trouble," which won a Grammy and two Country Music Association awards.

Martie married Gareth Maguire in 2001 and they have twin daughters, Eva Ruth and Kathleen Emilie, born on April 27, 2004.

NATALIE MAINES

OCTOBER 14, 1974 - LUBBOCK, TEXAS

Natalie is a songwriter and lead singer for the female country band Dixie Chicks. The group has won thirteen Grammys since 1998.

Natalie Louise Maines' musical career evolved very naturally. Her father, LLOYD MAINES, had already made a name for himself as a well-known steel guitarist and producer. Natalie began singing at the age of three. By the time she was fifteen, she had mastered both the acoustic guitar and the piano. Natalie played in a band during her years at Lubbock High School, but after a few performances the group broke up. Among the colleges Natalie attended was the prestigious Berklee School of Music. She had earned a scholarship with her vocal skills. Natalie also attended South Plains College in Levelland, Texas, where she played alternative rock. She is known to be a bit of a rebel. Natalie says, "[I] loved not thinking in the way I knew the majority of people thought."

In 1995 Natalie had her first commercial success as a backup singer on an album her father produced, *Dancehall Dreamer,* for country singer, PAT GREEN. Later that year, she auditioned as lead singer for the DIXIE CHICKS replacing LAURA LYNCH. The sisters, Martie and Emily, liked what they heard and at the age of twenty-one, Natalie joined the Dixie Chicks. From 1998 to 2007, the group won thirteen Grammys.

In March 13, 2003 issue of the London newspaper *The Guardian,* Betty Clarke wrote that the Dixie Chicks have been called "the good-time girls the country establishment loves to hate." With sales of over twenty-five million albums since their debut record, *Wide Open Spaces* in 1998, they must be doing something right. They have continued to earn Grammys as well. The CMA honored them as Vocal Group of the Year in 2002. The group was again nominated as Group of the Year in 2007.

Natalie says, "I'm a country girl in that I love the mountains, and I like the honesty and pride of people in the country..."

Barbara **Mandrell**

DECEMBER 25, 1948 - HOUSTON, TEXAS

Barbara was one of country music's most successful artists in the 1970s and 1980s. One of her biggest hits was "Sleeping Single in a Double Bed."

Born on Christmas Day in 1948 to Irby and Mary Ellen Mandrell, hers was a musical heritage. Barbara could read music and play the accordion by age five. Six years later she was so accomplished at playing the steel-pedal guitar that her father took her to a music trade convention in Chicago where she caught the attention of CHET ATKINS and JOE MAPHIS. Soon she was a regular at Maphis' nightclub in Las Vegas where she was known as the "Sweetheart of Steel." At twelve Barbara went on tour with JOHNNY CASH and performed with the likes of PATSY CLINE, JUNE CARTER, and GEORGE JONES. That tour inspired Barbara's father to form a family band. Barbara was fourteen and accompanied her singing father on the pedal-steel and saxophone. Her father played the guitar and her mother played bass. Also in the band was Barbara's future husband, KEN DUDNEY. The band toured the United States and Asia.

After her marriage, Barbara retired to become a homemaker but soon returned to her music career. She signed with Columbia in 1969 and had her first chart hit with OTIS REDDING'S "I've Been Loving You Too Long." The next year, she had her first Top Forty hit with "Playin' Around with Love." It was the first of many.

Calling themselves the DO-RIGHTS, Barbara's sisters, LOUISE and IRLENE, joined her to sing and play backup. In 1979 Barbara was the CMA Female Vocalist of the Year and NBC asked her to star in a musical variety show, *Barbara Mandrell and the Mandrell Sisters*.

In 1997 Barbara began an acting career and has appeared in *Diagnosis Murder; Dr. Quinn, Medicine Woman;* and had a starring role in the TV movie, *The Wrong Girl*. Barbara has won numerous awards over the years, including two Grammy Awards for her gospel albums.

LOUISE MANDRELL

JULY 13, 1954 - CORPUS CHRISTI, TEXAS

In 1983 Louise had a Top Fifteen hit with "Runaway Heart." "I Wanna Say Yes" was number five in 1985.

Louise Mandrell had some success as a country artist before the variety show she shared with her sisters, BARBARA and IRLENE. From 1997 through 2005, she performed at the Louise Mandrell Theater in Pigeon Forge, Tennessee. Although she never became the country music icon, recognized around the world, as her sister is, she still enjoyed much popularity in her own right throughout the 1980s.

Born into a musical family, Louise got her start as a member of the MANDRELL FAMILY BAND. The band toured in the United States and in Asia. In the 1970s, as BARBARA MANDRELL'S career was flourishing, Louise joined her sister's band, the DO-RIGHTS, while still seeking her own place in the ranks of country singers. Louise also toured with MERLE HAGGARD and in 1978 she signed with Epic Records.

In 1979 Louise married country singer R. C. BANNON and the two did well with the single, "Reunited," a cover of the number one smash hit by PEACHES AND HERB. The song rose to number thirteen. When it began in 1980, the television variety show, *Barbara Mandrell and the Mandrell Sisters*, became a showcase for Louise's singing as well as her instrumental and comic talents.

1983 was a big year. Louise had a Top Fifteen hit with "Runaway Heart" as well as two Top Ten spots with "Save Me" and "Too Hot to Sleep." In 1985 her biggest hit, "I Wanna Say Yes," made it to number five on the country charts.

In the early 1980s, Louise was a headliner at the Grand Palace in Branson, Missouri, with KENNY ROGERS, and sometimes joined sister Barbara, SAWYER BROWN, and other top country and pop stars at the Grand Palace. After Louise opened her own theater in Pigeon Forge, her show became the best attended (non-dinner) of all those in the Smokies.

NEAL MATTHEWS JR.

OCTOBER 26, 1929 - NASHVILLE, TENNESSEE - APRIL 21, 2000

Neal became part of country music's premier backup group, the Jordanaires, known for working with Elvis Presley, Patsy Cline, and George Jones.

Little credit has been given to the man who was instrumental in helping to create the "Nashville Sound." Neal developed a shorthand version for the chords known as the Nashville Number System in which numbers are used to denote chord intervals and harmonic relationships. GORDON STOKER, a member of the JORDANAIRES since 1949, explains that, "We were using it a few years before everybody else found out about it and started using it." It helped session players learn a song more quickly.

In 1953 Neal was discharged from the army, where he served in the Korean War and earned a Bronze Star Medal, and joined the Jordanaires as second tenor. In 1956 the group began a fifteen-year association with ELVIS PRESLEY. It was Neal who came up with "doowah, doowah, doowah" as the backup sound that has been copied often, even today. Some of the songs on which the Jordanaires sang backup with Elvis were, "All Shook Up," "Teddy Bear," "Don't," "Are You Lonesome Tonight?," and "Can't Help Falling in Love."

A Nashville native, Neal graduated from Hume-Fogg High School and attended Belmont College where he studied psychology. He married the former Charlsie Stewart. His daughter, Lisa Matthews Doster says, "He was a wonderful father and husband. He treated Mom with the upmost respect and love."

Neal wrote arrangements for JACK SCOTT'S "What in the World's Come Over You," JIM REEVES' "Four Walls," JOHNNY HORTON'S "Battle of New Orleans," and JIMMY DEAN'S "Big Bad John."

Elvis once told the Jordanaires, "Let's face it, if it hadn't been for you guys, there might not have been me." In 2001 Neal Matthews was inducted posthumously into the Country Music Hall of Fame® as a member of the Jordanaires.

MARTINA **MCBRIDE**

JULY 29, 1966 - SHARON, KANSAS

Martina has collected one gold album, three platinum CDs, and one triple platinum CD. She has earned CMA's Female Vocalist of the Year three times.

Reared on a dairy farm in southern Kansas, Martina, along with her brothers and sister, joined their father's band, the SCHIFTERS, when she still in high school. By the time she was eighteen, Martina was working at the local Dairy Queen and playing at night in her own rock band, the PENETRATORS. She soon moved the sixty miles to Wichita and formed another band. Finding that singing rock was hard on her soprano voice, Martina returned to her country music roots. She met her future husband, John McBride, a sound engineer, when she rented his warehouse for her band to rehearse. Martina and John were married May 15, 1988. Two years later they moved to Nashville to pursue careers in country music.

Martina's first job was selling T-shirts at Garth Brooks concerts. After landing a record contract with RCA, Martina began touring with Tim McGraw as a singer. Her debut album, *The Time Has Come*, in 1992, was a disappointment. Martina's first hit was "My Baby Loves Me" but it took her 1995 title track from *Wild Angels* to land a number one hit. Other top selling singles include, "Wrong Again," and "Broken Wings."

Martina became her own producer and writer and in a span of fifteen years sold over sixteen million albums. Her crossover pop hits include "Independence Day," "Valentine," and "I Love You." In 2003 Martina recorded what she has called a labor of love, her *Timeless* album. Regarding this project she says, "I had always wanted to do an album that would pay tribute to the music that shaped who I am as a country music fan."

Martina recorded a powerful song, "Concrete Angel," that deals with child abuse. She serves as the national celebrity spokesperson for the National Network to End Domestic Violence.

Martina was inducted into the Grand Ole Opry in 1995. She and John have three daughters, Delaney, Emma, and Ava Rose.

REBA MCENTIRE

MARCH 28, 1955 - MCALESTER, OKLAHOMA

Each year from 1984 to 1987, Reba won the Country Music Association's award for Female Vocalist of the Year.

Reba Nell grew up on a 7,000 acre ranch in southeastern Oklahoma. Her father, CLARK MCENTIRE, was a world champion steer roper. On the long car rides between rodeos, Reba's mother, Jacqueline encouraged the three children to sing in harmony. The trio soon became know as the SINGING MCENTIRES and performed at rodeos. Reba enrolled in Southeastern Oklahoma State University in 1973, and while in Oklahoma City at the National Rodeo Finals, she was asked to sing the National Anthem. Country and western singer, RED STEAGALL, encouraged Reba to record a demo for his publishing company in Nashville. During her spring break in 1975, she made the trip to Nashville see if she could get a record contract. Mercury liked what they heard and by fall she had signed her contract. Reba's first single, "I Don't Want to Be a One Night Stand," made it into the *Billboard* country charts at eighty-eight.

On September 17, 1977, Reba had her debut at the Grand Ole Opry. She recorded other songs but her next two, "(There's Nothing Like Love) Between a Woman and a Man" and "Glad I Waited Just for You" made it into the country charts that same year. It wasn't until 1984 that the singles, "How Blue" and "Somebody Should Leave" topped the charts from the album *My Kind of Country*. Its songs were predominately covers of old songs performed by RAY PRICE, CARL SMITH, CONNIE SMITH, and FARON YOUNG. Reba was now on her way to superstar status by winning Female Vocalist of the Year from the Country Music Association in 1984. Reba went on to win that award for three consecutive years and picked up her first Grammy in 1987 for "Whoever's in New England." The album, her first crossover to the pop charts, sold over three million copies. Her first crossover pop hit to make it to number one was "Because of You," a duet with KELLY CLARKSON, released in 2007.

126

TIM McGRAW

MAY 1, 1967 - DELHI, LOUISIANA

Tim has had nine consecutive albums debut at Number One on Billboard *with twenty-six of his singles reaching number one.*

Samuel Timothy (Tim) McGraw grew up enjoying the music of CHARLEY PRIDE and JOHNNY PAYCHECK. He started using his musical talent at church and in school but seriously considered a career as a professional baseball player like his father, Tug. Not long after enrolling on a baseball scholarship at Northeast Louisiana University, Tim bought a guitar and soon headed for Tennessee. He arrived in Nashville on May 8, 1989, and began playing the clubs in Printers Alley. It was four years before Tim got a record contract with Curb Records. His first album, *Tim McGraw,* was not successful, but a live performance of "The Joker" got the attention of future fans. The next year was 1994 and Tim released the controversial single, "Indian Outlaw." Some radio stations refused to play the song because of its lyrics. A year later, Tim's *All I Want* album produced his first hit, "I Like It, I Love It."

In 1996 Tim's career caught fire with the concert tour, "Spontaneous Combustion" that featured FAITH HILL as the opening act. Tim and Faith were married on October 6 that same year. A duet with Faith on his *Everywhere* album produced the number one single, "It's Your Love," and sold four million copies. Other major hit albums include, *A Place in the Sun, Set This Circus Down,* and *Greatest Hits.* Tim received his first Grammy for Best Country Vocal Collaboration for "Let's Make Love" on Faith's *Breathe* album. Tim has had additional number one hits while teaming up with other female artists including JO DEE MESSINA on "Bring on the Rain" and "Please Remember Me" with PATTY LOVELESS.

Tim has been one of the most consistent country singers in the last decade winning eleven ACM awards, ten CMA awards, and three Grammys. He has also had acting roles in *Friday Night Lights* and *Flicka.*

Tim and Faith have three daughters, Gracie, Maggie, and Audrey.

Jo Dee **Messina**

Jo Dee had three number one hits in 1998, "Bye Bye," "I'm Alright," and "Stand Beside Me." Burn was her first number one album released in 1999.

Coming from New England posed no problems for Jo Dee in following her dream. When she heard the music of ALABAMA and HANK WILLIAMS JR., she was hooked. Jo Dee formed a band when she entered her teens and gained experience playing in clubs throughout the northeast. In the late 1980s, she arrived in Nashville with only a desire to sing. With no prior contacts, she met another struggling singer, TIM MCGRAW. He would be a very helpful connection later in her journey to a successful music career. In the meantime, Jo Dee landed a regular spot on the Nashville radio show, *Live at Libby's.*

By the early 1990s, Tim McGraw's career had started to blossom and during a Curb's Fan Fair show, Jo Dee was introduced to an executive from Curb Records. With no inhibitions, she jokingly said, "I was thinking...y'all need a redhead on this label." Not long after that she received a contract to sign. Tim co-produced her first self-titled album which landed two Top Ten hits. In 1999 her first number one album, *Burn,* was released. Three years later, she launched her second number one album, a *Greatest Hits* collection. With hits such as "Bye Bye," "I'm Alright," "Stand Beside Me," "Lesson in Leaving," and harmonizing with Tim McGraw on the crossover hit "Bring on the Rain," Jo Dee earned the CMA's Horizon Award in 1999.

Jo Dee has enjoyed touring with VINCE GILL, GEORGE STRAIT, and on the JUDDS' reunion tour. Jo Dee spread her wings into acting with two TV appearances on *Touched by an Angel* in 1999 and 2002. The first episodes was called "Bring on the Rain" from her hit record.

Jo Dee says, "My greatest hope is that somewhere, somebody will hear this record, and find in it what I've found in music my entire life. Reassurance, understanding, inspiration, strength, and compassion."

ROGER **MILLER**

JANUARY 2, 1936 - FORT WORTH, TEXAS - OCTOBER 25, 1992

Roger's signature song, "King of the Road," was a major hit in 1965. He won eleven Grammys plus Broadway's Tony for "Big River."

R oger Dean Miller was born poor. As they say in Oklahoma, "dirt poor." Since his father died when Roger was a year old, and his mother was too ill to care for him, his uncle and aunt, Elmer and Armelia Miller reared him on a cotton farm near Erick, Oklahoma.

By the time Roger was ten, he bought his first guitar from the money he had earned picking cotton. Roger had grown fond of country music from listening to the Grand Ole Opry. Another source of this love was his cousin's husband, SHEB WOOLEY, creator of the 1958 novelty song, "Purple People Eater." Sheb gave Roger a fiddle and encouraged him to consider a musical career. After Roger had mastered the guitar, banjo, piano, drums, and the fiddle, he dropped out of school and became a rodeo rider.

At seventeen Roger joined the army and was sent to Korea. He would quip that his "education was Korea, Clash of '52." Roger got his dreams back in order after his discharge and headed to Music City. His first job was at the Andrew Jackson Hotel as a bellhop. In the mid-1950s, he had jobs playing the fiddle for MINNIE PEARL'S band and as a drummer for FARON YOUNG. Later he was hired by RAY PRICE to replace VAN HOWARD in the CHEROKEE COWBOYS. When BUDDY KILLEN of Tree Publishing hired Roger for $50 a week as a songwriter, Roger had found his calling, at least a portion of it. Song hits came pouring out, "Dang Me," "Chug-a-Lug," "England Swings," "Walkin' in the Sunshine," and his signature song, "King of the Road." In 1974 he composed and sang the songs for the animated Disney movie, *Robin Hood*. A number one fan of Roger's, Rocco Landesman, suggested that Roger should write a Broadway score for Mark Twain's *Adventures of Huckleberry Finn*. In 1985 *Big River* opened at Broadway's Eugene O'Neill Theatre. Roger received a Tony, the only country artist to achieve this high honor.

RONNIE **MILSAP**

JANUARY 16, 1943 - ROBBINSVILLE, NORTH CAROLINA

Ronnie was one of country music's most popular singers in the 1970s and 1980s and its first blind superstar.

Being born blind has not stifled Ronnie Lee Milsap's dreams of becoming a successful musician. He was reared by his father and grandparents near the Great Smoky Mountains. At the age of six, he was placed in the Governor Moorehead State School for the Blind. It was there that his teacher discovered Ronnie's extraordinary talent for music when he was only seven. Ronnie found solace in the compositions of BEETHOVEN and MOZART, but began to broaden his interest in other genres. He would listen to country, gospel, and blues on late night radio. After mastering several musical instruments including the violin, piano, guitar, and various woodwinds, Ronnie became almost obsessed with pop music. He started his first rock band, the APPARITIONS, while he was still in school.

Ronnie was offered a full scholarship to attend Emory University, but the desire to start his musical career became uppermost in his plans. In 1965 Ronnie married Frances Joyce Reeves, formed his own band, and recorded his first single for Scepter Records in New York. "Never Had It So Good" climbed to the Top Five on the *Billboard* soul chart. Four years later, he moved with his family to Memphis to become a session player.

When Ronnie came to the realization that he should stick with country music, he moved his family to Nashville on the day after Christmas in 1972. His first job was playing at the King of the Road Hotel. Four months after arriving in Music City, he became a client of JACK D. JOHNSON and signed with RCA Records. His first number one hit single, "I Hate You," began a string of forty number one hits.

Ronnie has said, "The only music I heard for the first six years of my life was country...I have played, and can play, any kind of music, but you must do what your heart feels is right, and to me that's country."

In 1977 Ronnie received CMA's Entertainer of the Year.

BILL MONROE

SEPTEMBER 13, 1911 - ROSINE, KENTUCKY - SEPTEMBER 9, 1996

Bill is considered the Father of Blue-grass Music. In 2003 he ranked number sixteen on CMT's 40 Greatest Men of Country Music.

"**T**here's not a prettier name in the world," mused Bill Monroe of the term *bluegrass.* The youngest of eight children, William Smith Monroe had lost both of his parents by age sixteen. Bill was already a seasoned performer by age twelve, playing his mandolin with his Uncle Pendleton. One of Bill's classic hits would be called "Uncle Pen."

Bill and his brothers, CHARLIE and BIRCH, traveled to the "Windy City" to perform on Chicago's WLS *National Barn Dance.* By 1935 the MONROE BROTHERS were gaining popularity and they moved to Charlotte, North Carolina's WBT. After the brothers split up in 1938, Bill formed the KENTUCKIANS, but a year later changed the name of the band to the BLUE GRASS BOYS, which would include banjo player, EARL SCRUGGS, singer-guitarist, LESTER FLATT, and CHUBBY WISE on the fiddle. More than 150 musicians played in the Blue Grass Boys in the almost sixty years of Bill's musical career.

With the fan base he had built, Bill was invited to join the Grand Ole Opry in 1939. He was only twenty-eight. Some of his compositions include, "Raw Hide," "Blue Moon of Kentucky," "Jerusalem Ridge," and "I Want the Lord to Protect My Soul." Although Bill didn't write JIMMIE RODGERS' standard, "Mule Skinner Blues," it became his signature song.

ELVIS PRESLEY included Bill's "Blue Moon of Kentucky" on the flip side of the first single he recorded at Sun Records, and Bill was inducted into the Rock and Roll Hall of Fame in 1997 for his contribution to that genre. In 1970 Bill was inducted into the Country Music Hall Fame®, and in 1989 his *Southern Flavor* album received the first Grammy given for bluegrass music. In 1993 he received a Grammy for Lifetime Achievement. In 2003 Bill Monroe was listed number sixteen on CMT's 40 Greatest Men of Country Music.

Patsy Montana

Patsy's self-penned song, "I Want to Be a Cowboy's Sweetheart," became the first record by a female country singer to sell a million copies.

Ruby Rebecca Blevins was the eleventh child and only girl in the Blevins home. JIMMIE RODGERS was her biggest influence as she learned to yodel and play the guitar, organ, and violin. In 1930 she moved to California with her brother. Patsy won a talent contest and landed an appearance on KMIC with STUART HAMBLEN. There was another singer with a similar name, and to prevent confusion, at Stuart's suggestion, she changed to Patsy and later added Montana. She sang with a trio of ladies who were billed as the MONTANA COWGIRLS.

When the trio broke up in the early 1930s, Patsy moved back to Arkansas and began performing on Shreveport's KWKH where she got the attention of JIMMIE DAVIS. She played the fiddle for Jimmie in her first recording session. A most unlikely event sent Patsy to Chicago to add another chapter to her singing career. Her brothers were entering the contest for the biggest watermelon at the Chicago World's Fair and Patsy decided to make the trip with them. She heard the KENTUCKY RAMBLERS of the WLS *National Barn Dance* and after the show learned that they needed a female singer. She was eventually hired. In 1935 she recorded "I Want to Be a Cowboy's Sweetheart" which became her biggest hit as well as her signature song. Other hits with the ARC label were "Rodeo Sweetheart," "Montana Plains," and "I Want to Be a Cowboy's Dream."

Between 1941 and 1945, Patsy recorded a dozen singles with Decca Records. After the war, she spent a couple of years with ABC radio on the *Wake Up and Smile* program. For several years she spent time in her home state with her husband, PAUL ROSE, and their two children. Patsy remained active in music into the 1990s and recorded several gospel albums.

Patsy Montana ranks number eighteen on CMT's Greatest Women of Country Music and was elected to the Country Music Hall of Fame.®

EDDIE **MONTGOMERY**

SEPTEMBER 30, 1963 - DANVILLE, KENTUCKY

Eddie teamed up with Troy Gentry to win Vocal Duo of the Year at the Country Music Association Awards in 2000.

When Eddie Montgomery joined forces with TROY GENTRY, an important new style of music had begun. Their sound has been described as "redneck country rock," which is an honest approach dealing with the working class. Other singers have come on board with the same authentic themes, such as HANK WILLIAMS JR., GRETCHEN WILSON, and BIG AND RICH.

Gerald Edward "Eddie" and his brother JOHN MICHAEL were part of a family band which played in honky-tonks during their formative years. Eddie says, "When you came in the house, you sat down on a guitar amp for a chair. My dad was a guitar player, my momma [Carol or 'Snookie'] was a drummer, and the bartenders were our babysitters." By the time Eddie was in his teens, he replaced his mother on the drums in his father's band, HAROLD MONTGOMERY AND THE KENTUCKY RIVER EXPRESS.

Eddie and John Michael left the family group while they were still teenagers to form their own band, EARLY TYMZ. Later TROY GENTRY joined the group and they changed their name to YOUNG COUNTRY. John Michael left to start a solo career and Troy soon left also. After Troy won the Jim Beam National Talent Contest in 1994, he toured with PATTY LOVELESS but soon rejoined Eddie to form MONTGOMERY GENTRY.

In 1999 the duo released their raucous debut album, *Tattoos and Scars,* which struck gold. Their next album, *Carrying On,* in 2001 sold 500,000. Montgomery Gentry's goal is to keep traditional country music alive in an era when pop country music seems to be taking over the airwaves. Eddie with his long coat and broad hat says, "Our sound isn't very polished...when you see us live, you're seeing a bunch of friends who grew up together, listening to the same records and same dream—and we found a way to keep going towards it."

John Michael **Montgomery**

JANUARY 20, 1965 - DANVILLE, KENTUCKY

Younger brother of Eddie Montgomery, John Michael's debut album, Life's a Dance, *in 1993 was the only album by a new artist to sell a million that year.*

John Michael and EDDIE grew up playing in the family band which also included their sister, Rebecca, mother, Carol, and father, Harold. By the time John Michael was five he was performing in the local clubs of Lexington, Kentucky. After his parents were divorced when he was seventeen, he became the lead singer in his father's band, the KENTUCKY RIVER EXPRESS.

John Michael and Eddie started their own band, EARLY TYMZ, but after TROY GENTRY joined the band they changed the name to YOUNG COUNTRY. When John Michael began his solo career, he went through some rough times in the late 1980s. His big break came in 1990. While he was singing at Austin City Saloon in Lexington, Atlantic Records liked what they were hearing and signed him to a record contract in January 1991.

John Michael's debut album, *Life's a Dance*, was released in 1992. From this album, "I Love the Way You Love Me," was a number one hit, while the title song hit the number four spot on the country charts. His next album, *Kickin' It Up*, scored big and produced four more hits, "I Swear," "Be My Baby Tonight," "If You Got Love," and "Rope the Moon." In 1994 John Michael was awarded the Country Music Association's Horizon Award, which profiles up-and-coming new artists.

In 1998 he released *What I Do Best*. After recovering from throat surgery, he released *Leave a Mark*. In 1999 *Home to You* would be followed with *Brand New Me* in 2000. John Michael switched his record label to Warner Brothers after Atlantic Records terminated its country division. In 2002 he released *Pictures* and a year later, *The Very Best of John Michael Montgomery*.

Staying close to his hometown of Nicholasville, Kentucky, John Michael spends quality time with his wife Crystal and two children.

George **Morgan**

JUNE 28, 1924 - WAVERLY, TENNESSEE - JULY 7, 1975

George's "Candy Kisses" stayed three weeks at number one on the country charts. He is the father of country singer, Lorrie Morgan.

George Morgan has been known as the "Candy Kid" since his first hit, "Candy Kisses," had three weeks at the top of the country charts. George, a country crooner much like EDDY ARNOLD, was born in Waverly, Tennessee. His family soon moved to Barberton, Ohio, where he grew up listening to the Grand Ole Opry. Although he had his first band in the 1940s and played sometimes on local radio, his career didn't grow until he wrote "Candy Kisses." It was then that WWVA in Wheeling, West Virginia, hired him on the *Wheeling Jamboree*. Not long after that the Opry called on George to replace Eddy Arnold and Columbia Records contacted him in 1948.

"Candy Kisses" was George's only number one hit, but six of his next seven singles made it to the country Top Ten. Three singles in the Top Ten and one that came close was a remarkable feat for a debut artist and his performances on the Opry kept his reputation alive. George was also known for his rose-themed songs including "Room Full of Roses," "Red Roses for a Blue Lady," and "Red Roses from the Blue Side of Town."

In 1956 George left the Opry for a time to host a Nashville television program at WLAC but came back to the Opry three years later. In 1974 it was George who had the distinction of being the last person to sing on the stage of the Ryman Auditorium.

The legacy of George Morgan lives on in his daughter, LORRIE MORGAN, a country artist in her own right. Thanks to today's technology, Lorrie has recorded a duet with her late father entitled "I'm Completely Satisfied with You" in 1979.

George Morgan is number forty-six on the list of Top 100 Country Artists of All Time.

LORRIE MORGAN

JUNE 27, 1959 - NASHVILLE, TENNESSEE

Lorrie has charted more than twenty-five singles on Billboard's Hot Country Singles. She is the daughter of country singer George Morgan.

Growing up backstage at the Grand Ole Opry as the daughter of GEORGE MORGAN should give one a good head start to a career in country music. Loretta Lynn Morgan was one of the lucky ones, but there is something to be said about maintaining star-power. At sixteen Lorrie lost her father and was catapulted into leadership of his band for the next two years.

Lorrie made her debut at the Opry when she was only thirteen, singing MARIE OSMOND'S "Paper Roses." It was the beginning of her professional ability to stand on her own and take on projects that have made her the successful artist she has become today. In her mid-twenties, Lorrie was invited to join the Grand Ole Opry. She has toured with GEORGE JONES and opened for a number of acts, including JACK GREENE.

Lorrie has always considered the Grand Ole Opry to be home. She says, "The Opry gave me my start in country music. It's a place we all need to go from time to time to remember why we're here and what gave us the opportunity to be here."

In 1979 Lorrie had a minor hit with "I'm Completely Satisfied" in which her father's voice was electronically dubbed. Nine years later, she had her first hit single, with "Trainwreck of Emotion." Her first number one single, "Five Minutes," was from her debut album, *Leave the Lights On*, in 1990. Lorrie was a superstar by then with two more number one hits, "What Part of No" and "I Didn't Know My Own Strength." Other albums that have struck gold are *Something in Red* and *Watch Me*.

Lorrie has appeared with pop legends such as the BEACH BOYS, and has recorded duets with ANDY WILLIAMS, FRANK SINATRA, JOHNNY MATHIS, and DOLLY PARTON.

Lorrie has a daughter, Morgan, and a son named Jessie.

ANNE **MURRAY**

JUNE 20, 1945 - SPRINGHILL, NOVA SCOTIA, CANADA

Anne's second album, This Way Is My Way, *featured "Snowbird" and launched her career in 1969. Her biggest hit was "You Needed Me."*

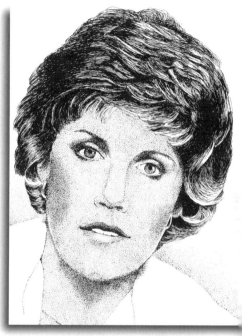

At seven years of age, Morna Anne Murray was discovering her gift as Canada's songbird. Little did she know that she would pave the way for other female singers such as CÉLINE DION, SHANIA TWAIN, and K.D. LANG. A couple of years later, Anne's aunt-to-be heard her singing with the car radio and told her mother that she had a beautiful voice. Anne says, "I later found out that Aunt Kay was tone deaf, but I guess it doesn't mean she couldn't detect talent!" In her late teens, Anne became interested in rock and roll with some of her favorite singers being BUDDY HOLLY, BOBBY DARIN, and CONNIE FRANCIS. She was also influenced by the likes of gospel, folk, and country musicians.

By the time Anne was fifteen, she was taking classical voice lessons and after high school, she attended Mount Saint Vincent University in Halifax. Although she failed the first audition for the CBS television show, *Sing-Along Jubilee,* two years later they remembered her unique voice and she got the job. Capitol Records signed Anne to a contract in the fall of 1969. In 1970 Anne became the first Canadian female in country music with a gold record. The album was *This Way Is My Way.* She received the Juno, Canada's Grammy equivalent, in 1971 for Best Female Vocalist. Her first Grammy came in 1974 for her hit, "A Love Song." It wasn't long until she became a regular on *The Glen Campbell Goodtime Hour.*

Anne's biggest hit was "You Needed Me" which earned her second Grammy. In 1999 Anne recorded twenty-six classic hymns on *What a Wonderful World.* She has had eleven number one hits on the country charts and twenty-five of her albums have sold more than a half million copies. Anne Murray ranked number twenty-four in the CMT's 40 Greatest Women of Country Music in 2002. She is married to Bill Langstroth and they have two children, William and Dawn.

WILLIE **NELSON**

APRIL 30, 1933 - ABBOTT, TEXAS

Two of Willie's best known songs are "Crazy" and "Hello Walls." He achieved success in the early 1970s in a genre called "outlaw country."

Growing up in the small farming town of Abbott, Texas, during the Great Depression, Willie and his sister Bobbie Lee were reared by their paternal grandparents. Willie's first musical training came from a mail order course. By the time Willie was ten, he had played for a dance and five years later he had a regular gig in local honky-tonks. Before he graduated from high school, Willie had his own radio show. As a songwriter, his first song sold was "No Place for Me." By 1959 he was writing songs while holding down a full-time job as a disc-jockey. After he sold "Night Light," Willie could afford to try his luck in Nashville. By 1961 he had scored two number one hits for FARON YOUNG'S "Hello Walls" and PATSY CLINE'S "Crazy." BILLY WALKER also did well with Willie's "Funny How Time Slips Away."

In 1965 Willie signed with RCA Records and joined the Grand Ole Opry. His singing career has included more than eighty duos with such artists as JULIO IGLESIAS, RAY CHARLES, ROGER MILLER, PORTER WAGONER, DOLLY PARTON, MERLE HAGGARD, BRENDA LEE, SHERYL CROW, and NEIL YOUNG. In 1985 three other heavyweights joined Willie to create the HIGHWAYMEN, which included WAYLON JENNINGS, JOHNNY CASH, and KRIS KRISTOFFERSON. They scored a number one hit single with JIMMY WEBB'S song, "Highwayman."

Willie has won nine of his forty-three nominations from the Country Music Association. The first country music album to be rated platinum was his *Wanted: The Outlaw*. In 2002 he earned a Grammy for his duet with LEE ANN WOMACK, "Mendocino County Line."

Willie's signature song, "On the Road Again," was from one of his films, *Honeysuckle Rose*. He ranks number four on the 40 Greatest Men in Country Music.

JENNIFER **NETTLES**

SEPTEMBER 12, 1974 - DOUGLAS, GEORGIA

As lead singer for Sugarland, Jennifer is a Grammy winner with Bon Jovi. They were nominated in the Best New Artist category.

From the early age of seven, Jennifer has been performing for her church and for school functions. Before she graduated from Coffee County High School in 1992, she had completed several music compositions. Jennifer and her high school friend, CORY JONES, began writing songs together, and by 1995 they had started their own band called SOUL MINER'S DAUGHTER. The duo released two albums in 1996 and 1998, *The Sacred and Profane* and *Hallelujah*. A year later, as Jennifer was changing her focus and dealing with more personal material, she started her own band, the JENNIFER NETTLES BAND.

Jennifer's voice has been compared to a young and gutsy REBA MCENTIRE with the sass of GRETCHEN WILSON. *Story of Your Bones*, her first album, earned the Independent Musician of the Year Award in 2000 from Musician's Atlas. KRISTEN HALL and KRISTIAN BUSH offered Jennifer the lead singer position in their country band, SUGARLAND. From their first album, *Twice the Speed of Light*, Sugarland picked up their first big hit, "Baby Girl." In 2005 they won Favorite Breakthrough Artist and were nominated for a Grammy as Best New Artist. After Kristen left the group, Jennifer and Kristian released *Enjoy the Ride* which sold more than three million copies.

BON JOVI joined Jennifer to record "Who Says You Can't Go Home?" The song soared to number one on the *Billboard* Hot Country Singles chart and to the Top 25 on the *Billboard* 100 chart. Jennifer also earned her first Grammy Award for Best Country Collaboration in 2007. ABC's *Good Morning America* has been using Sugarland's song, "Everyday America" as its theme, so millions can hear Jennifer's voice each morning.

In 2008 Sugarland won the CMA Award for Duo of the Year. At the same event, Jennifer also won Song of the Year for Sugarland's "Stay." With perfect harmony, Sugarland is enjoying a wave of sweet success.

BOB NOLAN

APRIL 13, 1908 - WINNIPEG, MANITOBA - JUNE 16, 1980

Bob was an original member of the Sons of the Pioneers. He is best known for his songs "Tumbling Tumbleweeds" and "Cool Water."

Clarence Robert Nobles, later Robert Clarence, was born in the Canadian province of Manitoba. He had little exposure to music except for the twice-a-year old-fashioned camp meetings held nearby. Robert was sent to Boston for his schooling and there was introduced to American folk music. At age fourteen, Robert (now Bob) joined his father, a army officer, who had retired to the Southwest. Bob's father felt that a name change was in order at this point in his life. He thought the name Nobles wasn't American enough and since he liked the Irish, he chose Nolan.

Bob graduated from high school in Tucson and attended the University of Arizona where he studied music and poetry. While in college, Bob began writing poetry about the desert, that later became lyrics for his songs. In 1927 he caught a train going East and feeling restless took the next train going back West. Not finding satisfaction, Bob traveled the country several times simply drifting and writing songs. In 1931 he turned to a career in music. He went to an audition conducted by none other than LEONARD SLYE (the future ROY ROGERS). The two joined with TIM SPENCER to form the ROCKY MOUNTAINEERS. The group became the PIONEER TRIO and then the SONS OF THE PIONEERS.

While train sounds haunt the lyrics of Bob's early songs, "Way Out There" and "One More Ride," he is best known for his cowboy melodies, "Cool Water" and "Tumbling Tumbleweeds." Not only were these songs standards, but they became classics of the western style. Bob's love of the desert can be heard through much of his work.

In 1971 Bob was elected to the Nashville Songwriters Hall of Fame. The Sons of the Pioneers were inducted into the Country Music Hall of Fame® in 1979.

ROY **ORBISON**

APRIL 23, 1936 - VERNON, TEXAS - DECEMBER 6, 1988

Known as "The Big O," Roy was a Grammy Award-winner. Songs he is known for include "Only the Lonely," "It's Over," and "Pretty Woman."

Because he was known for wearing his trademark dark glasses, Roy's fans originally thought he was blind. He suffered from myopia or near-sightedness requiring thick corrective lenses. Young Roy's family moved to a small oil town in western Texas called Wink. After his father taught him how to play the guitar, Roy began performing on the radio. He formed his first country band, the WINK WESTERNERS, while he was still in high school. At North Texas State College in the mid-1950s, his style of music changed with the times to rock and roll. His new band was called TEEN KINGS and got noticed from western Texas to Memphis, Tennessee. Sun Records recorded his first hit "Ooby Dooby" in 1956. Two years later the EVERLY BROTHERS recorded, "Claudette," one of Roy's songs.

By 1959 Roy had disbanded the group and signed a record contract with Monument in Nashville. Roy wrote some of his best-loved songs from 1960 to 1964, including "Only the Lonely," "Blue Angel," "Running Scared," "Blue Bayou," "It's Over," and "Pretty Woman." While Roy was on tour in England in 1963, his opening act was the not-yet-famous BEATLES. Tragedy struck in the mid-1960s for the Orbisons. Roy's wife, Claudette, was killed in a motorcycle accident; two years later in 1968, his home in Nashville caught fire and two of his three sons died. Roy married Barbara Wellnoener-Jacobs in 1969 and had two more sons.

In 1980 Roy recorded "That Loving You Feeling Again" with EMMYLOU HARRIS. The album earned them a Grammy. He recorded *The Traveling Wilburys Volume One* with BOB DYLAN, GEORGE HARRISON, TOM PETTY, and JEFF LYNNE. Near the end of his life, he recorded a version of "Crying" with K.D. LANG.

ELVIS PRESLEY once said that Roy Orbison was "the greatest singer in the world" and BARRY GIBB referred to Roy as the "Voice of God."

Marie Osmond

OCTOBER 13, 1959 - OGDEN, UTAH

At thirteen Marie's "Paper Roses" shot up to number one on the country charts. It ranked number five on pop charts in 1973.

ANDY WILLIAMS once introduced three-year-old Marie as "the youngest Osmond Brother." Ten years later, she released her smash hit, "Paper Roses," and to a sold-out crowd in Madison Square Garden performed with her brothers. Marie was the only girl born to George and Olive Osmond, causing the OSMOND BROTHERS to change their group's name to the OSMONDS. Her "Paper Roses" not only struck gold but Marie received a Grammy nomination for Best Female Country Vocal Performance and Best New Artist in 1974. Her duet with brother DONNY, "I'm Leavin' It All Up to You," climbed to number four on the pop charts. In January of 1976, when ABC launched the weekly variety show, *The Donny and Marie Show*, Marie would sing "I'm a little bit country," and Donny would answer "I'm a little bit rock 'n' roll." The show ran until 1981 and set fashion standards with hair styles and wardrobes throughout the world.

Marie's acting career began in 1979 with the TV movie, *The Gift of Love*. She followed it up three years later portraying her mother in *Side By Side: The Story of the Osmond Family*. In 1985 she co-hosted the television series, *Ripley's Believe It or Not*. The same year she provided her voice-over and singing to *The Velveteen Rabbit*.

With two more number one country hits from the album, *There's No Stopping Your Heart*, including the title track and "Meet Me In Montana," Marie was back racking up awards once more. In the 1990s, Marie landed on Broadway with leading roles in both *The Sound of Music* and *The King and I*. In season five of *Dancing with the Stars*, twenty-five million viewers tuned in to see her go all the way to the finals.

This mother of eight is a proud co-founder with JOHN SCHNEIDER of the *Children's Miracle Network* which has raised 3.4 billion dollars.

PAUL **OVERSTREET**

MARCH 17, 1955 - NEWTON, MISSISSIPPI

Paul is best known as a country singer and songwriter. His "Forever and Ever, Amen" was a huge hit for Randy Travis.

It was scripted from the beginning of time that Paul would become one of the most successful songwriters in Music City, U.S.A. In his early life in Mississippi, he met with hardship when his mother and father were divorced. His family had to rely on assistance from the government until his mother remarried. Paul and his siblings learned to harmonize while their mother played the piano. The radio became an important part of Paul's life as he listened to his favorite singers, including JIM REEVES, JOHNNY HORTON, HANK WILLIAMS, CHARLIE PRIDE, MARTY ROBBINS, and MERLE HAGGARD. Paul was inspired to pursue a career in songwriting after seeing the 1964 film, *Your Cheatin' Heart,* that told the story of Hank Williams. He spent summers with his father in California learning to play most of CREEDENCE CLEARWATER REVIVAL'S songs.

After his high school graduation in 1973, Paul drove his 1968 Ford Fairlane to Nashville seeking a successful career in the music industry. Finding more success as a songwriter, he eventually scored big with twenty-five Top Ten songs that were recorded by other singers. In 1982 GEORGE JONES recorded "Same Ole Me" which climbed to number five on the country charts. Paul was now on his way! With RANDY TRAVIS recording and scoring big with "On the Other Hand" and his Grammy winner, "Forever and Ever, Amen," Paul was now a writer to be taken seriously.

In 1982 Paul fulfilled his dream of becoming a singer. His first release was "Beautiful Baby." In the early 1990s, Paul turned to Christian songwriting, labeled by *Billboard* as "Positive Country." He founded Scarlet Moon Records in 1999 as a sub-label to Integrity. Paul and his wife, Julie, live near Nashville with their six children. He is involved with Samaritan's Place, a relief ministry helping people in crisis worldwide.

RANDY OWEN

DECEMBER 13, 1949 - FORT PAYNE, ALABAMA

Randy was lead singer for the group ALABAMA. They released twenty-one gold albums and sold seventy-three million records.

The state of Alabama can be proud of three cousins who got together to make a little music in 1969. The group was called YOUNG COUNTRY and the young men were TEDDY GENTRY, JEFF COOK, and RANDY OWEN. In 1972 the name changed to WILDCOUNTRY. In 1977 the group became ALABAMA. They had just signed a record contract with GRT and released a minor hit single, "I Wanna Be With You Tonight."

When lead singer Randy and company released "My Home's In Alabama," they were invited to sing at the Country Music New Faces show where they were noticed by RCA who released their single, "Tennessee River." It was the beginning of twenty-seven number one hits.

Randy writes in his autobiography, *Born Country,* about his father's death just before ALABAMA gained national notice. He says, "I really didn't have a chance to mourn. Some of the most successful days I had as an entertainer were some of the saddest days for me..."

Little did Randy know while he was growing up on a cotton farm on Lookout Mountain that he and his cousins would become the Country Group of the Century. ALABAMA earned 150 industry awards plus a star on the Hollywood Walk of Fame. Randy's hometown is also proud of Randy, Teddy, Jeff, and their drummer, MARK HERNDON. A larger-than-life bronze statue honors the group in Fort Payne, Alabama.

In June of 2008, Randy received an NAB Education Foundation's Celebration of Service to America Award on behalf of Country Cares for St. Jude Kids. Thanks to his role in establishing a radio fund raising event in 1989, County Cares has raised over $340 million.

Randy writes in his book, "God had a big plan for me and guided me through the good and the bad."

BUCK **OWENS**

AUGUST 12, 1929 - SHERMAN, TEXAS - MARCH 25, 2006

Buck co-hosted the Hee Haw *TV show with Roy Clark for seven years. Known as a songwriter and singer, he helped create the Bakersfield Sound.*

Alvis Edgar Owens Jr. got his nickname from a mule on the north Texas farm where his family were sharecroppers. The Owens family of ten had planned a move to the West Coast in 1937, much like the family in John Steinbeck's *The Grapes of Wrath*. They made it to Arizona before they had transportation problems and decided to settle in Mesa. By 1945 Buck had mastered the guitar and mandolin and began performing on the radio and in local clubs. Six years later, he moved to Bakersfield, California, a locale that was becoming a haven for country-western musicians.

Buck began working in recording sessions in Los Angeles and played at the Blackboard Club at night. He was twenty-eight in 1957 when he signed a contract with Capitol Records. Buck had his first two hits in 1959 with "Second Fiddle" and "Under Your Spell Again." Big changes were on the horizon. Buck moved back to Bakersfield and formed his first band, the BUCKAROOS. "Crying Time," recorded by RAY CHARLES, was just one of many songs Buck wrote that were popularized by other artists. In all, he had over forty songs in the Top Ten on country charts. Included are "I've Got a Tiger by the Tail," "Act Naturally," "Love's Gonna Live Here," "Together Again," and "Waiting in Your Welfare Line." According to *Billboard*, Buck had twenty-one number one hits in twenty-five years.

With the help of his old buddy, ROY CLARK, Buck agreed to co-host *Hee Haw*, the country version of the comedy show, *Laugh-In*. He also hosted his own syndicated television show, *Buck Owens' Ranch Show*.

Buck performed at Carnegie Hall, the London Palladium, and at the White House. He was elected to the Country Music Hall of Fame® and the Nashville Songwriters Hall of Fame in 1996. Buck ranks number twelve in CTM's 40 Greatest Men of Country Music.

PATTI **PAGE**

Patti's legendary "Tennessee Waltz" reached number one concurrently on the pop and country charts and sold more than ten million records.

Grammy Award-winner Patti Page is one of America's true musical icons. In the course of her remarkable seven-decade career, Patti has sold over one hundred million records, making her one of the biggest selling female recording artists in history. She has charted a staggering 111 hits on pop, country, and R&B charts, with fifteen gold singles and four gold albums.

Patti's silky-smooth voice engulfed the airwaves during the 1950s and 1960s, as she became the first crossover artist to take country music onto the pop charts with such million-record sellers as "Mockin' Bird Hill," "Mister and Mississippi," and "I Went To Your Wedding." Her legendary, ten million seller, "Tennessee Waltz," reached number one concurrently on both pop and country charts.

Born Clara Ann Fowler, this Oklahoma girl began her professional career at KTUL in Tulsa, Oklahoma, as an on-air singer. On weekends she performed with another KTUL personality, AL CLAUSER and his OKLAHOMA OUTLAWS. This was also where she was chosen as host of "Meet Patti Page," a program sponsored by the Page Milk Company, and her name became Patti Page forever thereafter.

As a Mercury Records artist, Patti changed the way pop music was recorded. On New Year's Eve in 1947, with the help of the studio engineer and a revolutionary new technique that permitted Patti to echo her own voice, she recorded "Confess." The song climbed to number twelve on the charts in 1948. Patti's success continued with "I Don't Care If the Sun Don't Shine" and her first million record seller, "With My Eyes Wide Open I'm Dreaming."

After nearly seventy years, Patti's accomplishments remain unparalleled. Today, she continues to use her sweet, tranquil voice to touch the hearts of many generations with new recordings and live performances.

Brad **Paisley**

OCTOBER 28, 1972 - GLEN DALE, WEST VIRGINIA

Brad has charted nineteen singles on Billboard's Hot Country Songs, *nine of which reached number one. "He Didn't Have to Be" was his first hit.*

Brad's first big influence in preparing for a music career is etched in his mind. He recalls, "My earliest memory is of running down the road to my grandfather's house. He was a railroad worker who worked the night shift. So he'd be at home all afternoon playing guitar." Brad was eight when his grandfather gave him a Sears Danelectro Silvertone guitar with an amp. He soon began playing and singing at church and for civic clubs. Brad formed his first band, BRAD PAISLEY AND THE C-NOTES, before he had reached his teens. "Born on Christmas Day" was the first song he wrote at age twelve. Brad's principal asked him to play the song at the next Rotary Club meeting. By chance the program director for radio WWVA, TOM MILLER, was present.

With Miller's recommendation, Brad was invited to perform for the station's Saturday night show, JAMBOREE USA. Brad played for the show for eight years as an opening act for ROY CLARK, JACK GREENE, and LITTLE JIMMY DICKENS. During the show's outdoor summer festival, Brad became a seasoned performer playing to crowds of sixty thousand.

Brad attended the local college, West Liberty, but transfered to Belmont University in Nashville. His internship was served at ASCAP and later he signed with EMI Music Company as a songwriter. Brad debuted on the Grand Ole Opry, May 28, 1999, and two years later he became a member. After signing with Arista Records as a singer, Brad released his debut album, *Who Needs Pictures,* which produced two hit singles, "He Didn't Have to Be" and "We Danced." Brad received the Country Music Association's Horizon Award and the Academy of Country Music's Best Male Vocalist Award in 2000. With other albums following, *Part II, Time Well Wasted,* and *Brad Paisley Christmas,* Brad has become one the favorite country singers of the twenty-first century.

DOLLY **PARTON**

JANUARY 19, 1946 - LOCUST RIDGE, TENNESSEE

Dolly is a Grammy winner, an Oscar nominee, musician, singer, songwriter, author, and actress. Her song, "I Will Always Love You," was a mega hit.

From the backwoods of Tennessee, Dolly Parton has become one of the most successful international female country stars. Dolly says, "As a child, I was always around music, and all of my people played fiddles, mandolins, banjos, and guitars. I was especially in love with the banjo." She was inspired by pioneer female singers, such as KITTY WELLS, BRENDA LEE, and PATSY CLINE. Dolly first sang in church, and by the age of ten, she was on television appearing on *The Cass Walker Program* out of Knoxville. The Grand Ole Opry was the next big venue where Dolly performed at the age of twelve. In 1960 she debuted on The *Porter Wagoner Show* and released the album, "Hello, I'm Dolly."

Dolly moved to Nashville and signed with Monument Records the day after she graduated from high school in 1964. Her first minor hit was "Dumb Blonde." She recorded several country hits, including "Just Someone I Used to Know," "Daddy Was an Old Time Preacher Man." Her first number one solo hit came in 1970 with "Joshua" and a year later, "Coat of Many Colors" climbed to number four. "Jolene" became her second number one hit in 1974. When she left the *Porter Wagoner Show* that same year, Dolly wrote "I Will Always Love You." The song became a hit for LINDA RONSTADT in 1975, a hit for Dolly in 1980, and in 1992 was a mega hit for WHITNEY HOUSTON. Dolly scored another number one hit with the song "Nine to Five" from her debut movie in which she co-starred with LILY TOMLIN and JANE FONDA. She was nominated for an Oscar in 2006 for the song "Travelin' Thru" from the film *Transamerica*.

Dolly's humorous quotes: "I would have been very tall had I not gotten so bunched up at the top." "It takes a lot of money to look this cheap." There is nothing cheap or lacking from this international superstar with her humble beginnings in a one-room cabin in Locust Ridge.

LES **PAUL**

JUNE 9, 1915 - WAUKESHA, WISCONSIN

Les is one of the most talented music innovators of the twentieth century. He invented the solid-body electric guitar and the first eight-track tape recorder.

The "Wizard of Waukesha" was playing the harmonica and guitar at an early age. Lester William Polsfuss shortened his name for the stage because "that leaves more time for guitar playin'." When he was thirteen, Les was already performing as a country music guitarist and working with sound-related inventions. In 1932 Les and JOE WOLVERTON, known as the OZARK APPLE KNOCKERS, were playing on KMOX in St. Louis and WBBM in Chicago. Les also played with RUBE TRONSON'S COWBOYS and WOLVERTON'S RADIO BAND.

Les was soon experimenting with amplifying his guitar. He understood that an acoustic guitar uses its hollowness to get the vibration of sound, but with electricity a solid body created a purer sound quality. Les built his first electric guitar from a four inch square chunk of pine with a microphone pickup attached. He called it "The Log." In the early 1940s, Les experimented with electronically amplified guitar strings and modified his tape recorder to produce "sound on sound" or what today is known as overdubbing. It was Les who introduced the first eight-track tape recorder in 1952.

Four years earlier, Les was in a near fatal automobile accident which shattered his right arm and elbow. The surgeon set his arm at an angle to allow him to continue holding and playing the guitar. After his recovery, Les teamed up with country singer, COLLEEN SUMMERS. Les changed her name to MARY FORD and they were married in 1949. *The Les Paul and Mary Ford at Home Show* was broadcast from 1953 to 1960. The couple recorded dozens of hits for Capitol Records, including "Vaya con Dios" and "How High the Moon." In 1975 Les and CHET ATKINS recorded an album, *Chester and Lester,* featuring a guitar duet. They earned a Grammy for Best Country Instrumental Performance.

JOHNNY PAYCHECK

MAY 31, 1938 - GREENFIELD, OHIO - FEBRUARY 19, 2003

Although Johnny is best known for the song "Take This Job and Shove It!," his ballad, "Someone to Give Love To," is closer to his stylistic range.

For the first twenty-seven years of Johnny Paycheck's life, his name was Donald Eugene Lytle. At the age of nine, Johnny first realized his dream to be a singer when he billed himself the "Ohio Kid" and began playing in talent contests. At fifteen, Johnny caught a freight train out of town to fulfill the dream. After a few years of playing in honky-tonks, he joined the navy in the mid-1950s. This proved to be a mistake. Johnny was court-martialed and served two years in a military prison for striking a superior officer.

After his release, Johnny was trying to get his life back on track and decided to take a chance in Nashville. BUDDY KILLEN of Tree Publishing hired him as a writer. Johnny signed a contract with Decca Records and changed his name to Donny Young. His debut album, *Shakin' the Blues,* failed to make it into the charts. After other failed attempts, Johnny began playing with well-known bands including those backing PORTER WAGONER, RAY PRICE, FARON YOUNG, and GEORGE JONES.

In 1966 Johnny legally changed his name to Johnny Paycheck after a Chicago boxer. That same year he met producer AUBREY MAYHEW. The two formed Little Darlin' Records. Johnny got his first Top Ten hit with "The Lovin' Machine." "Apartment #9," co-written with CHARLES "FUZZY" OWEN and BOBBY AUSTIN, earned the ACM Song of the Year Award. Johnny signed with Epic Records and "She's All I Got" peaked at number two by the end of 1971. During the "outlaw country movement" of the 1970s, Johnny fit right in. "Take This Job and Shove It!" became the anthem of dissatisfaction in the workplace and earned Johnny his only number one single.

Johnny served two more years in prison and was released in 1991. He remained clean and sober and gave anti-drug talks to young kids until his death. Johnny became a member of the Grand Ole Opry in 1997.

150

MINNIE **PEARL**

OCTOBER 25, 1912 - CENTERVILLE, TENNESSEE - MARCH 4, 1996

Sarah Colley Cannon, better known as Cousin Minnie Pearl, greeted her fans at the Grand Ole Opry with "How-dee! I'm just so proud to be here!"

Born Sarah Ophelia Colley, the daughter of a well-to-do lumberman in Centerville, Tennessee, Minnie Pearl fell in love with vaudeville and drama at an early age. She often would sneak into tent shows, much to her parents' displeasure. She attended Ward-Belmont College in Nashville where she majored in theater and planned to be a serious actress. As a young woman she liked classical music rather than country and in college she especially focused on her classes in dance.

After graduation, Sarah taught dance for a time until she took a job as drama coach with an Atlanta-based traveling theater group. While performing with the group in Baileyton, Alabama, Sarah met a young mountain woman on whom she based her much-beloved character of Minnie Pearl. In 1939 Sarah gave her first stage performance as Minnie Pearl in Aiken, South Carolina. It was her introduction to the audience at the Grand Ole Opry that sent her career sky rocketing to stardom in 1940. When cards and letters began pouring in, Minnie Pearl's place as a cast member was assured. The character of Minnie Pearl continued to be a part of the Opry until Sarah's death in 1996, a span of over fifty years. She also entertained around the world for charitable events and received many awards for her contributions to humanity.

As Minnie Pearl, Sarah was inducted into the Country Music Hall of Fame® in 1975. She received the American Cancer Society's Courage Award in 1987, the National Medal of Art in 1991, and was voted Country Music Woman of the Year in 1996.

Sarah had little in common with the brash country bumpkin that was Minnie. Says CHARLES K. WOLFE, country music author, "She was the epitome of the old gentrified Nashville." Sarah was married to Henry Cannon, a pilot and businessman, for more than fifty years.

KELLIE **PICKLER**

Kellie, country singer and songwriter with an effervescent personality, finished sixth on the fifth season of the Fox television series, American Idol.

We've come to know her as the blonde roller-skating waitress from the local Sonic Drive-In who placed sixth in season five of *American Idol.* Kellie was born to a teen mother who abandoned her at age two to be raised by Clyde and Faye Pickler, her paternal grandparents, in tiny Albemarle, North Carolina.

Kellie graduated from North Stanly High School in nearby New London where she was a cheerleader and a dancer and sang, "On the Side of Angels," at her commencement. Kellie was only an average student but her beauty set her apart from the rest. She was Miss Stanly County at age seventeen before she entered the Miss North Carolina pageant. From the pageant she earned a scholarship to Stanly Community College to study cosmetology but later changed to paralegal studies.

After receiving her associate's degree, Kellie put her education on hold to audition for *American Idol.* From her stint on the show, she was signed to a recording contract with BNA Records, a division of Sony BMG. Kellie's first album, *Small Town Girl,* was released on October 31, 2006. It placed ninth on the *Billboard* Top 200 and first on the Country Album Chart. The album sold seventy-nine thousand copies in its first week. Kellie wrote five of the songs on the album along with producer BLAKE CHANCEY. A video was made from the debut single, "Red High Heels." In its third week, the video reached number two on the GAC Top Twenty Countdown. Kellie's older sister also appears in the video.

With a vivacious and effervescent personality, Kellie is known for her Southern charm. She says, "A good attitude and being positive can make a huge difference in one's life." Hers is a life that could be the stuff of a good country song.

During 2008 Kellie toured with BRAD PAISLEY.

WEBB **PIERCE**

AUGUST 8, 1921 - WEST MONROE, LOUISIANA - FEBRUARY 24, 1991

Webb was known as the "King of Honky-Tonk Music" in the 1950s with thirteen number one hits and ninety-one charted singles.

Growing up in northern Louisiana, Webb Michael Pierce was influenced by the Cajun sound familiar in his hometown. He also loved the music of JIMMIE RODGERS and GENE AUTRY. Webb was motivated to learn to play the guitar before he reached his teens and by the age of sixteen, he landed his own radio show as a singer on Monroe, Louisiana's KMLB. After serving in the army for three years, he moved to Shreveport in 1944 where he was a shoe salesman for Sears and Roebuck.

Webb gradually began singing in his honky-tonk style in area nightclubs, and by the late 1940s, he was hired to sing on the *Louisiana Hayride*. He became a major star for the powerful radio station KWKH that had developed the *Hayride*. In 1951 Webb signed with Decca Records and released his first number one hit single, "Wondering." The band he formed, the WONDERING BOYS, included FLOYD CRAMER and FARON YOUNG.

With his new-found success, Webb moved to Nashville in 1952. There he met Audrey Greisham and the two were soon married. Webb soon had another number one hit, "That Heart Belongs to Me." After HANK WILLIAMS left the Grand Ole Opry, Webb was invited to replace him as a member of the cast. Webb's number one hits began piling up including, "There Stands the Glass," "Slowly," and "In the Jailhouse Now."

Webb and JIM DENNY, manager of the Opry, started their own music publishing company and began investing in radio stations. Webb left the Opry in 1955 and became a featured performer on the *Ozark Jubilee*. He rejoined the Grand Ole Opry the following year.

Webb's illustrious career charted fifty-five Top Ten songs, thirteen of which became number one singles. He was the number one singer of the 1950s with records sales of over sixty-five million. He was inducted posthumously into the Country Music Hall of Fame® on October 5, 2001.

153

Elvis **Presley**

JANUARY 8, 1935 - TUPELO, MISSISSIPPI - AUGUST 16, 1977

Before 1955 Elvis sang locally as the "Hillybilly Cat." The "King of Rock 'n' Roll" has sold over one billion records world-wide.

After graduating from Humes High School in 1953, Elvis drove a truck for the Crown Electric Company. No one could guess that soon this poor rockabilly singer would send shockwaves throughout the world with his music. Elvis had been attending the Assembly of God church since the family moved to Memphis and the gospel music he heard there had a profound effect on his life. In 1954 Elvis began his singing career at Sun Records and on October 2, 1954, he sang on the Grand Ole Opry for the first and only time. By 1955 he had a record contract with RCA. In his first recording session, BEN and BROCK SPEER along with GORDON STOKER and the JORDANAIRES sang backup.

Elvis' love for gospel, black rhythm and blues, and country music congealed into a fresh genre of music. He recorded his first single, "Heartbreak Hotel," in March 1956. The song spent seventeen weeks on *Billboard's* country chart and ten weeks on the Hot 100. It also became the number one country song of 1956. His last number one single on the pop charts, "Suspicious Minds," was recorded in September 1969. Elvis' best selling singles of the 1950s were "Hound Dog" and "Don't Be Cruel." The best selling single of the 1960s was "It's Now or Never" in 1960. The week of his death in 1977, his recording of "Way Down" was the number one song on *Billboard's* country singles chart.

Elvis was honored with induction into the Rock and Roll Hall of Fame, the Gospel Music Hall of Fame, and the Country Music Hall of Fame®. In 1993 the U.S. Postal Service sold more of the twenty-nine cent commemorative stamp that honored Elvis than any other stamp in history. All of these accolades show that his talent and charisma endeared him to countless fans around the world, as did the kindness he demonstrated throughout his short life.

RAY **PRICE**

JANUARY 12, 1926 - PERRYVILLE, TEXAS

Ray was elected to the Country Music Hall of Fame® in 1996. He is considered to be a country-western singer, songwriter, and guitarist.

Dividing his time between his father's farm and his mother's home in Dallas, Ray dreamed of a career as a veterinarian. Following high school graduation, he enrolled at North Texas Agricultural College in Abilene. After serving in WWII as a marine, Ray returned to Dallas. He began to travel down a different path while singing at Roy's House Cafe. JIM BECK, a record entrepreneur, liked what he heard and recorded Ray for the Nashville based Bullet label. Through his appearances on the *Big D Jamboree*, TROY MARTIN made the connection for Ray to sign a contract with Columbia Records. He recorded a song by HANK WILLIAMS called "Weary Blues," from *Waitin'* which sold enough records to secure his membership in the Grand Ole Opry in 1952.

Hank's influence on Ray could be heard on his first charted hit, "Talk to Your Heart." The two became close friends and Ray even used Hank's DRIFTING COWBOYS as his backup band. By 1956 Ray had developed his own sound and recorded his honky-tonk rendering of "Crazy Arms" which became his first number one hit. Ray had developed the "Ray Price beat," an experiment with a 4/4 shuffle beat. The new beat is an integral part of country music today.

Ray's band, the CHEROKEE COWBOYS, included singers WILLIE NELSON, ROGER MILLER, and JOHNNY PAYCHECK. Ray had already scored big hits with "Heartaches by the Number" and "City Lights" when he recorded the pop ballad, "Make the World Go Away." Some of his fans preferred his honky-tonk style to his 1967 version of "Danny Boy." Ray's huge crossover to the pop charts was "For the Good Times" in 1970.

Ray became one of the best innovators in country music. As DON HELMS of the Drifting Cowboys once said, Ray Price created an era."

Ray was inducted into the Country Music Hall of Fame® in 1996.

CHARLEY **PRIDE**

MARCH 18, 1938 - SLEDGE, MISSISSIPPI

· ·

During his career, Charley has had thirty-six number one hits. One of these hits came in 1971 with "Kiss an Angel Good Morning."

With his rich baritone voice, Charley Pride has appealed to all races and generations since his early days of playing ball with the Negro American League's Memphis Red Sox. Self-taught on a guitar purchased at fourteen from Sears and Roebuck, Charlie would sing and play on the team bus as they rode between ballparks. He also had gigs to play onstage with several bands as his team traveled the country. With encouragement from RED FOLEY and RED SOVINE, Charley took a trip to Nashville where he met JACK CLEMENT and was asked to learn some songs. Charley cut a demo that reached the hands and ears of CHET ATKINS. Atkins was so impressed with Charley's renditions that he signed him to RCA Records.

From his first number one hit, "All I Have to Offer (Is Me)," in 1969, until he last hit the top in 1984 with "Every Heart Should Have One," Charley had more than thirty-six number one country singles. In sales at RCA, Charley has sold over seventy million albums, second only to ELVIS PRESLEY. Dozens of Charley's songs that topped the charts have become today's classics. "Kiss an Angel Good Morning" was a million-selling crossover single that won him Entertainer of the Year from the CMA in 1971, as well as Top Male Vocalist in 1971 and 1972.

In his autobiography, Charley tells of his humble beginnings, a long-lasting marriage to Rozene, whom he met in his baseball days, his first singing engagement that led to an amazing career as the first and only African American superstar in country music. When Charley joined the Grand Ole Opry in 1993, it was twenty-six years since he first played there as a guest, the first African American in the Opry's seventy-year history. Charley ranks number eighteen in CMT's 40 Greatest Men of Country Music.

EDDIE **RABBITT**

NOVEMBER 27, 1941 - BROOKLYN, NEW YORK - MAY 7, 1998

During his career, Eddie scored twenty-six number one hits. As a songwriter, his biggest hit came in 1971 when Elvis recorded Eddie's "Kentucky Rain."

One of the most innovative country musicians of all time was reared in East Orange, New Jersey. Christened Edward Thomas, Eddie took his musical heritage from his father who loved to play the fiddle in Manhattan dance halls. In the late 1950s, Eddie had quit school and was working as an attendant in a mental hospital during the day and singing at night in a club, the Six Steps Down. His mother, Mae, told *People* that "his head was always full of music."

In 1964 Eddie signed with Twentieth Century Records and released his first single, "Next to the Note," with little notice. The next year, he headed to Nashville with high hopes and a thousand bucks in his pocket. He had no contacts there but he soon found that the industry needed some good songs. While picking fruit and working at other odd jobs, he was finally hired as a staff writer at Hill and Range Publishing Company making $37.50 a week. Five years later, he struck gold when ELVIS PRESLEY recorded "Kentucky Rain." Four years later, RONNIE MILSAP recorded "Pure Love," which became Ronnie's first number one hit.

By the late 1970s, Eddie was making his own number one hits with "Rocky Mountain Music," "Two Dollars in the Jukebox," "Drivin' My Life Away," and "I Just Want to Love You." In 1977 the CMA named Eddie Top Male Vocalist of the Year. He wrote "Every Which Way But Loose," for CLINT EASTWOOD's movie of the same name. The song made it onto the pop charts. "Suspicions" was named Song of the Year by BMI and Eddie's "I Love a Rainy Night" topped both country and pop charts.

After the death of his son, Timmy, Eddie became a spokesman for several charities including the American Council on Transplantation, Easter Seals, and Special Olympics. The legacy of this good man just may be that his country music compositions were taken to a wider audience.

157

MARTY RAYBON

DECEMBER 8, 1959 - SANFORD, FLORIDA

As lead singer for Shenandoah, Marty received a Grammy in 1990. Gary LeVox of Rascal Flatts says that Marty is "the greatest singer on the planet."

Show business has been part of Marty Raybon's DNA since he entered a local talent contest at the age of eight. As a teenager, Marty was a part of a family bluegrass band with his father and two of his brothers. After hearing MEL STREET on the radio at fifteen, he knew music was his calling. Influenced by the founder of bluegrass, BILL MONROE, and by the OSBORNE BROTHERS, Marty moved to Nashville in 1984 where he signed a publishing contract as a songwriter. He was soon pursuing his dream when he joined the award-winning country group SHENANDOAH as lead singer. The group was known for their number one hit singles, "The Church on Cumberland Road," "Sunday in the South," "Two Dozen Roses," "Next to You, Next to Me," and "If Bubba Can Dance (I Can Too)." In 1990 Shenandoah won Vocal Group of the Year from the ACM. Not long after the group disbanded in 1997, Marty and his brother Tim recorded an album with "Butterfly Kisses," a song that had already won a Grammy.

There are few male singers with a tenor voice as fine as that of Marty Raybon. After his time with Shenandoah, it took several attempts to find his niche once more. Finally, he partnered with Doobie Shea Records on the album, *Full Circle*, once again in the bluegrass genre, hence the title. This followed a restless period when Marty increasingly felt the need to return to the spiritual realm. The result was his return to bluegrass. *Full Circle* contains newly-composed songs along with standards from his early days.

Others in the business recognize Marty's gift. Says country music historian, ROBERT K. OERMAN, "Marty Raybon's voice is truly one of Nashville's greatest treasures." Grammy-nominated singer, JOSH TURNER, calls Marty "one of the best soul singers in music."

JIM **REEVES**

AUGUST 20, 1923 - PANOLA COUNTY, TEXAS - JULY 31, 1964

Jim was known as a crooner because of his warm, rich baritone voice. Songs such as "He'll Have to Go" showed his talent.

Gentleman Jim best fits the kindly crooner who made country-pop an important music genre on an international scale. James Travis Reeves was the eighth child of Mary and Thomas Reeves. After the death of his father when Jim was a baby, his mother managed to hold the family together on their farm near Carthage, Texas. At five Jim received a hand-me-down guitar and after hearing his older brother's records by JIMMIE RODGERS, he became enthralled with country music. Shreveport, Louisiana, was the nearest large city to Jim's home and by the time he was twelve, he had made the forty-mile trip to sing on a radio show.

Jim also had a love of baseball. He won an athletic scholarship to the University of Texas and at twenty-one was playing for the St. Louis Cardinals. After years with the pros, an injury to his ankle ended Jim's baseball career. He considered music as a career, but only after working at several blue-collar jobs. Jim became the lead singer for MOON MULLICAN'S band. By 1952 Jim was back in Shreveport hosting the *Louisiana Hayride*. When HANK WILLIAMS failed to show up one night, Jim made his singing debut with an enthusiastic response. Abbot Records quickly signed Jim to a contract after hearing him sing. His recording, "Mexican Joe," soared to number one by the spring of 1953.

In 1955 Jim signed a long-term contract with RCA and joined the Grand Ole Opry. That was also the year when Jim began recording a string of forty hit singles, many of which were crossover hits on the pop charts. Some of his number one hits include "Four Walls," "Billy Bayou," "He'll Have to Go," and "I Guess I'm Crazy." "Welcome to My World" made it to number two. With his fame reaching around the world, he was considered country music's foremost international ambassador. His "I Won't Come in While He's There" ranked number one three years after his death.

159

DON REID

JUNE 5, 1945 - STAUNTON, VIRGINIA

Don was lead singer and the main songwriter for the legendary group, the Statler Brothers. He has co-authored three books since retiring in 2002.

Born and reared in Staunton, Virginia, Donald Sidney Reid was the spokesman for the STATLER BROTHERS and their primary songwriter. Don has written such songs as "Class of '57" and "Do You Know You Are My Sunshine?" during times of contemplation. He says the BLACKWOOD BROTHERS and the STATESMEN QUARTET were big influences.

IN 1964 JOHNNY CASH took notice of the Statler Brothers and hired them as the opening act for his road tour. They stayed on for eight years. In 1965 the Statlers outlasted the BEATLES and the SUPREMES to win the Grammy for best pop song, "Flowers on the Wall." "I'll Go to My Grave Loving You" is one of Don's songs that captures a sense of deep abiding love which he writes about so well. The Statlers were voted Group of the Year every year from 1972 to 1979 by the CMA. The group, which also included PHIL BALSLEY, JIMMY FORTUNE, and Don's brother, HAROLD, has received over five hundred awards in their forty years of entertaining, including three Grammys and nine Country Music Association Awards. Many folks will remember their highly rated television show on TNN in the early 1990s.

The origin of the group's name has always brought a chuckle. While staying in a hotel, Harold saw the name of a local brand of tissue and recommended it as the name of the group. Don reported to the *Los Angeles Times*, "We could just as easily be known as the Kleenex Brothers."

The Statler Brothers placed second, just behind FRANK SINATRA, in the 1996 National Harris Poll of America's favorite singers. Novelists KURT VONNEGUT and ALEX HALEY have referred to the Statler Brothers as "America's poets."

Don and his family still live in his hometown of Staunton, Virginia, where he is enjoying retirement.

HAROLD **REID**

AUGUST 21, 1939 - STAUNTON, VIRGINIA

Harold sang bass for the legendary vocal group, the Statler Brothers. He is now retired after their farewell concert tour in 2002.

Harold Wilson Reid was born in August County, Virginia, and reared in Staunton. He and his brother were the writers for the STATLER BROTHERS TV show that aired on TNN in the early 1990s. Harold supervised all of the group's album covers and coordinated their bookings. The Statlers have recorded fifty albums and have earned thirteen gold and eight platinum albums.

Harold's musical influences began with the singing cowboys: ROY ROGERS, GENE AUTRY, and TEX RITTER. Later Southern gospel quartets came along such as the BLACKWOOD BROTHERS and the STATESMEN QUARTET. Harold was greatly encouraged and impressed by his high school choir director, GEORGE SARGENT. Also influential were BING CROSBY, DEAN MARTIN, and TENNESSEE ERNIE FORD, but Harold always came back to gospel music. He declares, "To this day there is still more talent buried in that industry than is evident in any other."

Before the Statlers had a full-time singing career, Harold sold men's clothing. JOHNNY CASH'S trademark black frock coat was designed by Harold. "It just tickled him. Up to that time, he just wore [a] shirt and pants that were black. This sort of added to his image and looked good for television," he recalls. Harold used his experience and talent to design concert clothing for the Statlers.

The Statlers were instrumental in nurturing new artists by inviting them to open for their shows. Included have been BARBARA MANDRELL, REBA MCENTIRE, RICKY SKAGGS, and GARTH BROOKS.

The Statlers were invited to the White House to sing at a state dinner as guests of PRESIDENT JIMMY CARTER. Harold talked freely with the President and with PRESIDENT ANWAR SADAT about their common love of American movies. Harold and his wife, Brenda, have five children, Kim, Karman, Kodi, Kasey, and Wil.

CHARLIE **RICH**

DECEMBER 14, 1932 - FOREST CITY, ARKANSAS - JULY 25, 1995

Charlie had two singles in 1973 that sold a million copies, "Behind Closed Doors" and "The Most Beautiful Girl in the World."

Known as the "Silver Fox," Charlie Rich was born into a poor family in the eastern part of Arkansas. Young Charlie learn to play the piano from C. J. ALLEN, a black tenant farmer. Charlie's quest for an eclectic mix of jazz, gospel, blues, and country was part of his make-up from the beginning. After serving in the U.S. Air Force, in 1956 Charlie formed a jazz and blues band, the VELVETONES, which featured his future wife, MARGARET-ANN GREENE.

About this same time, Charlie had begun writing material for future projects and was hired as a session musician for Judd Records. The owner, JUDD PHILLIPS, was the brother of the founder of Sun Records, SAM PHILLIPS. Sam heard Charlie perform at the Sharecropper Club in Memphis and invited him to cut a demo at Sun. At first Sam thought Charlie's music was too jazzy, but after hearing JERRY LEE LEWIS, Sam had second thoughts and invited Charlie to become a regular session player in 1958.

It wasn't until 1960 that Charlie's single, "Lonely Weekends," landed in the Top Thirty. In 1964 Charlie signed with Groove Records, a subsidiary of RCA, but a year later, Groove was out of business and Charlie was without a contract. Smash Records was Charlie's next record label with JERRY KENNEDY producing his next Top Thirty hit, "Mohair Sam." It was the summer of 1972 when Charlie had his first Top Ten hit, "I Take It on Home." Persistence paid off with his mega hit, "Behind Closed Doors," which soared to number one on the country charts and into the Top Twenty on pop charts. With his release of "The Most Beautiful Girl," Charlie made it to the top of both charts and earned a Grammy. He won three awards from the CMA, including Entertainer of the Year in 1974. His duet with JANIE FRICKE, "On My Knees" was his last number one in the fall of 1978.

JOHN **RICH**

JANUARY 7, 1974 - AMARILLO, TEXAS

John, with his partner, Kenny Alphin, created the duo Big & Rich. Their hit, "Save a Horse (Ride a Cowboy)" rated double-platinum status.

While John was playing the bass and singing with LONESTAR, the band's 1995 self-titled album earned an Academy of Country Music Award for Best New Vocal Group or Duo. The band was known for their close harmony and expressive lyrics. In 1998 after recording a second album, John left the group. He stayed with BNA Records and released two singles, but neither made the Top Forty.

John became frustrated with the industry and decided to collect some of those who might be considered outsiders. With this group, he formed what became known as MuzikMafia (Musical Artistic Friends In Alliance). After meeting KENNY ALPHIN, aka Big Kenny, the two decided to meet together and write. The first song they collaborated on was "I Pray for You." They also wrote "She's a Butterfly" for MARTINA MCBRIDE. The two had met a teen with brain cancer at Vanderbilt Children's Hospital and were inspired to pen the song.

John and Kenny joined two other singer/songwriters, JAMES OTTO and JON NICHOLSON. The jam sessions met weekly on Tuesday nights at a small Nashville club called the Pub of Love. John said, "We wanted to do it on the worst night of the week in the weirdest place in town, so that if anybody showed up, they'd be there because they wanted to hear music, not because they wanted to schmooze." The Mafia started as a group of twenty and grew to three or four hundred.

In 2007 John became the host of CMT's *Gone Country* with the intent of matching non-country celebrities with Nashville songwriters. Some of the guests were BOBBY BROWN, JULIO IGLESIAS JR., and *Brady Bunch* actress, MAUREEN MCCORMICK.

This talented musician and songwriter has created a niche for his creative juices to flow.

JEANNIE C. RILEY

OCTOBER 19, 1945 - STAMFORD, TEXAS

Jeannie is best known for her 1968 hit, "Harper Valley PTA." She was the first woman to have country and pop number one hits at the same time.

She was born Jeanne Carolyn Stephenson and was reared in a small west Texas town, Anson. Jeannie's father was an automobile mechanic, her mother, a nurse, and the home she grew up in had no foundation but concrete-block pillars. A hot wind blew under it in summer, and in the winter, "blue northers" howled until the family nearly froze to death. Jeannie dreamed of growing up to be somebody, somebody big, and having a big house where her parents would come to live with her. Jeannie spent her teenage years memorizing country music. Her first taste of performing in public came when she sang on her uncle's jamboree show.

After graduation from high school, Jeannie married Mickey Riley. The two moved to Nashville to further her career as a musician. With a job as a secretary at Passkey Music, as Jean Riley, she recorded some unsuccessful demos. In 1967 Jeannie's boss, PAUL PERRY, introduced her to SHELBY SINGLETON, for whom she recorded TOM T. HALL's "Harper Valley P.T.A." The recording was an instant hit, reaching number one on both country and pop charts, and in 1968, Jeannie first appeared on the Grand Ole Opry.

With her success came offers from Hollywood. Jeannie appeared with BING CROSBY, DEAN MARTIN, BETTE DAVIS, TOM JONES, ED SULLIVAN, and others. While other recordings with MGM Records and later Mercury and Warner Brothers didn't fair as well, Jeannie was in demand as a concert artist into the 1980s.

Jeannie turned to gospel music in the 1970s, forming her own band in 1974, RED RIVER SYMPHONY. The band had a minor hit in 1976 with "The Best I've Ever Had." Her autobiography, *From Harper Valley to the Mountain Top*, came out in 1980 and was followed in 1981 by a recording with the same name. Jeannie's popularity continued into the 1990s.

LeAnn **Rimes**

LeAnn's debut single, "Blue," was released when she was thirteen. At twenty-four, she had sold over thirty-seven million albums.

The father of Margaret LeAnn Rimes was a guitarist part-time and he gave encouragement to LeAnn at an early age. By two she was singing and tap dancing. At five she won a talent contest. When she was six, the family moved to Garland, Texas, where LeAnn grew up. She sang "The Star-Spangled Banner" at Dallas Cowboys games and also at the National Horse Cutting Championships in Fort Worth.

LeAnn's parents sold copies of her singing at these events, and at the age of eleven, she made a recording of "All That." The demo was heard by MIKE CURB who signed her to a contract with Curb Records. LeAnn's first release was a duet with seventy-eight-year-old EDDY ARNOLD of his hit, "Cattle Call." She also did a revamped version of "Blue," a long-time favorite in all genres. It was a great success, climbing to the top of the country charts.

LeAnn was the youngest nominee in 1996 at the CMA Awards, but it wasn't until 1997 that she won the Horizon Award. She also won Grammys that same year for Best Female Country Singer and Best Country Song for her rendition of "Blue." In 2000 LeAnn could be heard singing "I Need You" on the soundtrack of the movie *Jesus* as well as in *Coyote Ugly* with "Can't Fight the Moonlight." LeAnn also appeared in *Coyote Ugly*.

LeAnn has an extraordinarily rich voice that has been likened to that of PATSY CLINE, making her seem older than her years. Her career has remained successful in her adult years and she has managed to handle her fame and fortune with maturity.

In 2001 LeAnn met DEAN SHEREMET when he was cast as a dancer to appear during her performance at the Academy of Country Music Awards. The two were married in 2002.

Tex Ritter

JANUARY 12, 1905 - MURVAUL, TEXAS - JANUARY 2, 1974

Tex, best known for starring in forty "singing cowboy" movies, was involved with the formation of the Country Music Association (CMA).

One of the best-known singing cowboys in Western movies was born Woodard Maurice Ritter. His young life was spent on the family ranch in Beaumont, Texas. After Tex graduated from high school at the top of his class, he majored in law at the University of Texas in Austin. In college he became interested in acting. In 1928 Tex moved to New York where he found work on several Broadway plays, including *Green Grow the Lilacs*. Ten years later, ROGERS and HAMMERSTEIN adapted that play into the musical, *Oklahoma!* After being the featured singer at a rodeo in Madison Square Garden, Tex was dubbed the "singing cowboy." In 1932 he was cast in the starring role on *The Lone Star Ranger*. This was one of the first Western radio shows to air in New York.

With Gene Autry's acclaim growing as a singing cowboy in the mid-1930s, Grand National Pictures signed Tex to star in *Song of the Gringo* in 1936. He went on to star in eighty-five movies, seventy-eight of which were Westerns. Tex sang traditional Western folk songs in his movies including "Rye Whiskey," "Boll Weevil," and "Wayward Wind." As his acting career began to decline, he became the first country artist to sign with Capitol Records in 1942. Some of Tex's hits were "I'm Wastin' My Tears on You," "There's a New Moon Over My Shoulder," "Jealous Heart," "I Dreamed of a Hillbilly Heaven," and "You Two-Timed Me One Time Too Often." He recorded the theme song to *High Noon* which secured his job as MC of the television show *Town Hall Party* for seven years in the late 1950s.

Tex married actress Dorthy Fay on June 14, 1941, and they had two sons, Thomas and television star, the late JOHN RITTER.

Tex became a founding member of the Country Music Association, and in 1964 became the fifth person and the first singing cowboy to be inducted into the Country Music Hall of Fame®.

Marty **Robbins**

SEPTEMBER 26, 1925 - GLENDALE, ARIZONA - DECEMBER 8, 1982

Marty's "A White Sport Coat (And a Pink Carnation)" was a huge hit, but "El Paso" became his signature song and biggest hit.

One of the most versatile singers of all time is this man from Glendale, Arizona. Martin David Robertson changed his name to Jack Robertson when he began performing in nightclubs around Glendale to keep his disapproving mother from knowing of his endeavors. While he was in the navy, he learned to play the guitar and began writing songs. Around 1950 he landed his own television show, the *Western Caravan,* in Phoenix on KPHO. At that time, he changed his name to Marty Robbins. LITTLE JIMMY DICKENS was a guest on the show and saw Marty's potential. Through this contact, Marty landed a contract with Columbia.

Success didn't come for Marty until his third record release, "I'll Go On Alone," in January 1953. After this blockbuster hit, he landed a publishing contract with Acuff-Rose and was invited to join the Grand Ole Opry. In 1955 Marty scored big again with "That's All Right" and "Maybellene." Then "Singing the Blues" made it to number one in the fall of 1956. RAY CONNIFF'S orchestra helped Marty stay on top with "A White Sport Coat (And a Pink Carnation)." The song stayed at number one on the country charts for five weeks in the spring of 1957 and peaked at number two on the pop chart. Two years later, Marty scored again with his biggest hit and signature song, "El Paso." On his recording of "Don't Worry" he introduced fuzztone guitar in 1961.

Marty co-starred in movies, including these Westerns, *Raiders of Old California, Badge of Marshal Brennan, A Man and a Train,* and *Guns of a Stranger.* The title track of "Honkytonk Man" was used in the CLINT EASTWOOD movie of that name. Marty's recording career lasted thirty-one years with ninety-four songs on *Billboard's* country charts, sixteen of which scored in the number one slot. He had thirty-one on the Hot 100. Marty was inducted into the Country Music Hall of Fame® in 1982.

JULIE **ROBERTS**

FEBRUARY 1, 1979 - LANCASTER, SOUTH CAROLINA

In 2004 Julie scored a Top Twenty hit with the song, "Break Down Here." That same year, she gained success with "The Chance."

Julie Roberts has been singing her whole life, a life that began in Lancaster, South Carolina. In pre-school, she was in plays and later in school choirs. She even had a part in *My Fair Lady* at a summer camp for singers. During her junior and senior high school days, her mother and aunt drove her around for performances at area festivals. Julie learned to love the blues when she performed for nursing homes with a group of men in their sixties and seventies. Summers were spent in music shows at Carowinds in North Carolina and later at Dollywood. Julie began college at the University of South Carolina and graduated from Belmont University in Nashville where she formed a band that played small clubs and at events such as Nashville Predators hockey games.

After graduation, Julie got a job with Mercury Records and worked her way up from receptionist to assistant to the label head, LUKE LEWIS. She worked on her music at night, never telling Luke of her dreams and ambitions. Luke was meeting with BRENT ROWAN who played a demo of Julie's for him. Luke asked who this girl was and wanted to meet her. Rowan responded that it was the girl down the hall, his assistant. Julie signed a contract with Mercury and released her debut album in 2004. It was followed by *Men and Mascara* in 2006 with four songs written by Julie.

Julie has given two unforgettable performances on the *Tonight Show* and was chosen from artists in all music genres to sing "Good to Go," the theme for *Good Morning America.*

Of her life and success Julie says, "I'm happiest on the road. That is my salvation and people get that when they come to my shows. I love playing; that is what I have always loved. It's what I've dreamed about my whole life. When I step on the bus and into that back room, something comes over me."

EMILY **ROBISON**

AUGUST 16, 1972 - PITTSFIELD, MASSACHUSETTS

Emily is a founding member of the country music band, Dixie Chicks. She plays multiple instruments and is a singer and songwriter.

Emily Burns Erwin was born in Pittsfield, Massachusetts, but was raised in Addison, Texas, outside of Dallas. At the age of seven, she learned to play the violin. Emily says that her mother was a classical pianist, but that her father was a true country music fan. "He loved all the old stuff." At ten Emily taught herself to play the banjo by learning the chord progressions from books. This was followed by the dobro and other acoustic instruments. With sister Martie she toured the country with a teen bluegrass group, BLUE NIGHT EXPRESS, for several years.

In 1989 Emily and Martie formed their own band, DIXIE CHICKS, that eventually included NATALIE MAINES as lead singer and composer. When they were starting out, the Dixie Chicks sang on the street corners of Dallas. In the early years, the threesome paid their dues by booking their own dates, hiring the necessary equipment and lugging it to and from their gigs themselves. Much has changed in their lives since then. Their debut album, *Wide Open Spaces*, in 1997 sold twelve million copies. In 1998 the group received CMA's Horizon Award as new artists.

In 1999 Emily married CHARLIE ROBISON, a country singer from Texas, and changed her name. When the couple was courting, Martie wrote the hit song, "Cowboy Take Me Away." Emily and Charlie now have three children, Charles Augustus "Gus" born November 11, 2002, and twins Julianna Tex and Henry Benjamin, born April 14, 2005.

The Dixie Chicks have continued with two more recordings. *Fly* sold nine million copies and eventually had six Top Ten singles including "Ready to Run," "Cowboy Take Me Away," and "Without You." *Home* was equally successful with "Long Time Gone," "Landslide," and "Travelin' Soldier." All three recordings from the Dixie Chicks have won Grammys for Country Album of the Year.

JIMMIE **RODGERS**

SEPTEMBER 8, 1897 - MERIDIAN, MISSISSIPPI - MAY 26, 1933

Jimmie is known as the Father of Country Music. In 1961 he was the first person elected to the Country Music Hall of Fame®.

Losing his mother Eliza at the age of five, James Charles Rodgers was reared by various relatives near Meridian, Mississippi, and Mobile, Alabama, until his father, Aaron, remarried. Jimmie's dream of performing was a part of him from an early age. By age thirteen, he had run away twice and organized traveling shows. His father worked as a foreman on the Mobile and Ohio Railroad and was able to track him down. Aaron was able to get Jimmie a job as a waterboy. Later his brother found him a job as a brakeman for the New Orleans and Northeastern Railroad. At twenty-seven Jimmie contracted tuberculosis. The disease gave him the opportunity to get back to what he loved, entertaining. He traveled to Arizona hoping the climate would help his tuberculosis.

In 1927 with his wife Carrie and daughter Anita, he returned to Meridian. Also that year, Asheville, North Carolina, got its first radio station and Jimmie performed for the first time on the radio at WWNC. His new band, the TENNEVA RAMBLERS joined him weekly. The members were from Bristol, Tennessee. The group heard that RALPH PEER from the Victor Talking Machine Company was holding auditions in Bristol. On August 4, 1927, history was made. From 2:00 to 4:20, Jimmie recorded "Sleep, Baby Sleep" and "The Soldier's Sweetheart" and received $100. After this modest success, he traveled to Camden, New Jersey, and recorded four more songs. Two of the songs became major hits selling nearly half a million copies, "Blue Yodel No. 1 (T for Texas)" and "Away Out on the Mountain." On July 16, 1930, Jimmie recorded "Blue Yodel No. 9," also known as "Standin' on the Corner" with LOUIS ARMSTRONG on the trumpet. Jimmie recorded his last song, "Mississippi Delta Blues," on May 17, 1933. He died thirty-six hours later. Jimmie was the first person to be inducted into the Country Music Hall of Fame® in 1961.

Kenny **ROGERS**

AUGUST 21, 1938 - HOUSTON, TEXAS

In 1977 Kenny achieved huge success with his single, "Lucille." Another memorable success was "Coward of the County."

Reared in the poorest section of Houston, Texas, Kenneth Donald Rogers has become one of the most esteemed singers of pop and country music. He was the fourth of eight children and learned to play the guitar and fiddle before he graduated from high school. Kenny joined a rockabilly group called the SCHOLARS. One of their first two singles, "That Crazy Feeling," earned them a spot on *American Bandstand.*

Kenny attended the University of Texas briefly but dropped out to play bass in a jazz combo, the BOBBY DOYLE THREE. From there Kenny went on to join the NEW CHRISTY MINSTRELS in 1966. The next year, several of the members followed Kenny in forming the FIRST EDITION which soon became KENNY ROGERS AND THE FIRST EDITION.

The group scored a Top Ten hit with "Ruby, Don't Take Your Love to Town" in 1969. After Kenny left the group in 1974, he recorded the pop song, "Love Lifted Me," on the United Artist label. "Lucille," considered his biggest breakthrough hit, was recorded in 1977. Kenny had five straight number one hits between 1978 and 1980 with, "Love or Something Like It," "The Gambler," "She Believes in Me," "You Decorated My Life," and "Coward of the County." He recorded three number one hits with DOTTIE WEST, including "Every Time Two Fools Collide." Number one hits followed in the 1980s with "Don't Fall in Love with a Dreamer" with KIM CARNES, "We've Got Tonight" with SHEENA EASTON, and "Islands in the Stream" with DOLLY PARTON. "Lady" became one of the biggest hits of his career.

In 2003 Kenny received the CMA Lifetime Achievement Award for his career that has spanned six decades. In CMT's 40 Greatest Men of Country Music, Kenny Rogers ranks number nineteen.

Roy **Rogers**

NOVEMBER 5, 1911 - CINCINNATI, OHIO - JULY 6, 1998

With his wife, Dale Evans, Roy as "King of the Cowboys," was featured in over one hundred movies. "Happy Trails" was their signature song.

For his first twenty-six years, Roy Rogers was known as Len Slye. The date was Wednesday, October 13, 1937, when Roy signed a seven-year contract with Republic Pictures and renamed himself to star in his first movie, *Under Western Stars.*

Roy's parents, Mattie and Andy Slye, lived in Cincinnati for the first few months after Roy's birth. Roy would joke that he was born at second plate before their house was torn down to build Riverfront Stadium. In 1912 the family moved a hundred miles from Cincinnati to live on a houseboat at Portsmouth, Ohio. After seven years, they moved to a farm in Duck Run.

Mattie communicated with her kids by yodeling and she had different tones to tell when it was time for lunch or a storm was coming. Young Roy became a skilled square dance caller and played the mandolin while developing his yodeling style. After he graduated from high school, the family moved to southern California. By 1931 Roy was picking peaches in the same labor camps that JOHN STEINBECK made famous in his novel, *The Grapes of Wrath.* Roy began singing and playing on radio KMCS in Inglewood and soon joined a country music band called the ROCKY MOUNTAINEERS. He met BOB NOLAN and TIM SPENCER and the three formed the PIONEER TRIO. The name was changed one night when they were introduced as the SONS OF THE PIONEERS. The announcer thought they were too young to be *just* pioneers. The group made their first feature film, *The Old Homestead,* in 1935.

Roy's big break came when GENE AUTRY, unhappy with his contract, left Republic Pictures. A singing cowboy was needed to fill the bill. By 1944 Roy had made thirty-nine films for Republic before DALE EVANS joined him in *The Cowboy and the Senorita.* Dale's song, "Happy Trails," has been more than their signature song. It's everyone's hope.

Lulu **Roman**

MAY 6, 1947 - DALLAS, TEXAS

Lulu is best remembered for her comic relief on the long running television show Hee Haw. *She now tours as a gospel singer.*

After her mother became ill, Bertha Louise Hable was sent to live with her great-grandmother. When it became too much of a challenge to handle a youngster, the family placed young Lulu in an orphanage. Because of a thyroid dysfunction which caused a weight problem, Lulu was often teased by other children. She learned to mask her pain by using comedy as a defense.

After graduation from high school, Lulu began running with a wild crowd. At about that same time, she became a go-go dancer and changed her name to Lulu Roman. Once she had introduced comedy into her act, Lulu was prepared for her role as a cast member on *Hee Haw*. She became the most requested female character on the show.

Success and wealth proved poisonous to Lulu. Drug addiction led to her arrest and temporary removal from the show in 1971. After she became a Christian and straightened out her personal life, Lulu was invited to rejoin the cast. The positive change in her life resulted in a full pardon from the governor of Texas. Lulu continued to maintain her changed life and was a part of the show until it was cancelled in 1993. In 2001 Lulu appeared on *Touched by an Angel* in the season's final episode.

In 1985 Lulu earned a Dove Award for the song, "The King of Who I Am." She continues to tour as a gospel singer. In 2008 Lulu received a Doctor of Sacred Music degree from the North Carolina College of Theology. In 1999 Lulu was inducted into the Country Gospel Music Hall of Fame. Three years later, she released her sixteenth album, *Lulu Inspired,* containing a collection of her hits and favorites. It was nominated for a Dove Award.

Lulu Roman has had many hurdles to cross, but her spirit is strong and the future looks bright for her and her many fans.

Joe Don **Rooney**

SEPTEMBER 13, 1975 - BAXTER SPRINGS, KANSAS

Joe Don plays the guitar and sings harmony for Rascal Flatts. The group won the CMA Horizon Award in 2002.

Growing up in the tiny town of Picher, Oklahoma, Joe Don knows firsthand what it's like to watch your hometown slowly die. Years of mining there have destroyed the land and water. Joe Don brought his bandmates, JAY DEMARCUS and GARY LEVOX, to see his crumbling town while they were on tour at nearby Buffalo Run Casino in Miami. Joe Don has said that the town is part of who he is and he doesn't hide his roots.

Joe Don tried out several music genres with his older brother and sisters before he settled on mainstream country. He tells of an experience he had in Grove, Oklahoma, "There was a show called the *Grand Lake Opry*...kind of like the Grand Ole Opry. When I was nineteen, I worked there and every month we'd have a Grand Ole Opry star...like PORTER WAGONER, MERLE HAGGARD, and CONNIE SMITH." While playing in CHELY WRIGHT's band, Joe Don met Jay DeMarcus. When Jay and his cousin Gary needed a guitarist for a gig in Nashville's Printers Alley, Jay remembered Joe Don and invited him to fill in for the night. When Joe Don started to sing, the group realized that the magic that they had been looking for had just materialized.

RASCAL FLATTS recorded some demos. Lyric Street liked their sound and signed the group to a record contract. The year was 2000. Their self-titled debut album spawned three Top Ten songs, "Prayin' for Daylight," "This Everyday Love," and "While You Love Me." Two years later, their second album, *I Melt,* produced their first number one hit, "These Days." They won the CMA Horizon Award and toured with Toby Keith in 2002. The number one hits kept coming with "Mayberry" and "Bless the Broken Road." In 2008 Rascal Flatts won the Academy of Country Music Award for Top Vocal Group.

Joe Don is married to TIFFANY FALLON, Miss Georgia USA.

174

JOHN SCHNEIDER

APRIL 8, 1960 - MOUNT KISCO, NEW YORK

John is best known for his television role as Bo on The Dukes of Hazzard. *His 1986 "What's a Memory Like You" topped the country charts.*

By the time John was eight, he had mastered the guitar and had taken part in several plays in New York. John and his mother moved to Atlanta where he became involved in local theater. His love for auto racing and his endeavors to become a professional race car driver were short lived.

PHIL MANDELKER, one of the producers of *The Dukes of Hazzard,* discovered John and got him to play opposite TOM WOPAT. He stayed with the series, with a brief interruption in 1982, until it was cancelled in 1985. John wrote and directed several of the episodes and performed many of his own stunts. He also appeared in films and television movies in the early days of his music career.

In 2001 John landed the role as Clark Kent's father in WB's *Smallville.* He has also appeared in two of the *Dukes of Hazzard* reunions and in recurring roles on the popular drama, *Dr. Quinn, Medicine Woman,* as well as in *Diagnosis Murder, Veronica's Closet,* and *Touched by an Angel.*

John's first country album, *Now or Never,* spawned the single, "It's Now or Never," which climbed to the Top Five on both country and contemporary charts. He then recorded *White Christmas* before signing with MCA Records where he recorded five albums and racked up four number one singles, "I've Been Around Enough to Know," "Country Girls," "What's a Memory Like You (Doing in a Love Like This)," and "You're the Last Thing I Needed Tonight" between 1984 and 1987.

John, with MARIE OSMOND, co-founded the Children's Miracle Network in 1983. Its purpose is to raise funds and bring attention to the needs of suffering children around the world. John, a born-again Christian, has founded FaithWorks Productions which endeavors to produce family-oriented videos and recordings. John lives outside of Los Angeles with his wife, Elly Castle. The couple has three children.

EARL SCRUGGS

JANUARY 6, 1924 - SHELBY (FLINT HILL), NORTH CAROLINA

Earl is noted for creating a banjo style, now called Scruggs Style, that is a defining characteristic of bluegrass music.

Surrounded by a musical family, young Earl Eugene Scruggs picked up the banjo and started playing with a two finger style at age four. When he was ten, Earl developed what is called "Scruggs Style Picking" using three fingers. His four siblings played the banjo and guitar. Earl was twelve when bought his own banjo from Montgomery Ward for $10.95. Earl said that his idol at the time, the main person he loved the most, was MOTHER MAYBELLE CARTER, so that was who he copied. Three years later, he was playing in his first band, the MORRIS BROTHERS. At the age of twenty-one, he replaced STRINGBEAN and joined the legendary BILL MONROE AND THE BLUE GRASS BOYS.

After his first recording with the group, "Heavy Traffic Ahead," on September 16, 1946, they followed it up with "Shining Path." Two years later, Earl left to take care of his ailing mother. LESTER FLATT left the group at about the same time, and Earl joined forces with Lester to start a new group called FLATT AND SCUGGS AND THE FOGGY MOUNTAIN BOYS. They made their first recording on Columbia in 1950. The songs included "The Old Home Town," "Come Back Darling," "I'll Stay Around," "We Can't Be Sweethearts Any More," and "I'm Waiting to Hear You Call Me Darling." The band earned a Grammy Award in 1969. Their recording was used as the theme song for the *Beverly Hillbillies* TV show. In the film, *Bonnie and Clyde*, it was their rendition of "Foggy Mountain Breakdown" that added to the action and comic relief. Earl's two sons joined him in the EARL SCUGGS REVUE in 1969 after his breakup with Lester Flatt.

Earl Scruggs and Lester Flatt became members of the Country Music Hall of Fame® in 1985. The two rank number twenty-four on CMT's 40 Greatest Men of Country Music. Earl has earned several Grammys and was also inducted into the Bluegrass Music Hall of Fame.

BLAKE **SHELTON**

JUNE 18, 1976 - ADA, OKLAHOMA

Blake's hit single, "Austin," stayed at number one for five weeks in 2001. His self-titled album stayed on the Top 40 country chart for seventy weeks.

When Blake reached his teens, writing songs and honing his musical style became his passion. His first performance at the age of eight was "Old Time Rock 'n' Roll." He moved from local talent shows to playing in honky-tonk bars. At sixteen he won the Denbo Diamond Award, which is Oklahoma's highest honor for young performers. The famous song-writer of "Heartbreak Hotel," MAE BOREN AXTON, saw the potental in Blake and told him he was good enough to secure a record contract. Two weeks after his high school graduation, Blake moved to Nashville. Mae opened doors for him to meet the right people, and soon he had a record contract. BOBBY BRADDOCK liked Blake's work and wanted to produce his first album.

In March of 2001, Blake released his first single, "Austin," on the Giant label. The song soared to the number one position on the *Billboard* country singles chart where it stayed for five weeks. The ballad is made up of messages left on a answering machine with the hopes of reclaiming lost love. Not long after the release of Blake's hit song, the Giant label went out of business. Warner Brothers picked up Blake's contract. His self-titled album was released at the end of July 2001 and climbed to number three. For seventy weeks, the album stayed on the Top Forty, going gold within the year. *The Dreamer,* Blake's second album, released in 2003, contains the sad story of a son returning home to be with his dying mother in the song, "The Baby." Also included is a number that shows his versatility, the country rock story song, "Playboys of the Southwestern World."

Many of Blake's dreams have come true. One was the night he stood on the stage of the Grand Ole Opry with JACK GREENE singing "Statue of a Fool." Also that night, he was presented a gold record for his debut album.

RICKY **VAN SHELTON**

JANUARY 12, 1952 - DANVILLE, VIRGINIA

Starting with his number one hit, "Someone Lied," Ricky became one of the biggest male country music stars of the late 1980s and early 1990s.

The town of Grit, Virginia, can be proud of their number one son, Ricky Van Shelton. With his three older siblings, Ricky first began singing in the Pentecostal Holiness Church. All four children were faithful members of the choir and were discouraged from singing secular music. As Ricky reached his teens, his interest in rock 'n' roll and country music became part of his life. After graduation from high school, he performed at lodges, clubs, and private parties. To support his dream of becoming a professional county musician, Ricky took on an array of odd jobs including house painter, plumber, car salesman, service station attendant, and even tobacco picking in rural Virginia.

In 1984 Ricky, with encouragement from his fiancee, Bettye Witt, moved to Nashville for a shot at his dream. Bettye got a job as a personnel manager, while Ricky checked out night clubs and distributed his demos. He spent many hours sweating over lyrics that he hoped would bring him closer to his dream. In 1986 Ricky and Bettye were married and Ricky signed a contract with CBS. After a long two years, it took a local newspaper columnist hearing his demo to help him land the record deal.

Ricky's debut album, *Wild-Eyed Dream,* was released in 1987 and produced the single "Crime of Passion." That first single made it into the Top Ten; his next two singles, "Somebody Lied" and "Life Turned That Way," climbed to number one. A follow-up album, *Loving Proof,* spawned three number one hits, "I'll Leave This World Loving You," "From Jack to a King," and "Living Proof." In 1991 Ricky and DOLLY PARTON recorded the hit, "Rockin' Years." In all Ricky has produced almost a dozen number one hits, as well as five platinum, and three gold records.

Ricky has authored a series of children's books, *Tales From a Duck Named Quacker,* which have sold more than 200,000 copies.

JEAN SHEPARD

NOVEMBER 21, 1933 - PAULS VALLEY, OKLAHOMA

Jean was one of country music's first major female stars. One of her biggest hits was "The Dear John Letter."

Known as "The Grand Lady of the Grand Ole Opry," in 2005 Jean Shepherd celebrated fifty years as a cast member. She is the first singing member to achieve that milestone. Ollie Imogene Shepard was born in Oklahoma but grew up in the area around Bakersfield, California. It has been said that to be called a legend in the enter-tainment world, one must first be a pioneer and then go on to accomplish many more firsts. Jean's firsts in country music include starring in the first network country music show, first female to sell a million records, first female vocalist to overdub her voice on records, first female to make a color TV commercial, and the afore-mentioned Opry first.

Jean grew up as one of ten children, all musically inclined. The family would save pennies to purchase one JIMMIE RODGERS record a year. It is not surprising that Jean helped form, was lead singer, and played bass for the MELODY RANCH GIRLS. In an early performance of the band, Jean had the good luck to be on stage with none other than HANK THOMPSON. Hank was instrumental in getting Jean a contract with Capitol Records, a relationship that lasted for twenty-one years and produced such number one hits as "The Dear John Letter," "Beautiful Lies," "Seven Lonely Days," "Satisfied Mind," and "Second Fiddle." Her forceful tunes set the pace for others who came later, including LORETTA LYNN, JEANNIE C. RILEY, and WANDA JACKSON.

Jean was married to HAWKSHAW HAWKINS, who was killed in the same plane crash that took the lives of PATSY CLINE and COWBOY COPAS, and is the mother of two sons. Today Jean is married to BENNY BIRCHFIELD but still keeps up a busy road schedule. The JEAN SHEPHERD SHOW consists of a four-piece group that Jean calls the SECOND FIDDLE and is known as one of the finest traveling bands touring today.

RICKY **SKAGGS**

JULY 18, 1954 - CORDELL, KENTUCKY

Since the early 1980s, Ricky has earned twelve Grammy Awards. Chet Atkins once credited Ricky with "single-handedly saving country music."

The son of a country and gospel singer, young Ricky was singing with his parents at age three. At five he was playing the mandolin on stage with his mom and dad. In the book, *The Big Book of Bluegrass*, Ricky says, "Me and my mom would do a lot of duets, and my dad would sing baritone or bass, so we would have lead and tenor and bass, and it would sound real haunting and neat."

Ricky's musical idols were RALPH and CARTER STANLEY, the STANLEY BROTHERS. Ricky met KEITH WHITLEY, who also loved the Stanley Brothers and the two traveled to West Virginia to hear RALPH STANLEY play in a concert. Ralph was late, so the club owners asked the two boys if they could play until Ralph showed up. They were playing, "Little Glass of Wine," when the main attraction arrived. Ralph could remember what it was like when he and his brother had just started out and was impressed by their caliber of music. He invited the two to join his band, CLINCH MOUNTAIN BOYS. Ricky toured with the band for two years in the early 1970s. Ricky says, "It was a good training ground.... I learned what *not* to play.... Those were really great days."

After Ricky played a key role on the debut album of J.D. CROWE AND NEW SOUTH, *The New South* became known as the most influential of all bluegrass albums. In 1978 Ricky was instrumental in helping EMMYLOU HARRIS in her musical career and played on her earlier albums.

The release of *Waitin' for the Sun to Shine* in 1981 was the signal that Ricky had moved back into mainstream county music. He entered the top of the charts and remained there for most of the decade.

Since joining the Grand Ole Opry in 1982, Ricky has been an exponent of bluegrass music. His band, KENTUCKY THUNDER, earned a Grammy in 2003 for his song "Simple Life" from his live album. Ricky ranks number thirty-seven in CTM's 40 Greatest Men of Country Music.

CARL SMITH

MARCH 15, 1927 - MAYNARDVILLE, TENNESSEE

Known as "Mr. Country," Carl was one of the most successful male artists of the 1950s. He was twice married to singers, June Carter and Goldie Hill.

Maynardville, Tennessee, must be proud of producing two giants of country music. ROY ACUFF was the first, and young Carl Smith came along a quarter of a century later. Carl idolized Roy and others who had made the big time in country music. By the time Carl reached his teens, he had taught himself to play the guitar. As the legend is told, Carl earned the cash to buy his first guitar by selling flower seeds. At fifteen, he joined a San Francisco-based country band, called KITTY DIBBLE AND HER DUDE RANCH WRANGLERS.

Knoxville's WROL radio was broadcasting the Grand Ole Opry while Carl was growing up and in 1944 CAS WALKER offered him a job singing and playing the guitar for the BREWSTER BROTHERS. After serving in the military for two years in the late 1940s, Carl landed back at WROL playing in ARCHIE CAMPBELL'S band. GEORGE KRISE made a demo of Carl's singing and sent it to TROY MARTIN in Nashville, a representative of Peer-Southern Music Publishing and a talent scout for DON LAW of Columbia Records. As a result, Carl was given a six-day-a-week morning show at WSM and a contract with Columbia. It was a year before Carl had his first hit with a string of love songs. "Let Old Mother Nature Have Her Way" became his first number one hit and biggest-selling single. He followed that with "(When You Feel Like You're in Love) Don't Just Stand There."

After several years as a member, Carl left the Grand Ole Opry in 1956 to become the star of the *Philip Morris Country Music Show*. He appeared on RED FOLEY's *Jubilee U.S.A.* and co-hosted its follow-up, *Five Star Jubilee*. Carl had his own *Carl Smith's Country Music Hall* on television between 1964 and 1969. Always an innovator, Carl was the first to include drums as part of his band. It soon became the standard.

In 2003 Carl was elected to the Country Music Hall of Fame®.

CONNIE SMITH

AUGUST 14, 1941 - ELKHART, INDIANA

Connie is best known for her 1964 hit song, "Once a Day," which spent eight weeks at number one on the Billboard Country Music Charts.

Constance June Meador was born into a poor family of fourteen children in Elkhart, Indiana, in 1941. Her family moved often and Connie spent her growing up years in West Virginia and Ohio. She married at an early age and was starting a family when she won a talent contest in Ohio and got the attention of BILL ANDERSON, country music singer and songwriter. It was 1963. Bill invited Connie to come to Nashville where in 1964, she signed a contract with RCA. Connie's first single, Bill Anderson's "Once a Day" made it to the top spot in September that year and stayed there for eight weeks. Connie's single was the most successful debut by a female country artist. The song became one of the biggest songs of the year and certainly made a name for Connie in country music.

Although Connie may have been overly compared with PATSY CLINE, over the years her popularity has endured. She is thought by many to be one of the best female singers in country history. DOLLY PARTON has said, "There are only three great singers..." She names Connie Smith as one of the three.

The mid-1960s were Connie's heyday but in 1972, she recorded three big hits for the Top Ten, "Just What I Am" at number five, number seven, "If It Ain't Love (Let's Leave It Alone)," and at number eight "Love Is the Look You're Looking For." Starting that year, Connie incorporated more gospel music into her concerts.

While Connie had many successes over the years, she never again had a number one hit after "Once a Day." She is considered one of the Grand Ladies of the Grand Ole Opry. She became a member in 1971 and has been making appearances on that stage ever since then. Connie is number nine on CMT's Greatest Women of Country Music.

HANK **SNOW**

MAY 9, 1914 - BROOKLYN, NOVA SCOTIA - DECEMBER 20, 1999

Hank's last top hit, "Hello Love," was on Billboard's Hot Country Singles chart in April 1974. He became the oldest country artist to have a number one song.

By the mid-twentieth century, a man by the name of Hank Snow became one of the most successful country music singers from Canada during the industry's developing years. Clarence Eugene Snow was eight when his parents divorced and he was sent to live with his paternal grandparents until his mother remarried. His stepfather turned out to be abusive and mistreated young Clarence. When Clarence reached his teens, he spent four years as a cabin boy on a fishing trawler and entertained the crew by playing his harmonica and singing. Clarence had fallen in love with the country music he had heard from an old Victrola. He especially liked JIMMIE RODGERS, and after purchasing a $5.95 mail-order guitar, Clarence was determined to learn to sing and play just like his hero. At nineteen he had acquired a fifteen-minute weekly radio show called *Clarence Snow and His Guitar* on CHNS, Halifax. He met and married Minnie Aalders, and the couple landed a full-time radio job with a laxative company. Clarence was billed as HANK THE YODELING RANGER in honor of JIMMIE RODGERS, after hearing that Jimmie was an honorary Texas Ranger.

In 1936 Hank traveled to Montreal to cut his first recordings for Canadian Bluebird, "Lonesome Blue Yodel" and "Prisoned Cowboy." The young couple cracked the U.S. market after traveling to the West Coast and back to Dallas appearing on the *Big D Jamboree*. ERNEST TUBB went to bat for Hank and got him on the Grand Ole Opry in 1949. At that event he was introduced by HANK WILLIAMS.

Hank's first number one RCA hit was "I'm Moving On." It stayed on the charts forty-four weeks and was followed by two more number one hits, "The Golden Rocket" and "Rhumba Boogie." Hank recorded over one hundred albums for RCA and sold more than seventy million albums. He was elected to the Country Music Hall of Fame® in 1979.

TIM **SPENCER**

JULY 13, 1908 - WEBB CITY, MISSOURI - APRIL 26, 1974

Tim was one of the original members of the Sons of the Pioneers. His composition, "Room Full of Roses," was number one on both pop charts and country charts.

Vernon "Tim" Spencer was the son of a mining engineer who loved to make music on his fiddle. Young Tim made his debut singing with his brothers at the local Methodist church. He soon found that he loved to entertain.

By 1913 the family of fourteen moved to the foothills of the Sangre de Cristo Mountains near Springer, New Mexico. The grandeur of this new area would become the inspiration for many compositions later in his life.

When the family later moved to Oklahoma, Tim bought a banjo ukulele on credit without his father's permission. He was only thirteen, but when his father insisted that Tim return it, he left home. Not long after, his father found him working at a hotel restaurant in Dallas. Because Tim was homesick, he agreed to return home with his father. He began working in the mine but an ore car accident caused a cracked vertebra. Unable to continue at the mine, Tim began playing his banjo and singing in a nightclub, the Bucket of Blood.

Tim moved to California in 1931 following his Western movie hero, GENE AUTRY. Arriving at his brother's, he read in the newspaper that the ROCKY MOUNTAINEERS were looking for a baritone who could yodel. Tim wasn't a baritone and had never yodeled, but he got the job replacing BOB NOLAN. Four months later, he left the group to join the INTERNATIONAL COWBOYS, a trio. In 1933 LEONARD SLYE (ROY ROGERS) suggested they invite Bob Nolan to join them and again create the trio. Bob agreed and the PIONEER TRIO, later the SONS OF THE PIONEERS, was born.

Tim stayed with the group until his retirement in 1949 except for two years in the mid-1930s. He continued to manage the group for three more years and assisted in their recordings until 1957. His composition, "Room Full of Flowers," became a number one hit on country charts in 1974. He was elected to the Country Music Hall of Fame® in 1980.

RICHARD **STERBAN**

APRIL 24, 1943 - CAMDEN, NEW JERSEY

Before joining the Oak Ridge Boys as their bass singer, Richard toured with J.D. Sumner and the Stamps Quartet.

"Oom pa pa mau mau" will always be remembered as the deep bass voice in the 1981 hit song, "Elvira." Richard Sterban has certainly left a mark on country music.

Young Richard remembers singing soprano in Sunday school. By the time he was in the glee club in the seventh grade, he was singing tenor and in the fall of his eighth grade year, he was a bass. Richard grew up loving sports but thought he had more talent in music. He set his goal high and said, "I wanted to be in the best vocal group in the world." Before joining the OAK RIDGE BOYS in 1972, he had been a part of various gospel groups. The most notable was singing backup for ELVIS PRESLEY as a member of J.D. SUMNER AND THE STAMPS QUARTET.

The Oak Ridge Boys have collected dozens of country hits and a number one pop mega hit. They have earned Grammy, Dove, and ACM awards. The group's history extends back to 1943 when its home base was Knoxville, Tennessee. Richard said, "I was a fan of the Oaks before I became a member. I'm still a fan of the group today. Being in The Oak Ridge Boys is the fulfillment of a lifelong dream."

The Oaks have backed many of the best country artists, including GEORGE JONES, BRENDA LEE, JOHNNY CASH, BILLY RAY CYRUS, and BILL MONROE. They have also backed up RAY CHARLES, and when PAUL SIMON needed help with his 1977 hit song, "Slip Slidin' Away," the Oaks were there with their well-blended voices.

Richard is also a weather buff. On November 15, 2000, he received an award from the National Weather Service for his efforts to educate the public by recording a series of public service announcements.

Richard and his wife, Donna, have two daughters, Lauren and Tori. Richard also has three sons from a previous marriage.

RAY STEVENS

JANUARY 24, 1939 - CLARKDALE, GEORGIA

Ray had several novelty hits including, "The Streak" and "Ahab the Arab." His first number one hit, recorded in 1977, was "Everything Is Beautiful."

Known for writing and singing novelty songs, Ray has a serious side to his music. As in "Mr. Businessman" and "Would Jesus Wear a Rolex?" only Ray Stevens can lay down a track that causes one to reexamine personal motivations.

Harold Ray Ragsdale was influenced by hearing the radio while swimming at the public pool. He was also exposed to the eclectic selections from the local jukebox. Ray had learned to play the piano by the age of six and formed a band at fifteen called the BARONS in his hometown of Albany, Georgia. The band's venues included the American Legion and private parties.

Ray met radio personality, BILL LOWERY, after a move to Atlanta. Ray had heard that Bill was looking for some new songs, and he went to Bill's home and said, "My name is Ray Ragsdale and I'm going to learn to write songs for you." Bill answered, "Okay lad, go to it." When Ray was still in high school, he had borrowed a tape recorder and recorded the sweet song, "Silver Bracelet." Bill liked it well enough to give Ray a contract with Prep Records. Ray finished high school and then studied classical piano and music theory at Georgia State University. In 1961 he left college in his junior year to give Nashville a try. Ray landed a record deal with Mercury and soon recorded his first hit, "Ahab the Arab," which reached number five on the pop charts in 1962. After he recorded "Harry the Hairy Ape," Ray left Mercury and was hired by Monument as a producer for upcoming stars such as DOLLY PARTON.

Ray received a Grammy for Male Vocalist of the Year with his number one hit, "Everything Is Beautiful," in 1970. Four years later, "The Streak," Ray's second number one pop hit, reached number three on the country charts. In 1975 Ray published ELVIS PRESLEY'S last hit song, "Way Down." His music spans comedy, pop, rock, and country.

GORDON **STOKER**

Gordon joined the Jordanaires in 1950. For fourteen years, the group backed-up Elvis Presley.

Hugh Gordon Stoker was born in the small town of Gleason, Tennessee, in the telephone office building where his family made their home. His mother, Willie, was the night operator and his dad, Ambus, known locally as H.A., was the repairman.

Gordon remembers playing an old Kimball organ when he was eight years old for the Jolley Springs Baptist Church. A coal oil lamp was the only light. He was called Hugh Gordon and was known, among singing circles, for his talented piano playing for the CLEMENT TRIO. Mr. Clement would introduce him saying, "He's not a banker, he's not a broker, he's just the world's greatest piano player, Hugh Gordon Stoker!"

JOHN DANIEL, of the DANIEL QUARTET, was so impressed with twelve-year-old Hugh Gordon that he wanted to take him to Nashville to make him a star. For two years, Gordon appeared with the quartet on WSM morning radio programs and at the Grand Ole Opry.

After serving three years in the Army Air Corps during World War II, Gordon enrolled at Oklahoma Baptist University. In 1948 he moved back to Tennessee to continue his studies at Peabody College. He played for the Daniel Quartet for another year, until an opportunity came knocking when the JORDANAIRES arrived in town. Shortly after that, Gordon met his wife, as well as a young man who would change his life forever, ELVIS PRESLEY.

For over fifty years, the Jordanaires have been known worldwide as one of the most versatile quartets. Their background harmony style became an integral part of hit records by Elvis, PATSY CLINE, and RICKY NELSON. With the Jordanaires, Gordon was inducted into the Gospel Music Association Hall of Fame, as well as the Country Music Hall of Fame® and was awarded several Grammys.

GEORGE **STRAIT**

MAY 18, 1952 - POTEET, TEXAS

George has been nominated for more CMA awards than any other artist. At their 2008 event, he won both Single and Album of the Year.

During George's teen years, he began playing in a rock 'n' roll garage band but always preferred country music. His primary influences were HANK WILLIAMS, BOB WILLS, MERLE HAGGARD, and GEORGE JONES. Soon after he graduated from Pearsall High School in the late 1960s, George enrolled in college. He soon left college and eloped with NORMA VOSS, his high school sweetheart. They made it official by repeating their vows a few weeks later on December 4, 1971. That same year, George enlisted in the military and was stationed in Hawaii where he played in an army-sponsored band called RAMBLING COUNTRY.

After his discharge in 1975, he enrolled at Southwest Texas University at San Marcos and formed his own country band called, ACE IN THE HOLE. The band had little success with the records they cut for D, a Dallas-based record label in the late 1970s. Club owner and former owner of MCA Records, ERV WOOLSEY, invited some of the executives from MCA to hear George play. They liked what they heard and George signed with the record company in 1980. His first single, "Unwound," climbed into the Top Ten. His third single, "If You're Thinking You Want a Stranger (There's One Coming Home)," in 1982 was the beginning of a chain of Top Ten hits that ran into the new century. His first number one hit came the same year with "Fool Hearted Memory."

By 1990 George had won CMA's Album of the Year, Male Vocalist in 1985 and 1986, and Entertainer of the Year in 1989 and 1990. In 2005 he recorded a duet with LEE ANN WOMACK, "Good News, Bad News," and won CMT's Vocal Event of the Year. He has sold sixty-two million recordings and garnered fifty-five number one country hits.

George was inducted into the Country Music Hall of Fame® in 2006. He is number nine on CMT's 40 Greatest Men of Country Music.

STRINGBEAN

David Akeman was better known as Stringbean and became the comedy relief at the Grand Ole Opry, as well as on the television show, Hee Haw.

David Akeman got his interest in country music from his banjo-picking father. Showing his ingenuity at seven, David made his own "banjo" using a shoebox and thread from his mother's sewing basket. At twelve he traded a pair of prize bantam chickens he had raised for a real banjo. With his reputation growing as a fine musician, David was in demand for local dances. Although he was available to entertain when asked, these were the days of the Great Depression and money was scarce. To make ends meet, David worked for the Civilian Conservation Corps, planting trees and building roads.

David won a talent contest judged by ASA MARTIN who invited him to join his KENTUCKY HILLBILLIES. On one occasion during a performance, Asa was trying unsuccessfully to remember David's name. Finally, Asa introduced David as "String Beans." With David's 6 foot, 5 inch, lanky physique, the name lasted throughout his career. He was pressured into singing when a band member failed to show up for a performance. David began his comedic shtick during this time. He divided his time between playing semi-pro baseball and his music career. It was Stringbean who helped keep the banjo as a part of country music during the late 1930s. When BILL MONROE was fielding his own semi-pro baseball team, he found out about David's musical talents and invited him to join his BLUE GRASS BOYS in 1943. David also teamed up with WILLIE EGBERT WESTBROOK as STRING BEANS AND COUSIN WILBUR, a comedy team. After two years with the Blue Grass Boys, Stringbean was replaced by EARL SCRUGGS. He soon teamed up with GRANDPA JONES and became a regular on the Grand Ole Opry wearing his long nightshirt and short pants that emphasized his height.

Stringbean became a instant hit in 1969 on the television show, *Hee Haw,* and remained a star on the Grand Ole Opry until his death in 1973.

MARTY **STUART**

SEPTEMBER 30, 1958 - PHILADELPHIA, MISSISSIPPI

Marty has six Top Ten hits, four Grammys, five gold records, and one platinum. He has toured with Lester Flatt and collaborated with Bob Dylan.

While lying in his crib listening to "Twinkle, Twinkle, Little Star" over and over again, young Marty fell in love with music. He got his first crank-up guitar at the age of three and at five was teaching himself to play a real one. A few years later, his mother, Hilda, loaned him the money to buy a mandolin because that was the instrument his heroes in country music were playing. He gave up on the BEATLES for the music of FLATT & SCRUGGS, BILL MONROE, and JOHNNY CASH. In 1971 Marty traveled to Indiana to Bill Monroe's Bean Blossom Festival to meet LESTER FLATT. He also met ROLAND WHITE, a member of Lester's band. Roland saw Marty's talent and opened doors for him to join Lester's band. It was Labor Day weekend in 1972. Marty was only fourteen years old.

Marty lost a mentor and hero when Lester died in 1979, but his love for the music kept him strong. He toured with BOB DYLAN and was a session player for WILLIE NELSON, EMMYLOU HARRIS, and BILLY JOEL. He joined Johnny Cash's band after Johnny heard Marty play the guitar. Marty married Johnny's daughter, Cindy, in 1983. They were divorced five years later. In 1997 he married songwriting partner, CONNIE SMITH.

After six years of playing for Johnny, Marty secured a contract with CBS Records and released a self-titled album in 1986. Despite disappointing sales, the first single, "Arlene" broke into the *Billboard* Top Twenty and earned him a nomination for Best New Male Vocalist by the ACM. Marty signed with MCA in 1989. Numerous hit singles followed.

Marty has served six terms as president of the Country Music Hall of Fame® and on the Museum's board of directors. He personally owns 20,000 different items including the handwritten manuscript of HANK WILLIAMS' "Your Cheatin' Heart." In 2003 he released his *Country Music* studio album and co-headlined a tour with MERLE HAGGARD.

TAYLOR **SWIFT**

DECEMBER 13, 1989 - READING, PENNSYLVANIA

In 2006 at the age of 16, Taylor had her first hit, "Tim McGraw." Since then, she has risen to fame, especially gaining a large internet following.

Included among those who have influenced Taylor's life and career are her grandmother, an opera singer, LEANN RIMES, and TIM MCGRAW. Taylor has been singing for her whole life, all eighteen years of it. She grew up on a farm in Wyomissing, Pennsylvania, and began singing locally at the age of ten in karaoke contests, and at county fairs and festivals. At eleven, she sang "The Star-Spangled Banner" at a Philadelphia 76ers basketball game. By twelve, she was playing the guitar and writing her own songs. Her parents peddled her work in Nashville, where at fourteen, she became the youngest person to land a songwriting deal with Sony/ATV.

It was then that her family decided to move to Hendersonville. At a showcase at the Bluebird Cafe, Taylor was heard by SCOTT BORCHETTA who signed her for his new label, Big Machine Records. Her self-titled debut album began at number three on the *Billboard* Country Album Chart. It went gold in only thirteen weeks and platinum in thirty-three. It wasn't long before stars including GEORGE STRAIT, BRAD PAISLEY, and RASCAL FLATTS were inviting her to tour with them.

And then came an offer from the namesake of her hit song, "Tim McGraw," to join the Soul2Soul Tour with Tim and FAITH HILL. The "Tim McGraw" digital version was certified gold by RIAA, something only eleven country artists have accomplished. Says the *Arizona Daily Star*, "Swift's quick rise is three parts chutzpah, one part determination, and a legacy of parents believing so strongly in their little girl's talents that they packed up and moved to give her a shot."

While the field of country music is slow to accept change, Taylor has become the first "bona fide country star of the MySpace generation" and with over twenty million song streams on her MySpace page, Taylor is clearly appealing to the younger generation of country fans.

GORDON TERRY

Gordon first gained national exposure at nineteen when he joined the Grand Ole Opry. He was instrumental in launching Barbara Mandrell's career.

Floyd Terry always loved country music. He had taught his oldest sons to play instruments and the day came when he decided to have them perform at the Grand Ole Opry. He arrived at the Opry office thinking he could sign his kids up but was told the filing cabinet was full of "white paper" applicants. Floyd asked for red paper to fill out his application so it would stand out from the rest. It wasn't long before he received a letter from the Opry and his gang was scheduled to play. That was June 9, 1941, and Gordon was nine years old. Ten years later, Gordon joined the Opry as a regular cast member.

In 1949 BILL MONROE was performing in Decatur, Alabama, when Gordon auditioned to be one of the BLUE GRASS BOYS. He was hired and toured with Bill Monroe for five years. Gordon then backed up FARON YOUNG until 1957. That same year, Gordon scored his biggest hit with "Wild Honey." In 1958 he moved to Los Angeles and appeared in the television series, *Sky King,* and the movies, *Hidden Gun, The Night Rider*, and *Honkytonk Man*. His manager turned down a role in one of the *Tarzan* movies while Gordon was on tour with JOHNNY CASH.

By 1964 Gordon had built a rustic resort and western theme park not far from his roots in Loretto, Tennessee. He sold Terrytown three years later due to his tour schedule.

One of Gordon's best signature novelty songs was "Johnson's Old Gray Mule," learned from CURLY FOX. Gordon recorded *Disco Country* in 1977 and four years later he released *Rockin' Fiddle*. With BOB WILLS, he was inducted into the Fiddlers Hall of Fame in 1981.

As a young man, Gordon Terry won the Alabama state fiddling title at fourteen and became one of the best to play the fiddle in Ryman Auditorium and anywhere that good country music was heard.

Hank **Thompson**

SEPTEMBER 3, 1925 - WACO, TEXAS - NOVEMBER 6, 2007

Labeled the "King of Western Swing," Hank was elected to the Country Music Hall of Fame® in 1989. He sold over sixty million records.

Born Henry William Thompson, Hank was captivated by BOB WILLS, JIMMIE RODGERS, and the singing cowboy, GENE AUTRY, at an early age. He soon learned to play the four-dollar guitar his parents bought in a secondhand store for his Christmas present. After Hank graduated from high school in 1943, he was billed as "Hank the Hired Hand" on Radio WACO. While serving in the navy, Hank often entertained the troops singing the songs he had written.

After his discharge from the service, Hank attended Princeton University to study electrical engineering through the G.I. Bill. Eventually he decided on a career in music and returned to Waco. Hank put his first band together and called it the BRAZOS VALLEY BOYS. The first single they recorded was "Whoa Sailor." With the help of TEX RITTER, Hank signed a contract with Capitol Records in 1947 that lasted for eighteen years.

"Humpty Dumpty Heart" was Hank's first mega hit in 1949. Five other singles climbed the country charts that year. KEN NELSON, who became Hank's producer in 1951, can take part of the credit for Hank's success. The next year, Hank recorded what would become his signature song, "The Wide Side of Life." The song stayed at number one for three months on the country charts. KITTY WELLS recorded and renamed the song "It Wasn't God Who Made Honky Tonk Angels." With that song, Kitty became the first female country artist to sell a million records.

Because of his background in electrical engineering, Hank became the first country artist to have elaborate sound and lighting for his concerts. In 1961 he recorded the first live country album, *At the Golden Nugget.* Hank turned to television in 1953 and *The Hank Thompson Show* eventually became the first color telecast of a variety show. Hank was inducted into the Country Music Hall of Fame® in 1989.

MEL TILLIS

AUGUST 8, 1932 - TAMPA, FLORIDA

Known by his speech impediment, Mel Tillis won the CMA Entertainer of the Year Award in 1976. He is the father of Pam Tillis.

It was the composition, "I'm Tired," that launched the musical career of Lonnie Melvin Tillis. The song was recorded by WEBB PIERCE in 1957 when Mel was achieving very little success in Nashville. When the song landed at number three on the country charts, Mel was offered a songwriting contract at Webb's Cedarwood Music. Mel tried his own wings by recording "It Takes a Worried Man to Sing a Worried Song" and "The Violet and a Rose," proving that he had singing talent as well.

In 1962 Mel released his first album, *Heart Over Mind,* and the next year teamed up with Webb to record "How Come Your Dog Don't Bite Nobody but Me." "Wine" became Mel's first Top Fifteen hit. More success was soon to follow with "Stateside" and "Life Turned Her That Way."

Mel's speech impediment was blamed on the malaria he contracted as a child. He discovered that while singing he didn't stutter. He entered and won a local talent show at eighteen. After graduating from high school, he joined the air force and was stationed in Okinawa, Japan, where he put his early training on the guitar to use in forming a band, the WESTERNERS.

In 1968 one of Mel's songs, "Ruby, Don't Take Your Love to Town," became a major hit for KENNY ROGERS AND THE FIRST EDITION. Four years later, Mel recorded his first major hit, "I Ain't Never." As a result, Mel was inducted into the Nashville Songwriters International Hall of Fame and won the Country Music Association's Entertainer of the Year Award. Mel won Comedian of the Year six times during the 1970s and was honored by BMI as Songwriter of the Decade for two decades. He has written over a thousand songs. Over five hundred have been recorded by major artists. He has had nine songs climb to number one with thirty-six being Top Ten singles. Mel was inducted into both the Grand Ole Opry and the Country Music Hall of Fame® in 2007.

PAM TILLIS

JULY 24, 1957 - PLANT CITY, FLORIDA

Since 1991 Pam has charted more than thirty singles on the Billboard *country charts, including her number one single, "My Crazy Life."*

Pam Tillis has done it all. As the child of country music royalty, MEL TILLIS is her father, she made her debut at the Grand Ole Opry at the age of eight. On that auspicious night she sang "Tom Dooley." Pam knows what it is like to top the singles charts frequently, to reach the goal of platinum, to sing at Nashville's Bluebird Cafe, to appear on Broadway, in movies, and on *Hollywood Squares*, to sing in San Francisco bistros, to hear the ovation at your own induction to the Opry. Through it all, she has never lost touch with her roots in country music, as is evident in the songs she writes and sings. She is especially in tune with the country sound she remembers from her early years.

While growing up, Pam recalls that there was music all around. Music was the only thing she took seriously. She enrolled in Belmont University and at that time formed her first band. In the late 1970s, she dropped out of college to continue her musical career. She got her start in San Francisco before returning to Nashville where she became a demo singer. After an unsuccessful pop album for Warner Brothers, she turned to songwriting at Tree Publishing. At about the same time, Pam was making regular appearances on TNN's *Nashville Now*, a variety show that RALPH EMERY hosted. Pam's songs have been recorded by a variety of artists, including CHAKA KHAN, MARTINA MCBRIDE, GLORIA GAYNOR, CONWAY TWITTY, JUICE NEWTON, and HIGHWAY 101. One of Pam's songs became the first number one hit for LORRIE MORGAN.

Pam's acting career includes roles on *Promised Land, Diagnosis Murder, L.A. Law,* and on Broadway in *Smokey Joe's Cafe.*

In 2007 Pam released *RhineStoned* on her own label, Stellar Cat Records. She ranks number thirty in CMT's 40 Greatest Women in Country Music.

TRENT **TOMLINSON**

JULY 3, 1975 - BLYTHEVILLE, ARKANSAS

Trent Tomlinson's debut album, "Country Is My Rock," produced three Top Forty singles on Billboard's Hot Country Songs.

Born in Arkansas, Trent was reared in SHERYL CROW's hometown of Kennett, Missouri. His father had plans for him to be the next basketball superstar, but Trent had different dreams. His friends in high school were the musicians. Trent's mother wanted him to play classical piano but Trent preferred the music of JERRY LEE LEWIS. After giving up the piano because of its limitations, Trent started playing the guitar. At night, he could be seen playing rock music in local bars, but slowly he changed to country and spent time writing his own songs.

After Trent lost first place in TNN's talent competition, *You Can Be a Star,* by a margin of two-tenths of a point, his father began to realize his son's talent. Trent started college, but after six months decided to give Nashville a try. His first job was cleaning carpet by day and at night he played at Barbara's in Printers Alley. Both the publisher and record label Trent signed with went out of business. Back home in Missouri, he learned that BUDDY KILLEN of Tree Publishing had bought his catalog of songs out of bankruptcy court and had a contract for him. After a year and a half, Trent went to work for MCA Publishing and in 2004 he signed with Lyric Records. His debut album, *Country Is My Rock,* was released in 2006. SARA EVANS included Trent's "Missing Missouri" on her album, *Real Fine Place,* in 2005. GEORGE STRAIT recorded Trent's "Why Can't I Leave Her Alone" on his album, *It Just Comes Natural,* in 2006.

Influenced by the outlaw county movement of WILLIE NELSON and country rockers, BIG AND RICH, Trent didn't spend almost a decade as a struggling songwriter and singer to become just another honky-tonker.

Trent says the message in his songs is "I have the ability to love you, to understand, and at the end of the day all that matters is Mama and Daddy and going to heaven. That pretty much sums everything up."

MERLE **TRAVIS**

NOVEMBER 29, 1917 - ROSEWOOD, KENTUCKY - OCTOBER 20, 1983

Merle wrote "Sixteen Tons" and his famous "Travis picking" influenced a generation of musicians including Chet Atkins.

The man who developed "Travis picking" was born in poverty. His father was a tobacco farmer who turned to the better paying job of a coal miner. Merle remembered the stories told by his father about life in the coal mines. These stories became the foundation for Merle's biggest hit, "Sixteen Tons." The first instrument young Merle mastered was a five-string banjo, but at twelve he was given a homemade guitar that set his path in a different direction. Just by chance, IKE EVERLY, father of DON and PHIL EVERLY, was a neighbor who shared with Merle a unique three-finger style of playing the guitar. Merle became proficient as he entered his teens and supplemented his income from the Civilian Conservation Corp.

At the age of twenty, Merle became a member of CLAYTON MCMICHEN'S GEORGIA WILDCATS. A year later, he joined DRIFTING COWBOYS with a permanent position to play at Cincinnati's Radio WLW. With this national exposure, Merle was invited to play with GRANDPA JONES and the DELMORE BROTHERS who were billed as a gospel quartet called the BROWN'S FERRY FOUR. After serving in the U.S. Marines during WWII, he headed for Los Angeles late in 1944. Merle appeared in Western movies as a member of RAY WHITLEY'S WESTERN SWING BAND. Nine years later, he appeared in his biggest film, *From Here to Eternity,* and sang "Re-Enlistment Blues."

In 1947 Merle started writing hit songs including, "Sixteen Tons," "Smoke! Smoke! Smoke! (That Cigarette)," "Dark as a Dungeon," "Over by Number Nine," and "Divorce Me C.O.D." After some turbulence in his life, Merle settled down in the mid-1970s. He married his fourth wife, Dorothy, who had been married to HANK THOMPSON, and concentrated on his music. CHET ATKINS teamed up with Merle in 1974 as the ATKINS-TRAVIS TRAVELING SHOW, and the two won a pair of Grammys.

RANDY TRAVIS

MAY 4, 1959 - MARSHVILLE, NORTH CAROLINA

Randy's single of Kim Williams' "Three Wooden Crosses," reached number one and won the CMA award for Song of the Year in 2003.

Ranked thirteen on CMT's Forty Greatest Men of Country Music, Randy has had a long and hard road to get to the top in his field. He was the second of six children born to Harold and Bobbie Traywick. Their folks dressed Randy and his three brothers in Western attire and billed them as the TRAYWICK BROTHERS. Later, Randy and Ricky performed as a duo and played at fiddler conventions and other crowd-drawing venues. Randy met his future wife and manager, ELIZABETH HATCHER, after he won a talent show hosted by Country City, USA in 1975. For the next five years, Randy worked at the club and recorded two singles, "Dreaming" and "She's My Woman." He changed his name to Randy Ray and moved to Nashville in the early 1980s.

In 1985 Warner Brothers finally signed Randy after he had been turned down by other labels. By now, record executives had changed his name to Travis. In the soundtrack for the movie, *Rustler's Rhapsody*, Randy's first recording with Warner, he sang "Prairie Rose." His first album, *Storms of Life,* was followed by two singles, "On the Other Hand" and "1982." His voice is reminiscent of such performers as GEORGE JONES, LEFTY FRIZZELL, and MERLE HAGGARD. In 1986 Randy won CMA's Horizon Award and a year later, Album of the Year with *Always and Forever*. By the end of the 1980s, Randy had sold more than thirteen million albums and was in demand for live performances. He ended his relationship with Warner Brothers and signed with DreamWorks in 1997. "Out of My Bones" was his first number one single with the new label.

Randy has twenty-two number one hits, six number one albums, five Grammys, and six Dove Awards. With his acting skills being seen on *Matlock, Touched by an Angel,* and on the big screen in *The Rainmaker,* Randy Travis is pleasing a huge fan base.

TRAVIS **TRITT**

FEBRUARY 9, 1963 - MARIETTA, GEORGIA

Travis roared onto the country music scene in the late 1980s with his southern country rock. His first number one hit was "Help Me Hold On."

With little encouragement from his family to pursue a career in music, young Travis taught himself to play the guitar and by the age of fourteen started writing his own compositions. While working for an air-conditioning company, he received encouragement from his employer who happened to be a guitarist. By nineteen, Travis was pursuing his dream of a music career full time. An executive at Warner Brothers, DANNY DAVENPORT, was the next important person on Travis' road to success. He recorded demo tapes at Danny's private studio and hit the honky-tonk circuit.

In mid-1989, Travis got his biggest break when he signed a contract with the Nashville division of Warner Brothers. By April of 1990, his debut album, *Country Club,* was released and Travis was on his way to fulfill his dreams as a respected country singer. The album produced two hit singles, "Help Me Hold On" and "I'm Gonna Be Somebody." Travis describes his music as a triangle, "On one side is a folk influence from people like JAMES TAYLOR, LARRY GATLIN, and JOHN DENVER. On the second side are GEORGE JONES and MERLE HAGGARD—that type of music...on the third side are the ALLMAN BROTHERS and the MARSHALL TUCKER BAND."

Travis was holding his own in the early 1990s against upcoming superstars such as GARTH BROOKS, CLINT BLACK, and ALAN JACKSON. His hits kept coming with his second album, *It's All About to Happen,* in 1991 and *T-r-o-u-b-l-e* in 1992 with a number one single, "Can I Trust You With My Heart." In 1991 Travis won CMA's Horizon Award and was invited to join the Grand Ole Opry. He earned a Grammy for "The Whiskey Ain't Working" in 1993 and is listed number forty on CMT's 40 Greatest Men of Country Music. Travis continues to tour. His most recent CD release was *The Storm* in 2007.

ERNEST TUBB

FEBRUARY 9, 1914 - (NEAR) CRISP, TEXAS - SEPTEMBER 6, 1984

Ernest was the sixth member elected to Country Music Hall of Fame®. "I'm Walking the Floor Over You" became his biggest hit.

No book of famous country singers would be complete without the great Ernest Tubb. He was the youngest child of a cotton sharecropper who farmed across the state of Texas. At fourteen, Ernest had fallen in love with the music of JIMMIE RODGERS. During his spare time he would practice playing the guitar and singing. In 1936 Ernest contacted Jimmie's widow, Carrie, and a friendship developed. She offered him advice including everything from the clothes he wore to finding new songs for him to sing. She also was instrumental in securing a record deal for Ernest with RCA. Ernest's goal was to yodel like his idol, but a tonsillectomy in 1939 lowered his voice and forever prevented him from yodeling.

By 1940 Ernest had become a full-time musician. His first success came after he recorded "Blue Eyed Elaine" and "I'll Get Along Somehow" for Decca Records. His biggest hit came the next year with "I'm Walking the Floor Over You." The next person to make an impact on Ernest's career was Nashville talent agent, J. L. FRANK. Through this contact, Ernest joined the Grand Ole Opry, began selling a series of songbooks on the radio, and with his band, the TEXAS TROUBADOURS, appeared in movies.

Ernest had several hits in the 1940s, including "Soldier's Last Letter," "Tomorrow Never Comes," "It's Been So Long Darling," "Rainbow at Night," and "Filipino Baby." In his spare time, he opened the first major all country radio shop and included a live show immediately following the Grand Ole Opry. The show became known as the *Midnight Jamboree* and continues today. In 1947 he brought the Grand Ole Opry to Carnegie Hall. Ernest Tubb's legacy includes his ability to boost the careers of many stars such as HANK WILLIAMS, HANK SNOW, CARL SMITH, PATSY CLINE, JOHNNY CASH, JACK GREENE, and LORETTA LYNN. In CMT's 40 Greatest Men of Country Music, Ernest Tubb ranks number twenty-one.

TANYA **TUCKER**

OCTOBER 10, 1958 - SEMINOLE, TEXAS

In 1972 Tanya had her first hit at the age of thirteen with "Delta Dawn." Her success extended into the 1980s and 1990s.

With much encouragement from her mother and father, Beau and Juanita Tucker, Tanya became a country music star when she was just entering her teens. While moving around the southwest, her father sought construction work while helping fulfill his daughter's dreams. Tanya has said, "I wasn't forced to do anything. My dad and I have always had an understanding. If I wanted something...he'd say 'well let's see what we can do.' He would never say 'No, that's impossible.' He would make it happen as long as I did my part." The family moved to Las Vegas where Tanya recorded a demo tape. BILLY SHERRILL heard the tape and signed Tanya to a record contract with Columbia. She turned down a chance to record the song, "The Happiest Girl in the U.S.A.," that made DONNA FARGO a superstar. Instead she chose "Delta Dawn," a song she had heard BETTE MIDLER sing on the *Tonight Show*. Tanya scored in the Top Ten with "Delta Dawn" but her first number one hit was "What's Your Mama's Name?" in the spring of 1973. By the time she reached her sixteenth birthday she had signed with MCA Records and was moving more to the country rock genre. Tanya became a star with more hits including, "Lizzie and the Rainman," "San Antonio Stroll," and "Here's Some Love." Although the cover of her 1975 *T.N.T.* album caused some controversy, she still struck gold.

During the 1980s, Tanya recorded singles with GLEN CAMPBELL, PAUL DAVIS, and PAUL OVERSTREET, giving her three number one hits. The first was "I Won't Take Less Than Your Love." The next two songs were "If It Don't Come Easy" and "Strong Enough to Bend." Tanya received the prestigious award, Female Vocalist of the Year from the Country Music Association in 1991. She ranks number twenty in CMT's 40 Greatest Women of Country Music.

JOSH **TURNER**

NOVEMBER 20, 1977 - HANNAH, SOUTH CAROLINA

Josh's self-penned song, "Long Black Train," became a hit in 2003. "Your Man" and "Would You Go With Me" are his first number one hits.

"**G**rowing up singing in the church choir" could be the beginning of many country musicians' biographical sketches. For Joshua Otis Turner nothing is typical. He says, "Growing up, traditional country music was always where my heart was at, because those songs were speaking about the life that I was living in rural South Carolina." Josh's smooth baritone voice has been compared to the sound of GEORGE JONES.

When Josh moved to Nashville to attend Belmont University, he received an invitation to sing at the Grand Ole Opry on December 21, 2001. There were several standing ovations when the crowd heard his self-penned song, "Long Black Train." Josh drew inspiration for the song while listening to his grandparents record collection. The album was produced by FRANK ROGERS at MCA Records. The title track became Josh's first hit and was certified platinum in December 2004.

Josh's next two singles, "Your Man" and "Would You Go With Me" were certified double platinum. *Your Man* was released in 2006 and soared to number two on the Top 200 charts and became one of only four country albums to hit the double-platinum range in 2006. With all his hits, Josh was invited to join the Grand Ole Opry on October 27, 2007, just shy of his thirtieth birthday. One of his favorite singers, VINCE GILL, formally inducted him as one of the youngest-ever members. On his next project, *Everything Is Fine*, Josh wrote seven songs including the fun-loving "Firecracker." "Trailerhood" continues the fun by telling you where you have arrived and "everyday's about feeling good."

Josh has had two successful collaborations. The first was a single, "Another Try" with TRISHA YEARWOOD, and next was the Grammy nominated single, "Nowhere Fast," with ANTHONY HAMILTON. Josh is married to Jennifer and they have a son, Hampton, born October 6, 2006.

SHANIA **TWAIN**

AUGUST 28, 1965 - WINDSOR, ONTARIO, CANADA

Shania's third album, Come on Over, *is the biggest-selling album by a female solo artist and the top-selling country album of all time.*

Shania in the Ojibwa Native American language means "I'm on my way." This superstar from Canada picked the correct name in the early 1990s. Born Eileen Regina Edwards she was reared by her mother, Sharon, and adoptive stepfather, Jerry Twain. To say that her parents encouraged her to develop her musical talent would understate their efforts. By the time Eileen was eight, her parents would wake her up and take her to nightclubs to sing. She started writing her own material early in her career and was inspired by TAMMY WYNETTE, WILLIE NELSON, STEVIE WONDER, the MAMAS AND THE PAPAS, and the CARPENTERS.

Tragedy stuck when Shania's folks were killed in an automobile accident in 1987. Shania had been working at Deerhurst Resort in Huntsville, Ontario, but returned home to help rear her four siblings. She continued to perform and recorded a demo tape of her songs. By 1993 Mercury Nashville had released her unsuccessful debut album. That same year, she met and married producer, ROBERT LANGE, and released her second album, *The Woman in Me.* Selling eighteen million copies, it broke all records for any other female country singer in history. From this album, Shania had three number one hits, "Any Man of Mine," "I'm Outta Here," and "No One Needs to Know." In 1997 her third album, *Come on Over,* sold thirty-four million copies worldwide. Although some dyed-in-the-wool country fans think she has taken country music too far toward rock, Shania has obviously captured a fan base.

Shania is the top-selling female artist of all time with seventeen Top Ten songs, half of which soared to number one. She ranks seventh as CMT's 40 Greatest Women of Country Music. Shania says, "All I ever intended was to make a living at what I do. Everything I've achieved since then is above and beyond."

CONWAY **TWITTY**

SEPTEMBER 1, 1933 - FRIARS POINT, MISSISSIPPI - JUNE 5, 1993

Conway had fifty-five number one hits, more than any other country artist. Conway also enjoyed success in Rock 'n' Roll.

Growing up in Mississippi and Arkansas, Harold Lloyd Jenkins was taught by his riverboat pilot father to play the guitar by the time he was four. He loved listening to the gospel singing from the local black congregation and on Saturday night the family always gathered around the radio to listen to the Grand Ole Opry. Harold's first band was the PHILLIPS COUNTY RAMBLERS. By the time he was twelve, Harold had his own radio show. He had a talent for baseball and almost signed with the Philadelphia Phillies but was drafted by the army instead and served during the Korean War.

After his discharge from the army, Harold headed for Sun Records to check out the latest music trends. At first he didn't try rockabilly but chose the smooth sounding ballad, "It's Only Make Believe." It became his first hit. By 1965 he had produced three gold records and had his first number one hit, "Hello Darlin'." He and LORETTA LYNN scored big with three hits, "After the Fire Is Gone," "Lead Me On," and "Louisiana Woman, Mississippi Man." In 1957 Harold's name change was based on the tiny towns of Conway, Arkansas, and Twitty, Texas. The 1963 Broadway musical, *Bye Bye Birdie,* was a parody based on the lives of Conway and ELVIS PRESLEY.

A part of Conway's legacy is the many artists to whom he gave a boost along the way. Although he did not talk during his concerts or give interviews, Conway was known to have the clout to speak on behalf of new artists coming onto the scene. He co-owned the United Talent Agency and he especially liked songwriters. He said about himself that he was "the best friend a song ever had." VINCE GILL, NAOMI JUDD, and REBA MCENTIRE are some of the artists he helped bring to the forefront. Conway was inducted into the Country Music Hall of Fame® in 1999. He is considered number six in CMT's 40 Greatest Men of Country Music.

CARRIE **UNDERWOOD**

MARCH 10, 1983 - MUSKOGEE, OKLAHOMA

Carrie won first place during the fourth season of American Idol. *She has since become a multi-platinum recording artist.*

SIMON COWELL'S prediction came true when he said that Carrie would win the fourth competition of *American Idol* in 2005 and that she would outsell all the previous winners. Carrie was the first country artist to win the competition. She has gone on to a successful musical career.

Carrie first sang for the congregation at the Free Will Baptist Church and for other social events in her hometown of Checotah, Oklahoma. In 1996 at thirteen, Carrie was close to having a contract with Capitol Records, but the management changed and the deal fell through.

While attending Northeastern State University in Tahlequah, Oklahoma, Carrie had a role in a country music show and learned about country legends, PATSY CLINE and the CARTER FAMILY. She majored in Mass Communications with an emphasis in broadcast journalism but kept her options open for a career in music. When Carrie decided to compete on *American Idol*, she went to St. Louis for the tryout. While it might have seemed like an upset to win over BO BRICE in the final competition, Carrie has proved to be worthy of the title.

Some Hearts, her debut album, sold more than six million copies, the biggest-selling *American Idol* album to date. The album spawned three hits on the country charts, including "Jesus, Take the Wheel," "Don't Forget to Remember Me," and "Before He Cheats." "Jesus, Take the Wheel" stayed at number one for six weeks and earned Single Record of the Year from the ACM. Carrie also won Female Country Artist of the Year and the Horizon Award for New Country Artist in 2006. Also that year, this intelligent singer graduated from college *magna cum laude*.

Carrie has toured with KENNY CHESNEY and BRAD PAISLEY and signed deals to promote Hershey's chocolates and Skechers shoes. Carrie Underwood has certainly shown that she's the real thing.

KEITH **URBAN**

OCTOBER 26, 1967 - WHANGAREI, NEW ZEALAND

Since 2004 two of Keith's albums have reached the Top Ten on the U.S. Billboard 200 albums chart. He has scored seven number one songs.

Whangarei, New Zealand, seems to be an unlikely place for a country singer to be born. Several conditions came together to contribute to Keith Lionel Urban's trek to the top of his profession. The first was his parents' love of American culture, especially country music. Next, there were guitar lessons at the age of six. Finally there was raw talent of which Keith had plenty. Winning talent contests by age eight, Keith was influenced by the music of DON WILLIAMS, GLEN CAMPBELL, DOLLY PARTON, DIRE STRAITS, and the songwriting of JIMMY WEBB.

In the early 1990s, country music was coming Down Under and in the center of this movement was Tamworth, Australia. Since his family had moved to Brisbane when Keith was two, it was natural for him to gravitate to his destiny. At twenty-four, Keith recorded his first album which sent four singles to number one on the Australian country charts. With dreams of moving to the epicenter of country music in the U.S., he arrived in Nashville in 1997. Keith drafted two of his mates from home to form his first band, the RANCH. With a record deal from Capitol, their debut album, *The Ranch,* received favorable revues, especially for Keith's guitar playing. He soon disbanded the trio and began his solo career.

By the turn of the century, Keith had duplicated his Australian success in the U.S. In 2000 his self-titled album produced his first number one hit in the U.S. market, "But for the Grace of God." In addition, Keith won CMA's Horizon Award in 2001. The next year, "Somebody Like You," from his *Golden Road* album stayed at number one for six weeks. Also, "You'll Think of Me" won Keith a Grammy. *Golden Road* went triple platinum, as did his 2004 album, *Be Here.*

Keith married fellow Australian, actress NICOLE KIDMAN, in 2006. Their daughter, Sunday Rose, was born July 7, 2008, in Nashville.

Porter **Wagoner**

AUGUST 12, 1927 - WEST PLAINS, MISSOURI - OCTOBER 28, 2007

Porter was elected to the Country Music Hall of Fame® in 2002. His eighty-one charted records include his number one hit "Satisfied Mind."

The "Thin Man from West Plains" contributed much to the country music scene for over fifty years. He became the unofficial spokesman for the Grand Ole Opry after the death of ROY ACUFF in 1992. Young Porter would pretend to introduce Roy while standing on a tree stump in his backyard. Then, Porter would "be" the King of the Hillbillies and sing "Wabash Cannonball." His older brother, Glenn Lee, taught him to play an eight-dollar National guitar from Montgomery Ward. By the time Porter was fifteen, the family farm was sold to pay off debts. He got a job pumping gas and working at a department store. The owner hired Porter to sing on the radio show he was sponsoring.

By 1951 Porter was hired by KWTO in Springfield, Missouri, on a show that later became the *Ozark Jubilee*. Three years later, he had signed with RCA and had a Top Ten hit with "Company's Comin'." In 1955 he scored his first number one hit with his self-penned, "A Satisfied Mind." Soon after, Porter moved to Music City, USA, and joined the Grand Ole Opry. *The Porter Wagoner Show* began on television in 1960 with singer NORMA JEAN. When Norma Jean left the show, she was replaced by a twenty-one-year-old blond from east Tennessee named DOLLY PARTON. Audiences eventually warmed up to the change because of the wonderful music created by Porter and Dolly.

Porter earned three Grammys with the BLACKWOOD BROTHERS QUARTET during the 1960s and was the first country musician to create the concept album with each track built around a theme. Other hit songs he wrote or co-wrote include, "Carroll County Accident," "Skid Row Joe," and "Green, Green Grass of Home." Porter always adhered to pure country tradition. WAYLON JENNINGS said of him, "He couldn't go pop with a mouthful of firecrackers."

BILLY **WALKER**

JANUARY 14, 1929 - RALLS, TEXAS - MAY 21, 2006

Billy's signature song, "Charlie's Shoes," was number one on the country charts in 1962. His "Just for the Hank of It!" honored his friends.

"The Tall Texan" was his nick-name. Billy Walker was born in rural Texas, just months before the stockmarket crash of 1929. Billy and his seven siblings were in jeopardy after their mother died when he was four. Young Billy and three of his brothers were sent to an orphanage for several years until his father, a Methodist minister, remarried. Billy won his first contest in New Mexico at age fifteen, but had no support from his dad in his quest to become a country musician. Because of his strict religious upbringing, Billy had some hard decisions to make. Should he pursue his dreams or obey his father? With his first taste of singing before a crowd, he knew he had made the right choice.

Billy's first big performance was at the *Big D Jamboree* in Dallas as "the masked singer," a gimmick he soon gave up. From there it was on to the *Louisiana Hayride* in Shreveport and then the *Ozark Jubilee* in Springfield, Missouri. He became friends with SLIM WHITMAN and the two began performing together. They decided to let an unknown singer, ELVIS PRESLEY, have his chance to sing. Elvis made a hundred and fifty dollars a day while touring with Billy.

After joining the Grand Ole Opry on January 1, 1960, Billy's career received a big boost. During his fifty years at the Opry, Billy landed thirty-two Top Ten hits including his signature song, "Charlie's Shoes," in 1962. Other hits were "Cross the Brazos at Waco" in 1964, and "When a Man Loves a Woman (The Way I Love You)" in 1970.

Billy and his wife Bettie were always accessible during the Grand Ole Opry fan club parties. Unfortunately, their lives and those of two band members ended on an Alabama highway on May 21, 2006.

Billy Walker was more than tall in stature, he was a kind and genuine singer who is missed by his fans and country music as a whole.

RAY **WALKER**

MARCH 16, 1934 - CENTREVILLE, MISSISSIPPI

Ray has served as bass singer for the renowned Jordanaires since 1958. For fourteen years, the Jordanaires sang backup for Elvis Presley.

Born in Centreville, Mississippi, Raymond Clinton Walker Jr., first lived in nearby Wilkinson. He was second of the five children of R.C. and Elizabeth. Ray's father was an evangelist and the family moved every two to four years. By 1952 when Ray entered David Lipscomb College in Nashville, the family had lived in seven states. Ray was chaplain of his high school graduating class in Jacksonville, Florida, as well as at David Lipscomb. With his smooth bass voice Ray became part of the college quartet. PAT BOONE had also been a member of this quartet. Since third grade, Ray had been singing in a quartet and it was natural for him to land a spot performing on television. In his junior year, Ray and Marilyn DuFresne were married. A year later, he dropped out of college to build a radio station in Centerville, Tennessee. By 1957 he had earned his degree and in April 1958, he was contacted by his former choral director about a job. GORDON STOKER of the JORDANAIRES was in need of a bass singer to replace HUGH JARRETT. Ray's audition was at 11:00 in the evening. He received a call the next day to fly to Hollywood for a recording session. He officially became the bass singer for the Jordanaires on June 1, 1958.

The Jordanaires began singing backup for ELVIS PRESLEY at the start of his career. After Elvis heard the group sing "Peace in the Valley" he commented to Gordon Stoker, "If I ever get a recording contract with a major company, I want you to back me up."

Ray remembers his first meeting with Elvis, "He was a real person. He gave you his full attention. He was the kindest, quietest, most courteous person you ever met in your life."

Ray and the Grammy-winning Jordanaires have been inducted into the Gospel Music, Country Music, and Rockabilly Halls of Fame.

STEVE **WARINER**

DECEMBER 25, 1954 - NOBLESVILLE, INDIANA

Steve is one of the most popular country artists with a string of number one hit singles. "Holes in the Floor of Heaven" was one of his winners.

Born on Christmas Day, Steven Noel Wariner knew what his life's career would be before he was nine years old. His parents, Roy and Ilene, surrounded young Steve and his four siblings with music. Roy had a "real" job during the day, but at night he played in a small country band. Young Steve would practice with his father's Danelectro bass guitar to the recordings of RAY PRICE, HANK THOMPSON, JIM REEVES, and his hero, CHET ATKINS. When he was ten, Steve made his debut playing with the new ROY WARINER BAND. Steve was also a fan of GEORGE JONES and MERLE HAGGARD. Into his teens, Steve played the electric guitar and drums for country and rock groups made up of family members. Before he had graduated from high school he was invited to open for DOTTIE WEST at the Nashville Country Club in Indianapolis.

After touring three years with Dottie, Steve joined BOB LUMAN'S band in 1975 as bass player. Two years later, Chet Atkins, his longtime idol, hired Steve as his bass player and signed him with RCA. His number one hits include, "All Roads Lead to You," "Some Fools Never Learn," "You Can Dream of Me," "Where Did I Go Wrong?," "The Domino Theory," "Tips of My Fingers," and "Holes in the Floor of Heaven."

Steve earned his first Grammy nomination in 1988 for Best Country and Western Vocal Performance-Duet with GLEN CAMPBELL for "The Hand That Rocks the Cradle." His first Grammy came four years later with Best Country Vocal Collaboration for "Restless." Grammy nominations kept coming. In 2001 Steve, with his son, Ryan, earned a Best Country Instrumental Grammy nomination for "Bloodline." In 2005 Steve released his twenty-fifth album entitled "This Real Life."

Composer, guitarist, singer, Steve Wariner, was inducted into the Music City Walk of Fame in 2008.

KITTY **WELLS**

In 1952 Kitty's recording of "It Wasn't God Who Made Honky-Tonk Angels" was the first by a female to sell a million copies.

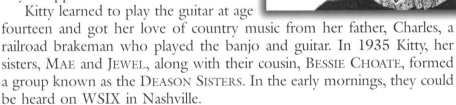

The "Queen of Country Music," Kitty Wells, was named Ellen Muriel Deason at birth. She created the role of "queen" for all future female country singers and was the first woman in the business to sell a million records and reach number one in country music. Kitty was voted the number one Country Female Artist fourteen straight years by all of the trade publications of the day. No other woman in country has as yet topped her achievements.

Kitty learned to play the guitar at age fourteen and got her love of country music from her father, Charles, a railroad brakeman who played the banjo and guitar. In 1935 Kitty, her sisters, MAE and JEWEL, along with their cousin, BESSIE CHOATE, formed a group known as the DEASON SISTERS. In the early mornings, they could be heard on WSIX in Nashville.

In 1937 Kitty married country legend, JOHNNY WRIGHT. Johnny and JACK AUGLIN were a duo act; Jack was married to Johnny's sister Louise. Kitty's career with Johnny and Jack lasted over sixty years. It was Johnny who gave Kitty her name, Kitty Wells, in 1943. It came from an old folk ballad recorded by the PACKARD FAMILY called "Sweet Kitty Wells."

In their early years Kitty, with Johnny and Jack, was heard on air in Raleigh, North Carolina; Knoxville, Tennessee; Bluefield, West Virginia; Decatur, Georgia; and on the *Louisiana Hayride* in Shreveport.

During the 1950s, Kitty accumulated twenty-three Top Ten hits. After Kitty's recording of "It Wasn't God Who Made Honky Tonk Angels" sold a million records, the three became regulars on the Grand Ole Opry.

In 1976 Kitty was elected to the Country Music Hall of Fame®, and in 1991 she received a Lifetime Achievement Award from the National Academy of Arts and Sciences.

DOTTIE **WEST**

OCTOBER 11, 1932 - MCMINNVILLE, TENN. - SEPTEMBER 4, 1991

Dottie's career began in the early 1960s with her Top Ten, Grammy winning, country hit, "Here Comes My Baby Back Again."

Dreaming of becoming a singer at an early age, Dorothy Marie Marsh began singing in the church choir and taking guitar lessons. The oldest of ten children, Dottie was committed to help her mother financially after her father deserted the family. She picked cotton and helped manage a small restaurant. After graduating from high school, Dottie majored in music at Tennessee Technological University in Cookeville. There she met BILL WEST, an engineering major and musician. They were married in 1952 and after graduation moved to Cleveland, Ohio, where both played in clubs and Bill worked for an electronics firm. They made regular appearances on local television in *Landmark Jamboree*.

On a 1959 trip to Nashville, Dottie was turned down by several record labels. Ready to leave town, she stopped at Starday Records and paid $511.00 to cut her first single, "Angel on Paper." It was heard by Opry manager, OTT DEVINE, and Dottie was invited to sing at the Grand Ole Opry. The biggest stars began recording her songs. JIM REEVES was the first to record "Is This Me?" It became a hit and Jim invited Dottie to record a duet, "Love Is No Excuse." She also recorded "Slowly" with JIMMY DEAN.

In 1964 Dottie signed with RCA and recorded "Here Comes My Baby Back Again." The song hit the Top Ten and won Dottie a Grammy, the first for a female country singer. It has since been recorded by over one hundred artists. Dottie will always be remembered for her duets with KENNY ROGERS such as, "Anyone Who Isn't Me Tonight" and "All I Ever Need Is You." A 1973 Coca-Cola commercial based on her song "Country Sunshine" won Dottie a Clio Award. This was a first for a country artist. Dottie's close friend, PATSY CLINE, once told her, "Hoss, if you can't do it with feeling, don't." It was advice that Dottie took to heart.

SLIM **WHITMAN**

Slim is one of the best-selling and most influential artists in country music history. One of his biggest hits was "Indian Love Call."

Once known as "America's Favorite Folk Singer," Ottis Dewey Whitman Jr. learned to yodel while listening to recordings by MONTANA SLIM and JIMMIE RODGERS. It wasn't until he was serving in the U.S. Navy during WWII that Slim learned to play the guitar. Being left-handed, he restrung the guitar upside-down. While on board the U.S.S. *Chilton*, Slim had his first taste of entertaining when he sang for the sailors. His navy buddies still remember the good times when Slim sang during "Happy Hour." After his discharge from the service in 1946, Slim returned to his home in Tampa to work at the shipyard. He also pitched for the Plant City baseball team. Slim's friends urged him to get on with his musical career and in 1948 he took their advice.

Slim began singing for several radio stations in the Tampa area and formed his own backup band, the VARIETY RHYTHM BOYS. His first big break came when COLONEL TOM PARKER heard him singing on Tampa Bay's WFLA Radio and helped him get signed with RCA in 1948. ELVIS PRESLEY was just beginning his career and he toured with Slim as Slim's opening act. Slim was paid $500 per show and Elvis received $50.

Slim released his first single, "I'm Casting My Lasso Toward the Sky," which became his signature song. In 1950 Slim joined the *Louisiana Hayride*. During this time, HANK WILLIAMS helped Slim with his stuttering. Slim's breakthrough hit was BOB NOLAN'S "Love Song of the Waterfall" but it was "Indian Love Call" that became one of his best-known songs. Slim's *All My Best* album sold four million copies and became the best-selling album in history to be marketed on television. Slim has been a regular on the Grand Ole Opry, but he is more famous in Europe than in the U.S. In 1956 Slim became the first country singer to sing at the London Palladium.

CHUCK **WICKS**

JUNE 20, 1979 - SMYRNA, DELAWARE

Chuck's "Stealing Cinderella" was nominated for CMT's award, USA Weekend Breakthrough Video of the Year, for 2008.

Perseverance must be the watch word for this young man from Delaware. Charles Elliot Wicks was reared on a farm near Smyrna. His first big dreams were to become a professional baseball player. His other love was music. Country music. After hearing the likes of ALAN JACKSON and KENNY ROGERS, he was hooked. Chuck began writing his own material and by the time he was a senior at Florida Southern College, his attraction for sports was overtaken by music.

Lacking only two classes until graduation, Chuck packed his bags and headed for Nashville. He eventually secured a recording contract with RCA Records, but not until he had persevered. Chuck spent years honing his craft with some of the most gifted Music Row writers, including GEORGE TEREN, RIVERS RUTHERFORD, NEIL THRASHER, MONTY POWELL, and WENDELL and MIKE MOBLEY. By day Chuck wrote down lyrics and seven nights a week he parked cars at Fleming's Steak House. His goal has been to compose about a hundred songs a year.

All that work paid off. Chuck got a contract with RCA and began working on his debut album. He could now appreciate his fortunate break. With his soulful baritone voice blending R&B and country, Chuck has listened well to his idols who have gone before him. *Starting Now* has many references to driving cars, reminiscent of the writing he did while parking the cars at Flemings. While his first single, "Stealing Cinderella," was climbing the charts, it became the CD to play for the father and daughter dance at weddings.

Chuck first appeared on the Grand Ole Opry in August 2007, and was a cast member on the short-lived reality show, *Nashville*. Chuck's vast collection of songs accompanied him on the road in 2008 as he toured with BRAD PAISLEY.

DOYLE **WILBURN**

JULY 7, 1930 - HARDY, ARKANSAS - OCTOBER 16, 1982

Doyle and his brother Teddy were billed as the Wilburn Brothers. Their weekly TV show helped launch Sonny James, Loretta Lynn, and Jean Shepherd.

The original WILBURN CHILDREN singing group was established out of necessity. Their father, who was disabled in WWI, bought musical instruments for his five children to use in earning an income for the family. From Sears and Roebuck, their recently purchased guitar, mandolin, and fiddle were put to work playing on a street corner in Thayer, Missouri, on Christmas Eve in 1937. The children took classes for six months in a one-room school in Hardy, Arkansas. The rest of the year was spent touring radio stations, school auditoriums, and churches throughout the South. In 1940 the group got their first break, meeting ROY ACUFF while singing on tour in Birmingham, Alabama. With his recommendation, the children were invited to join the Grand Ole Opry. As luck would have it, child labor laws forced the Opry to terminate their contract after six months. After their sister, Geraldine, married and left the group, the four brothers, Lester, Leslie, Doyle, and Teddy continued touring as THE WILBURNS. In 1948 the four brothers joined the *Louisiana Hayride*.

Doyle and Teddy began touring as the WILBURN BROTHERS after they were discharged from the army in 1953. They returned to the Grand Ole Opry and became the backup singers for WEBB PIERCE. That same year, they signed a contract with Decca Records for their first big hit, "I Wanna, Wanna, Wanna." With a first place win on *Arthur Godfrey's Talent Scouts*, the brothers received their first national exposure.

The brothers debuted their weekly syndicated television program in 1963, which boosted their record sales. The show helped launch newcomers to the country scene such as, SONNY JAMES, JEAN SHEPHERD, and especially LORETTA LYNN.

Virgil Doyle Wilburn died of cancer in 1982, ending one of the most successful brother performances to ever grace the Grand Ole Opry.

TEDDY **WILBURN**

NOVEMBER 30, 1931 - HARDY, ARKANSAS - NOVEMBER 24, 2003

Teddy and his brother Doyle, the Wilburn Brothers, appeared on Dick Clark's American Bandstand in 1957 performing "I Got Over the Blues."

Close harmony was not invented by the WILBURN BROTHERS, but Teddy and Doyle perfected it. The brothers grew up in northern Arkansas during the Great Depression. Their father, Benjamin, was injured in the First World War and was counting on his children to supplement the family's income by using their musical talents. After the five children were equipped with instruments, ordered by mail, their professional musical careers began sixteen miles away on a street corner in Thayer, Missouri. Their father became their manager, agent, and crowd collector. As the school was open only six months out of twelve, THE WILBURNS were free to tour the rest of the year. They were invited to become a regular performing act at the Grand Ole Opry with the recommendation of ROY ACUFF in 1940.

After Teddy and Doyle were honorably discharged from the army in 1953, they began touring with WEBB PIERCE, FARON YOUNG, and ERNEST TUBB. Decca Records signed the Wilburn Brothers to a contract, and in the mid-1950s they charted Top Ten hits on the country charts. In the early 1960s, they had three hits in the Top Five, "Trouble's Back in Town," "Roll Muddy River," and "It's Another World." They began hosting their own weekly television show in 1963 which featured a young LORETTA LYNN. The show also provided a stage for the OAK RIDGE BOYS, TAMMY WYNETTE, and BARBARA MANDRELL. Teddy and Doyle appeared on *American Bandstand* with DICK CLARK, performing "I Got Over the Blues" on November 14, 1957.

After Doyle died in 1982, Teddy said "It was like a 45-year marriage ended. There was a lot of adjusting to do." Teddy embarked on a solo career and continued appearing on the Grand Ole Opry until his death in 2003.

DON WILLIAMS

MAY 27, 1939 - FLOYDADA, TEXAS

Don is known as the "Gentle Giant." He has had seventeen number one hits, including "I Believe in You" and "Lord I Hope This Day Is Good."

A reluctant superstar, Don learned to play the guitar from his mother. Although he fell in love with the sounds of ELVIS and CHUCK BERRY, "country" is the music that made him famous as a songwriter and musician. As a teenager, Don played in several bands before forming his own, the STRANGERS TWO, with his friend, LOFTON KLINE. They soon recruited SUSAN TAYLOR and as the POZO-SECO SINGERS, the trio began singing folk-pop music in 1964. The next year, Columbia Records signed them to a contract. Two years later, their single, "Time," settled in the Top Fifty. After a couple more minor hits, the group disbanded in 1971.

Don decided to move the Nashville and become a songwriter. He initially signed with COWBOY JACK CLEMENT at Jack Music, Inc. A year later, Don signed as a solo artist with JMI. His debut song, "Don't You Believe," was a disappointment, but in 1973, his "The Shelter of Your Eyes" climbed the country charts to number fourteen. His first single with ABC/Dot Records, "I Wouldn't Want to Live If You Didn't Love Me," reached number one. CMA named Don Male Vocalist of the Year in 1978. His "Tulsa Time" won CMA's Single Record of the Year in 1979. Don has always recorded wholesome themes in his music, not dwelling on fighting, marital infidelity, or drinking.

Don appeared in two of BURT REYNOLD'S films, *W.W. & The Dixie Dance King* and *Smokey and the Bandit 2.*

Although Don has certainly left his imprint on country music in America, he has gained a large audience in Europe as well. His seventeen number one songs on the *Billboard* charts include, "Lord I Hope This Day Is Good," "You're My Best Friend," and "Turn Out the Lights and Love Me Tonight." Don's last Top Ten single was "Lord Have Mercy on a Country Boy" in 1992.

HANK **WILLIAMS**

SEPTEMBER 17, 1923 - MOUNT OLIVE, ALABAMA - JANUARY 1, 1953

Hank was one of the most influential musicians of the Twentieth Century. He ranks number two in CTM's 40 Greatest Men of Country Music.

Hiram King Williams was born with a spinal deformity and spent the latter part of his short adult life coping with pain. Young Hiram rarely saw his father, Lon, from age six until the early 1940s. His mother, Lillie, moved the family frequently, but in 1931 settled in Georgiana, Alabama, where she managed a boarding house. Two years later, at age ten, Hiram moved about forty miles away to live with his uncle and aunt, Walter and Alice McNell, in Fountain. Two events that would shape Hiram's life forever would take place in Fountain.

As a pre-teen, Hiram had his first taste of whisky. It was the beginning of a habit that would control his life. The one good occurrence that took place at his relatives was that his aunt taught him to play the guitar. A year later, Hiram moved back to Georgiana where he befriended a black blues singer, RUFUS PAYNE, who was called TEE-TOT. Hiram learned from Tee-Tot to sing the blues. This greatly influenced his songwriting.

By 1937 the family moved to Montgomery where Hiram continued writing songs and performing. It was around this time that he changed his name from Hiram to Hank. Still fourteen, Hank officially began his musical career when he won a talent show at the Empire Theater in Montgomery. The next year, he formed his first band, the DRIFTING COWBOYS, and landed a spot on the local radio station WSFA.

Hank married his manager, Audrey Mae Sheppard, in 1944. He became a local celebrity but the two had bigger dreams. On a visit to Nashville they made contact with FRED ROSE of Acuff-Rose Publishing. Fred became Hank's manager and record producer at MGM. Hank's first single was "Move It On Over" in 1947. He had eleven number one hits in his short career, starting with "Love Sick" in 1949. Hank's last single had the foreboding title, "I'll Never Get Out of This World Alive."

HANK **WILLIAMS** JR.

MAY 26, 1948 - SHREVEPORT, LOUISIANA

Son of an American music icon, Hank Jr. had his first two number one hits in 1970 and 1972 with "All for the Love of Sunshine" and "Eleven Roses."

Living up to a legend is difficult to do. Although he appreciates his father's contribution to the country music landscape, Hank Jr. grows weary of trying to clone him. Randall Hank Williams was born one month before his legendary father made his debut at the Grand Ole Opry. His father's nickname for him was "Bocephus," after the dummy belonging to country comic ventriloquist ROD BRASFIELD. With the encouragement of his mother Audrey, eleven-year-old Hank Jr. first appeared on the Grand Ole Opry. Audrey continued her support of Hank Jr.'s career. At fourteen he recorded one of his father's songs which became his first hit record, "Long Gone Lonesome Blues." The next year, he recorded all the songs on the soundtrack to his father's film biography, *Your Cheating Heart.* GEORGE HAMILTON was cast in the role of Hank Williams.

In 1969 Hank Jr. signed with MGM, the biggest recording contract in the history of the company. A year later, he adopted a southern rock style that can be heard on *Hank Williams Jr. and Friends.* Hank Jr. won CMA's Entertainer of the Year Award in 1987 and 1988. His only Grammy was presented in 1989 for a duet with his father's voice.

When Hank Jr. recorded "A Country Boy Can Survive," he speaks from experience. While mountain climbing in Montana in 1975, Hank Jr. had a tragic fall with severe injuries. With his face shattered, he began to fight back with an extended period of physical therapy and many reconstructive surgeries. RICHARD THOMAS was cast to play Hank Jr. in the film, *Living Proof: The Hank Williams Story.*

Hank Jr. is the first country singer to win an Emmy. He has earned four trophies for his theme song for ABC's *Monday Night Football* – "Are You Ready for Some Football?" He ranks number twenty in CTM's 40 Greatest Men of Country Music.

KIM WILLIAMS

JUNE 28, 1947 - KINGSPORT, TENNESSEE

Kim is one of the most prolific song-writers of hits in the country music genre. His work includes Randy Travis' "Three Wooden Crosses."

This country boy from eastern Tennessee was taught to love music by his parents. Kim mastered the guitar and began writing songs before he reached his teens. In 1974 Kim was critically burned in an industrial electrical accident. It took the next decade and over two hundred operations before he was able to pursue his first love of music. His first trip to Nashville in 1984 began his professional career and he honed his talent until landing a five-year contract with Tree International in 1989. It took five more years for Kim to be recognized as ASCAP's Songwriter of the Year. For the next fifteen years his songs became the number one singles recorded by GARTH BROOKS, REBA MCENTIRE, and RANDY TRAVIS. Other artists who have recorded Kim's songs include WILLIE NELSON, BROOKS AND DUNN, GEORGE STRAIT, GEORGE JONES, ALAN JACKSON, CONWAY TWITTY, HANK WILLIAMS JR., KEITH ANDERSON, BARBARA MANDRELL, KENNY CHESNEY, and the GAITHER VOCAL BAND.

Kim's song list is a treasury for today's country fans with songs such as "Three Wooden Crosses," "Papa Loved Mama," "Ain't Going Down (Till the Sun Comes Up)," "She's Gonna Make It," "The Heart Is a Lonely Hunter," "Who Needs You Baby," "Honky Tonk Truth," "While You Loved Me," and "Love Can Turn the World." Kim's "Overnight Male" was featured in the movie soundtrack of *Pure Country* starring George Strait. Kim also wrote the music for the animated children's movie *Wobots*.

Both country and Christian music fans have recognized the talent of Kim Williams in his ability to write great songs. Randy Travis recorded Kim's "Three Wooden Crosses" which topped both country and Christian charts. In 2003 it won Song of the Year from CMA, a GMA Dove Award, the NSAI, and the ACM.

Kim spends his creative time near his roots on Clinch Mountain.

BOB **WILLS**

Bob Wills and his Texas Playboys created a sound known as Western swing music. In 1950 he had a Top Ten hit, "Ida Red Likes the Boogie."

One of the most versatile bands of the mid-twentieth century was created by James Robert Wills, better known as Bob Wills. Young Bob was reared in a musical family that included his father who regularly won fiddling contests. Before he had reached his teens, Bob had mastered the fiddle and began entertaining at ranch dances. In 1923 he had his debut on the radio in Amarillo, Texas. By the early 1930s, Bob had formed a band called the ALADDIN LADDIES for the Aladdin Lamp Company. Later he was sponsored by Light Crust Flour and changed the band's name to LIGHT CRUST DOUGHBOYS.

As leader of the band, caught in the middle of the Great Depression, Bob knew he had to become resilient. The band left Waco and relocated in Oklahoma in 1933 and wound up playing live on Radio KVOO in Tulsa. They were now billed as BOB WILLS AND HIS TEXAS PLAYBOYS. The American Recording Corp, forerunner of Columbia Records, discovered the group. During the late 1930s and early 1940s, the band recorded the classics, "Steele Guitar Rag" and Bob's signature song, "New San Antonio Rose." The latter hit number three on the country charts and was one of two gold records for Columbia in 1944. Their other gold record was by FRANK SINATRA. For sixteen weeks in 1946, Bob's biggest hit to top the charts was "New Spanish Two Step." By mid-century, Bob and his band were exciting their audiences with a unique blend of jazz, hillbilly, blues, and big band swing. Typically the band consisted of nine to eighteen members and included steel guitar, horns, and fiddles.

Bob's last major hit was in 1960, "Heart to Heart Talk." The recording reached number five on the country charts. Bob was inducted into the Country Music Hall of Fame® in 1968 and ranks number twenty-seven in CTM's 40 Greatest Men of Country Music.

GRETCHEN **WILSON**

JUNE 26, 1973 - POCAHONTAS, ILLINOIS

Gretchen's 2004 debut album, Here for the Party, *topped the country charts and reached number two on the Billboard 200 Chart.*

In rural Pocahontas, Illinois, where Gretchen Wilson grew up, numerous trailer parks mingled with cornfields and pig farms. Gretchen's mother was sixteen when she was born; her father left when Gretchen was two. When her mother couldn't pay the rent, they packed their meager possessions and moved on to another trailer park. Gretchen quit school after eighth grade and at fourteen, along with her mother, cooked and tended bar at Big O's, five miles outside of town.

Gretchen's musical talent came from her father whom she met at her initiative when she was twelve. Gretchen says, "His family, I'm told, had a little traveling band. I think it was a gospel band." Gretchen could sing from an early age and before karaoke had been heard of, she sang, with a microphone and assorted CDs, for tips on the stage at Big O's. It wasn't long until she was fronting a small band and thought about a life in a place far from Bond County.

In 1996 Gretchen moved to Nashville but had little success for several years and earned her living at a bar in Printers Alley. One night, singer-songwriters, KENNY ALPHIN and JOHN RICH of BIG & RICH, came to the bar and heard Gretchen sing. John asked why she didn't have a record deal by now. Gretchen threw him a business card and homemade demo saying, "I'm busy. I'm working right now." She ignored calls from John for several months but eventually contacted him. John's friends began using Gretchen on demos. She became a member of MuzikMafia, and among her peers began to refine her style. She signed with Sony Music Nashville and in 2004 her debut single, "Redneck Woman," spent five weeks at number one on *Billboard's* country airplay chart. Gretchen's first album, *Here for the Party*, sold nearly five million copies. She received the CMA Horizon Award in 2004 and her autobiography, *Redneck Woman, Stories of My Life*, made the *New York Times* Bestseller List.

Lee Ann **Womack**

AUGUST 19, 1966 - JACKSONVILLE, TEXAS

Lee Ann is a Grammy Award winner and in 2005, earned three CMA awards, including Album of the Year.

Lee Ann Womack has been a student of real life and real country music for as long as she can remember. "Some people take voice lessons to learn how to sing, but I just sat and listened to country records, like GEORGE JONES, DOLLY PARTON and stuff like that... that's how I learned how to sing."

When she was little, Lee Ann's disc jockey father took her to work and had her pick out the tunes for him to play —favorites were RAY PRICE, BOB WILLS, and GLEN CAMPBELL. In high school she passed on her senior trip, asking that her parents take her to Nashville where she toured Music Row and went to TNN tapings. She studied at South Plains Junior College in Levelland, Texas, one of the first to give a degree in bluegrass and country music, where she traveled with the school band, COUNTRY CARAVAN. Eventually, she ended up at Belmont University and in 1990, she made a permanent move to Nashville. While at Belmont, Lee Ann married songwriter, JASON SELLERS.

As a songwriter, Lee Ann signed with Tree Publishing in 1995. A year later as an artist, she signed with Decca Records, the label of country legends. Her first album in 1997 only reached number twenty-two on the charts. However, with endorsements from ALAN JACKSON, GEORGE STRAIT, and others, four singles made it to number two. Two more albums did not excite the public, but when Lee Ann teamed with WILLIE NELSON on "Mendocino County Line," they won a Grammy and a CMA Award in 2002.

Lee Ann recorded a traditional country album in 2005, *There's More Where That Came From*, and won CMA's Album of the Year, as well as Single of the Year for "I May Hate Myself in the Morning." Divorced from Jason Sellers, she married her producer, FRANK LIDDELL in 1999. Lee Ann has two daughters, both of whom appeared in her video, *I Hope You Dance*.

TAMMY **WYNETTE**

Tammy was known as the "First Lady of Country Music." Her best-known songs were "Stand by Your Man" and "D-I-V-O-R-C-E."

Born Virginia Wynette Pugh on her maternal grandparents' farm, she changed her name to Tammy Wynette in 1966. Her musical father died when she was eight months old and her mother moved in order to work at a defense plant in Birmingham, Alabama. Young Tammy taught herself to play the musical instrument her father had left her and sang at the Providence Baptist Church. While picking cotton, Tammy dreamed of a musical career. Two of her girlfriends joined her in forming a trio that began singing gospel music on the local radio station.

Before she graduated from high school, Tammy married Euple Byrd. The marriage lasted six years. In 1965 she was a single mother of three children, with the youngest child afflicted with spinal meningitis. Her dreams of a career in music appeared to be slipping away. She was working as a beautician to pay for expensive medical bills when she landed a regular spot on Birmingham's WBRC-TV's MORNING SHOW. Tammy was featured on the COUNTRY BOY EDDY SHOW, a job that led to PORTER WAGONER'S syndicated show. With a move to Nashville in 1966, Tammy could begin to believe in her dreams again.

Tammy pitched some songs to producer-songwriter, BILLY SHERRILL, and soon was signed to record at Epic Records. Her first single, "Apartment #9," was a modest hit. Her subsequent recording of "Your Good Girl's Gonna Go Bad" soared to number three on the country charts in 1967. Tammy became one of the most successful female singers of all time starting with her number one solo hit, "I Don't Want to Play House." She married GEORGE JONES in 1969. They toured together with their hits, "We're Gonna Hold On" and "Golden Ring." Her autobiography, *Stand By Your Man,* became a movie in 1982. Tammy ranks number two in CTM's 40 Greatest Women of Country Music.

TRISHA **YEARWOOD**

SEPTEMBER 19, 1964 - MONTICELLO, GEORGIA

Ranked tenth on CMT's Greatest Women of Country Music, Trisha's first number one single, "She's in Love with the Boy," was released in 1991.

"**M**ost little kids ask Santa Claus for a doll or a bike for Christmas. I was asking for a tape recorder because I wanted to hear my voice on tape." Trisha has known from the age of five that she wanted to have a career in music. In her little community of Monticello, Georgia, that was like saying she wanted to be president of the United States. At sixteen, Trisha was too young to go into a bar in Macon for talent night. She begged her parents to come with her. They did. She won. Says Trisha, "...that $50 check is still hanging on my bulletin board in Georgia."

In her teens, Trisha convinced her parents to vacation in Nashville to visit the Grand Ole Opry. As they drove down Music Row the long-time dream seemed more real than ever. While attending Belmont University, Trisha worked as a guide at the Country Music Hall of Fame®. Her first job after graduation was as receptionist at MARY TYLER MOORE'S MTM Records. Trisha was often hired to sing on demos and in 1987, she caught the eye of GARTH BROOKS. Hired to sing backup for Garth, she then met GARTH FUNDIS. He had a song, "She's in Love with the Boy," in a drawer just waiting for the right singer to come along. Trisha's recording of the song topped the *Billboard* charts in August 1991. Her debut album was certified double platinum. Of the ten albums following, all went gold; six were certified platinum. Winner of numerous industry awards, Trisha was inducted into the Grand Ole Opry in 1999. She also has played a U.S. Navy forensic specialist on TV's *Jag*.

As two of the biggest stars of the 1990s, Trisha had maintained her friendship with Garth Brooks over the years. They began dating in 2000 and were married in 2005. A happy person these days, Trisha Yearwood says in her own words, "I feel really grateful and blessed to get to do what I love. I love, love, love to sing."

DWIGHT YOAKAM

OCTOBER 23, 1956 - PIKEVILLE, KENTUCKY

Dwight has won two Grammys and has sold twenty-three million albums. With Buck Owens, he recorded "Streets of Bakersfield" in 1988.

Born in the same town as country singer, PATTY LOVELESS, Dwight chose a different avenue to express his version of country music.

Dwight's family moved out of the coal mining town of Pikeville, Kentucky, to Columbus, Ohio, soon after he was born. While attending Northland High School, he became interested in drama and acted in several school productions, including Charlie, the lead role, in *Flowers for Algernon*. Country music was calling him and in 1977, he moved to Nashville to chase his dream of becoming a honky-tonk singer. At the time Dwight landed in Music City, a movement, influenced by the movie, *Urban Cowboy*, was going on in which country music was shifting away from the honky-tonk genre. Fans were looking for something new. Dwight soon met PETE ANDERSON, a guitarist who shared a mutual taste in music, and the duo headed for Los Angeles.

Dwight and Pete were welcomed by the nightclubs there and soon had a following called "cowpunks." In 1984 Dwight received significant airplay on college and alternative radio stations for his album, *A Town South of Bakersfield*. Reprise Records came calling. When *Guitars, Cadillacs, Etc., Etc.* was released in 1986, the first single was JOHNNY HORTON'S "Honky Tonk Man." By now the college stations across America were big fans, but more importantly, it became a hit on the country charts. Dwight then talked BUCK OWENS out of retirement and the two recorded "Streets of Bakersfield," Dwight's first number one hit. In 1993 he released his masterpiece, *This Time*. "Ain't That Lonely Yet" earned Dwight his first Grammy in 1996. Also that year, Dwight ventured into movies co-starring with BILLY BOB THORNTON in *Sling Blade*.

Dwight Yoakam has become one of the music industry's biggest stars, bringing back the traditional sound that has made country music great.

FARON YOUNG

FEBRUARY 25, 1932 - SHREVEPORT, LOUISIANA - DECEMBER 10, 1996

In the early 1950s, Faron had several number one hits including, "Live Fast, Love Hard." His last hit was "It's Four in the Morning" in 1971.

The first crowd that Faron played to was a herd of cows on his father's dairy farm. He said, "I'd get a guitar and sit on the back porch and start singing, and 50-60 cows would come up and watch me sing. I'd talk to them. 'Right now, friends and neighbors, another star of the Grand Ole Opry, Faron Young.'" He couldn't imagine that in a few years he would become one of the most popular singers ever to step on the stage at the Ryman Auditorium.

By the time Faron entered Fair Park High School, he had mastered the guitar and formed his first band. It was his high school football coach who encouraged him to sing country music at service clubs and nursing homes. By 1951 WEBB PIERCE invited Faron to join him on Shreveport's KWKH, which featured the *Louisiana Hayride*. The next year, Capitol signed Faron to a record contract that would last ten years. That same year, he released his first charted hit, "Goin' Steady." Uncle Sam came calling just as Faron's musical career was beginning. He was stationed at Fort McPherson, Georgia. Because of his recent celebrity status as a singer, he was snatched up to replace EDDIE FISHER as Special Services headliner. Faron was the first country singer to fill that post. He was backed up by GORDON TERRY on the fiddle as part of the CIRCLE 'A' WRANGLERS. With his natural charisma, Faron recorded weekly radio recruiting shows.

During the mid-1950s, Faron starred in several movies including *Hidden Gun*. Thereafter, he was dubbed "the Singing Sheriff." Capitol Records had plans for him also. Faron recorded some of the best honky-tonk classics including, DON GIBSON'S "Sweet Dreams" and WILLIE NELSON'S "Four Walls." Besides being one of the most popular musicians, Faron was also a shrewd businessman. He co-founded the *Music City News,* and yes, he did get to appear on the Grand Ole Opry.

"Country music is great music because it really comes from real life experiences. It is such a great haven for reality."

— Bryan White

INDEX

RESOURCES

In researching for this book, an attempt was made to reach a publicist or manager for the artists. When this became a formidable task, I perused the public library and found a few books dealing with country music that I found to be beneficial. *The Encyclopedia of Country Music* compiled by the staff of the Country Music Hall of Fame and Museum and edited by Paul Kingsbury was a valuable resource. However, the book was published prior to 2000 and since then the landscape of country music has had many changes.

A year's subscription to *Country Weekly* provided more current information. Watching the CMT channel was also valuable for observing upcoming and current talent. A wide range of web sites gave a variety of information. I soon found which web sites were trustworthy. Listed below are some of the resources that were helpful in writing the biographies.

Roy Acuff — xroads.virginia.edu; ctm.com - Stephen Thomas Erlewine; TNhistoryforKids.org; Findagrave.com; imdb.com **Trace Adkins** — traceadkins.com; starpulse.com - Steve Huey, *All Music Guide*; cmt.com
Gary Allan — cmt.com; mozilla.com - Johnny Loftus **Duane Allen** — oakridgeboys.com
Rex Allen — westernmusic.org rexallenmusic.org; cojoweb.com; imdb.com **Kenneth Alphin** — bigandrich.imeem.com; bigandrich.com; imdb.com; countrystandardtime.com; co-opliving.com
Bill Anderson — billanderson.com; cmt.com **Keith Anderson** — countrymusic.about.com; cmt.com
Lynn Anderson — cmt.com; countrypolitan.com **Eddy Arnold** — cmt.com; nndb.com
Ernie Ashworth — cmt.com - James Manheim, *All Music Guide*; alamhof.org; profile.myspace.com
Chet Atkins — bmi.com; misterguitar.com - Bob Oermann; misterguitar.com - Stephen Thomas Erlewine; misterguitar.com - Richard McVey II, *Music City News* **Rodney Atkins** — rodneyatkins.com; billboard.com; cmt.com; *Guidepost*, July 2007 p. 41-43 **Gene Autry** — cmt.com; adherents.com; geneautry.com; findagrave.com - Kit and Morgan Benson; The Associated Press, Robert Dose, Elfriede Frank, and Rick L. Rozar
Phil Balsley — thestatlerbrothers.com; musicianguide.com; countrymusic.about.com **Deford Bailey** — cmt.com; pbs.com - excerpts from *Deford Bailey: A Black Star in early Country Music* by David C. Morton and Charles K. Wolfe; answers.com - Eugene Chadbourne, *All Music Guide*; tnstate.edu - Linda T. Wynn
Bobby Bare — cmt.com - Stephen Thomas Erlewine, *All Music Guide*; sing365.com; musicianguide.com - Ken Burke
Clint Black — musicianguide.com - Anne Janette Johnson and Ken Burke **Dierks Bentley** — delafont.com; opry.com; countrymusic.about.com; mutigers.cstv.com; cmt.com; lycos.com **Joseph Bonsall** — hdw-inc.com; josephsbonsall.com **Boxcar Willie** — boxcarwillie.com; cmt.com - Stephen Thomas Erlewine, *All Music Guide*; tshaonline.org - Constance M. Bishop **Garth Brooks** cmt.com - Stephen Thomas Erlewine, *All Music Guide*; askmen.com **Kix Brooks** — cmt.com - Steve Huey, *All Music Guide* **Luke Bryan** — last.fm.com; capitolnashville.com; cmt.com **Glen Campbell** — query.nytimes.com; glencampbellshow.com
Mary Chapin Carpenter — cmt.com; marychapincarpenter.com - Michael Hill; imdb.com **A.P. Carter** — nashvillesongwritersfoundation.com; carterfamilyfold.org **Maybelle Carter** — carterfamilyfold.org; az.essortment.com; answers.com - David Vinopal, *All Music Guide* **Sara Carter** — carterfamilyfold.org; az.essortment.com; answers.com - David Vinopal, *All Music Guide* **Johnny Cash** — johnnycash.com; imdb.com; GMT - Patrick Luce **June Carter Cash** — imdb.com; johnnycash.com; junecartercash.com; thebaron84.tripod.com - Peter Cooper **Rosanne Cash** — rosannecash.com; rollanet.org; cmt.com **Ray Charles** — visionaryproject.org; raycharles.com **Kenny Chesney** — cmt.com; kennychesney.com; imdb.com; askmen.com; newsoxy.com - Jennifer Hong **Mark Chesnutt** — markchesnutt.com; cmt.com; music.msn.com; gactv.com **Roy Clark** — royclark.org; cmt.com - David Vinopal, *All Music Guide*; opry.com; great-music.net
Terri Clark — terriclark.com; geocities.com; thecanadianencyclopedia.com; ticketspecialists.com; cmt.com; opry.com; countrymusic.about.com **Patsy Cline** — patsycline.com; patsy.nu **Jeff Cook** — cookandglenn.com; thealabamaband.com - Stephen Thomas Erlewine; alamhof.org **Cowboy Copas** — cmt.com - John Bush, *All Music Guide*; patsyclinetribute.com; purecountrymusic.com; countrymusic.about.com
Floyd Cramer — countrypolitan.com - Sherry Anderson, nndb.com; cmt.com; Countrypolitan.com, (January 2001); rockhall.com; spaceagepop.com; euronet.nl/users/wvbrecht/floyd.htm; encyclopediaofarkansas.net;

arktimes.com **Billy Ray Cyrus** – cmt.com - Tom Roland & Stephen Thomas Erlewine; reality-tv-online.com; starplus.com - Tom Roland and Stephen Thomas Erlewine, *All Music Guide*; buddytv.com; images.google.com **Charlie Daniels** – cmt.com; charliedaniels.com; musicianguide.com - Anne Janette Johnson **Jimmie Davis** – cmt.com - John Bush, *All Music Guide*; nashvillesongwritersfoundation.com **Skeeter Davis** – takecountryback.com - Sherry Anderson. (June 2001) Article appears courtesy of countrypolitan.com; ronstadt-linda.com **Jimmy Dean** – tsimon.com; cmt.com - Steve Huey **Alton Delmore** – cmt.com - Richie Unterberger, *All Music Guide*; delmorebrothers.net; countrymusichalloffame.com; oldies.com, *The Encyclopedia of Popular Music* by Colin Larkin **Rabon Delmore** – cmt.com - Richie Unterberger, *All Music Guide*; delmorebrothers.net; countrymusichalloffame.com; oldies.com, *The Encyclopedia of Popular Music* by Colin Larkin **Jay DeMarcus** – bestprices.com luv2jdemarcusxrf.tripod.com **John Denver** – classicbands.com; imdb.com; findadeath.com **Little Jimmy Dickens** – cmt.com - Stephen Thomas Erlewine; countrymusic.about.com - Rick Kelly **Ronnie Dunn** – cmt.com - Craig Harris; superiorpics.com **Ralph Emery** – tv.com; tennesseeencyclopedia.net; countrymusichalloffame.com **Dale Evans** – archives.cnn.com; royrogers.com; cowgirls.com **Sara Evans** – gactv.com; starpulse.com - John Bush; saraevans.musiccitynetworks.com **Don Everly** – cmt.com - Kim summers, *All Music Guide*; history-of-rock.com; everlybrothers.com **Phil Everly** – cmt.com - Tim Sendra, *All Music Guide*; rollingstone.com; rockhall.com **Donna Fargo** – Thanks for information from Donna Fargo and Linda Cottingham; birthplaceofcountrymusic.org; cmt.com; musicweb-international.com; imdb.com **Lester Flatt** – cmt.com - David Vinopal; doodah.net; folkmusic.about.com; flatt-and-scruggs.com **Red Foley** – countrypolitan.com; countrymusichalloffame.com - John Rumble; cmt.com - Jason Ankeny, *All Music Guide* **Tennessee Ernie Ford** – ernieford.com; imdb.com; findagrave.com; cmt.com - James Manheim and Bruce Eder, *All Music Guide* **Jimmy Fortune** – jimmyfortune.com, thebaron84.tripod.com, cmt.com **Janie Fricke** – janiefricke.com; cmt.com - Steve Huey, *All Music Guide* **Lefty Frizzell** – cmt.com - Stephen Thomas Erlewine, *All Music Guide*; rockabillyhall.com; nashvillesongwritersfoundation.com **Larry Gatlin** – cmt.com - Steve Huey, *All Music Guide*; imdb.com; gatlinbrothers.musiccitynetworks.com; gactv.com **Crystal Gayle** – cmt.com - Steve Huey, *All Music Guide*; imdb.com **Teddy Gentry** – thealabamaband.com; clemson.edu; Biographies compiled by John W. Rumble; lyrics.mylnm.com; teddygentrymusic.com **Troy Gentry** – montgent.fuzzmartin.com; top40-charts.com; patientadovate.org; countryhound.com; imdb.com; tv.com; monsterandcritics.com **Don Gibson** – countrymusichalloffame.com, adapted from Country Music Hall of Fame® and Museum's *Encyclopedia of Country Music*; severing.nu; cmt.com; nashvillesongwritersfoundation.com **Vince Gill** – vincegill.com; cmt.com **William Lee Golden** – williamleegolden.com; oakridgeboys.com; nashvillemusicguide.com; alamhof.org **Josh Gracin** – joshgracin.com; cmt.com; gactv.com **Jack Greene** – jackgreeneopry.com; cmt.com - Tom Roland, *All Music Guide* **Lee Greenwood** – leegreenwood.com; cmt.com - Tom Roland, *All Music Guide*; musicguide.com - James M. Manheim **Andy Griffith** – biography.com; imdb.com; mayberry.com; tv.com; netglimse.com; movies.yahoo.com; answers.com **Merle Haggard** – cmt.com - Stephen Thomas Erlewine **Tom T. Hall** – cmt.com - Stephen Thomas Erlewine, *All Music Guide*; countrymusic.about.com - Wendy Newcomer **Emmylou Harris** – emmylou.net; imdb.com; askmen.com **Hawkshaw Hawkins** – cmt.com - Cub Koda, *All Music Guide*; oldies.com; bioandlyrics.com **Mark Herndon** – thealabamaband.com; thealabamaband.com **Faith Hill** – faithhill.com; cmt.com; starpulse.com - Steve Huey **Johnny Horton** – cmt.com - Stephen Thomas Erlewine; rockabillyhall.com **Ferlin Husky** – cmt.com - Stephen Thomas Erlewine, *All Music Guide*; members.triod.com **Alan Jackson** – cmt.com - Sandra Brennan and James Manheim, *All Music Guide*; countrymusicnews.ca **Sonny James** sonnyjames.com - John Bush, *All Music Guide*; cmt.com; alamhof.org **Waylon Jennings** – waylon.com; cmt.com **George Jones** – cmt.com; georgejones.com; opry.com **Grandpa Jones** – cmt.com - Bruce Eder, *All Music Guide*; everything2.com **Naomi Judd** – cmt.com; wma.com; dailycelebrations.com **Wynonna Judd** – starpulse.com - Steve Huey, *All Music Guide*; **Toby Keith** – cmt.com; biggeststars.com - *All Music Guide* **Doug Kershaw** – dougkershaw.com **Buddy Killen** – legacyrecordings.com - Ed Hogan, *All Music Guide*; songcitystudios.com; findagrave.com; imdb.com **Pee Wee King** – musicianguide.com - Lloyd Hemingway; cmt.com - Steve Huey, *All Music Guide*; imdb.com; reddstewart.com; Wade Hall, *The Encyclopedia of Country Music*, Ed. by Paul Kingsbury **Alison Krauss** – cmt.com **Kris Kristofferson** – imdb.com; cmt.com; ohboy.com; dailycelebrations.com; scaruffi.com **Miranda Lambert** – cmt.com; askmen.com **K.D. Lang** – amazon.com; divastation.com **Tracy Lawrence** – cmt.com; countrymusic.about.com **Brenda Lee** – brendalee.com **Gary LeVox** – rascalflatts.com; sing365.com - Corey Apar, *All Music Guide*; music.msn.com **Gordon Lightfoot** – gordonlightfoot.net; corfid.com; thecanadianencyclopedia.com **Hank Locklin** – cmt.com - Michael Erlewine; sing365.com; florida-arts.org **Charlie Louvin** – bonnaroo.com; cmt.com - Stephen Thomas Erlewine; nashvillesongwritersfoundation.com; charleslouvinbros.com; nashvillesongwritersfoundation.com **Ira Louvin** – cmt.com - Kim Summers; alamhof.org - David Vinopal; nashvillesongwritersfoundation.com **Patty Loveless** – cmt.com; starpulse - Steve Huey **Lyle Lovett** – starpulse.com - Stephen Thomas Erlewine, *All Music Guide*; newyorker.com - Alec Wilkinson (March 1, 2004); judiciary.senate.gov **Loretta Lynn** – lorettalynn.com; cmt.com - Stephen Thomas Erlewine **Martie Maguire** – chickoholic.tripod.com; superiorpics.com **Natalie Maines** – chickoholic.tripod.com, Interview by Nina Malkin; imdb.com; Betty Clark, *The Guardian*, March 12, 2003 **Barbara Mandrell** – cmt.com - Jason Ankeny; sing365.com; imdb.com; barbara-mandrell.com; **Louise Mandrell** – cmt.com -

All Music Guide; geocities.com **Neal Matthews** — jordanaires.net; findagrave.com; findarticles.com **Martina McBride** — cmt.com; biography.com; martina-mcbride.com; tv.com; countrymusic.about.com; sing365.com; imdb.com **Reba McEntire** — starpulse.com - William Ruhlmann; cmt.com **Tim McGraw** cmt.com; starpulse.com - Steve Huey - *All Music Guide*; askmen.com **Jo Dee Messina** — cmt.com; gactv.com **Roger Miller** — rogermiller.com - Adapted from the Country Music Hall of Fame® and *Museum's Encyclopedia of Country Music*, published by Oxford University Press - Daniel Cooper; cmt.com - Stephen Thomas Erlewine **Ronnie Milsap** — ronniemilsap.com; cmt.com - Sandra Brennan; musicguide.com - Anne Janette Johnson **Bill Monroe** — countrymusichalloffame.com - Adapted from the Country Music Hall of Fame® and *Museum's Encyclopedia of Country Music*, published by Oxford University Press.; rockhall.com; cmt.com **Patsy Montana** — cowgirls.com; musicguide.com; cmt.com - Sandra Brennan and James manheim, *All Music Guide* **Eddie Montgomery** — montgomerygentry.com; gactv.com; sing365.com; cmt.com **John Michael Montgomery** — johnmichael.musiccitynetworks.com; cmt.com; sing365.com; netglimse.com **George Morgan** — countrymusic.about.com; cmt.com - John Bush, *All Music Guide* **Lorrie Morgan** — cmt.com; countrymusic.about.com; starpulse.com - Sandra brennan, *All Music Guide* **Anne Murray** — annemurray.com; thecanadianencyclopedia.com; sing365.com **Willie Nelson** — geocities.com - Leon Russell; cmt.com **Jennifer Nettles** — jennifernettles.com; cmt.com; askmen.com; starpulse.com - Shawn M. Haney; ascap.com - Jon Bahr; bellaonline.com; associatecontent.com **Bob Nolan** — bobnolan.sop.net; imdb.com - Jim Beaver; sonsofthepioneers.org; b-westerns.com **Roy Orbison** — famoustexans.com - Ron Tyler, ed., *The New Handbook of Texas*, Vol. 4 (Austin, Texas: Texas State Historical Association, 1996) pp. 1164-65; findagrave.com - Kit and Morgan Benson; 8notes.com **Marie Osmond** — marieosmond.com; imdb.com; cmt.com - Steve Huey, *All Music Guide*; oprah.com **Paul Overstreet** — pauloverstreet.com; musicianguide.com; cmt.com - Sandra Brennan, *All Music Guide*; uk.real.com - Mike McGuirk **Randy Owen** — alamhof.com - Stephen Thomas Erlewine; gactv.com; thealabamaband.com, *The Times-Journal*, June 10, 2008 **Buck Owens** —countrymusichalloffame.com; cmt.com; findagrave.com - bio by: Donald Greyfield; imdb.com - Mini Biography - Brian Rathjen **Patti Page** — material from Patti Page's personal manager, Michael J. Glynn **Brad Paisley** — cmt.com; starpulse.com - Biography–Steve Huey **Dolly Parton** — infoplease.com; television.aol.com - bio - Sandra Brennan; rollingstone.com–From *The Rolling Stone Encyclopedic of Rock & Roll* (Simon & Schuster, 2001); sonynashville.com; icweb2.loc.gov (Library of Congress) **Les Paul** — The Encyclopedia of Country Music, Edited by Paul Kingsbury, p. 407; rockhall.com; answer.com; music.aol.com **Johnny Paycheck** — furious.com - Kurt Hernon, September, 2002; cmt.com; talentondisplay.com - Shaun Mather **Minnie Pearl** — cmt.com - James Manheim; countrymusichalloffame.com; findagrave.com - Bio by Jared Vaughn; imdb.com; grindersswitch.com **Kellie Pickler** — kelliepicklerforum.com; askmen.com - Steve Granitz; buddytv.com; cmt.com **Webb Pierce** — webbpierce.net; countrymusichalloffame.com; cmt.com - Stephen Thomas Erlewine **Elvis Presley** — elvis.com; imdb.com - Ed Stephan, Chris Holland; answer.com **Ray Price** — cmt.com; Dan Cooper, *All Music Guide*; countrymusichalloffame.com **Charley Pride** — charleypride.com; cmt.com; shs.starkville.k12.ms.us - *Biography of Charley Pride*, by Damien Allen **Eddie Rabbitt** — cmt.com - Tom Roland, *All Music Guide*; musicianguide.com; nndb.com; findagrave.com **Marty Raybon** — martyraybon.com; cmt.com; countrymusic.about.com - Reviewed by Matt Bjorke; nashvillemusicguide.com **Jim Reeves** — starpulse.com - David Vinopal; countrymusichalloffame.com **Don Reid** — statlerbrothers.com; members.aol.com; gmahalloffame.org; musicianguide.com; answers.com - Jason Ankeny; countrymusic.about.com; hebaron84.tripod.com; *This Is My Story*, published by Thomas Nelson, edited by David Liverett, page 231 **Harold Reid** — statlerbrothers.com; cmt.com - Edward Morris; members.aol.com; musicguide.com; jacksonsun.com; *This Is My Story*, published by Thomas Nelson, edited by David Liverett, page 233 **Charlie Rich** — charlierichjr.com; cmt.com; imdb.com - Stephen Thomas Erlewine, *All Music Guide* **John Rich** — cmt.com; guerillawomentn.blogspot.com; sing365.com **Jeannie C. Riley** — cmt.com - Sandra Brennan; kanabel.com; bipolar.about.com **LeAnn Rimes** — askmen.com; cmt.com - Stephen Thomas Erlewine **Tex Ritter** — famoustexans.com- *Bibliography: Ron Tyler*, ed., *The New Handbook of Texas*, Vol. 5 (Austin, Texas: Texas State Historical Association, 1996) p. 595.; countrymusichalloffame.com - Adapted from the Country Music Hall of Fame® and *Museum's Encyclopedia of Country Music*, published by Oxford University Press.; nashvillesongwritersfoundation.com; cmt.com - Jason Ankeny **Marty Robbins** — cmt.com - Hank Davis; countrymusichalloffame.com; martyrobbins.net - liner notes from *Marty Robbins - A Lifetime of Song 1951-1982* **Julie Roberts** — cmt.com; gactv.com; countrymusic.about.com - From Shelly Fabian **Emily Robison** — sing365.com; celebritywonder.com; chickoholic.about.com; imdb.com **Jimmie Rodgers** — jimmierodgers.com; rockhall.com; countrymusichalloffame.com; alamhof.org - David Vinopal; nativeground.com **Kenny Rogers** — kennyrogers.biz/biography.html; cmt.com - David Vinopal and Stephen Thomas Erlewine; starpulse.com **Roy Rogers** — royrogers.com - *Happy Trails: The Life of Roy Rogers*, By Laurence Zwisohn **Lulu Roman** — material from Lulu Roman's personal manager, Marc Giguere; luluroman.20m.com; imdb.com; billboard.com **Joe Don Rooney** gactv.com; cmt.com; sing365.com; umich.edu; luv2jdemarcusxrf.tripod.com **John Schneider** — cmt.com - Steve Huey, *All Music Guide*; superiorpics.com; tv.com; sweetlyrics.com **Earl Scruggs** — earlscruggs.com; cmt.com - David Vinopal; bmi.com; flatt-and-scruggs.com - *America's Music: BlueGrass* - Barry R. Willis; *Your Guide to Folk Music* - Kim Ruehl; bmi.com - MusicWold - Gerry wood **Blake Shelton** — cmt.com; musicianguide.com; countrymusic.about.com; starpulse.com **Ricky Van Shelton** — rickyvanshelton.com; cmt.com - Steve Huey, *All Music Guide*; sweetlyrics.com;

enormousrecords.com; musicianguide.com **Jean Shepard** — cmt.com - Dan Cooper and Stephen Thomas Erlewine; enormousrecords.com; opry.com; bakersfield.com **Ricky Skaggs** — skaggs.musiccitynetworks.com; cmt.com; opry.com; gibson.com **Carl Smith** — countrymusichalloffame.com - Ronnie Pugh - Adapted from the Country Music Hall of Fame® and *Museum's Encyclopedia of Country Music*, published by Oxford University Press; cmt.com - Stephen Thomas Erlewine **Connie Smith** — cmt.com; starpulse.com - John Bush; imdb.com; sweetslyrics.com; huxrecords.com; yahoo.com **Hank Snow** — countrymusichalloffame.com - Charles Wolfe — Adapted from the Country Music Hall of Fame® and *Museum's Encyclopedia of Country Music*, published by Oxford University Press.; cmt.com; hanksnow.com; thecanadianencyclopedia.com; WSWS: Arts Review: Music: December 31, 1999, Country music singer Hank Snow dead at 85 - Iva Bruce; the canadianencyclopedia.com **Tim Spencer** — sonsofthepioneers.org; cmt.com; imdb.com; mannamusicinc.com **Richard Sterban** — publicaffairs.noaa.gov; musicnewsnashville.com; smgray3.tripod.com; musicnewsnashville.com; sing365.com **Ray Stevens** — cmt.com - Steve Huey **Gordon Stoker** — gleasononline.com — Source: *The McKenzie Banner; This Is My Story*, published by Thomas Nelson, edited by David Liverett, page 267 **George Strait** — cmt.com; billboard.com - Stephen Thomas Erlewine; imdb.com **Stringbean** — cmt.com - Bruce Eder, *All Music Guide*; findeagrave.com; imdb.com - Jon C. Hopwood **Marty Stuart** — martystuart.com; martystuart.net **Taylor Swift** — cmt.com; gactv.com; billboard.com - Megan Frye **Gordon Terry** — cybergrass.com; imdb.com; answers.com; findagrave.com; doodah.net; music.msn.com - Johnny Loftus, *All Music Guide*; tv.com; windowsmedia.com **Hank Thompson** — countrymusichalloffame.com - John Rumble - Adapted from the Country Music Hall of Fame® and *Museum's Encyclopedia of Country Music*, published by Oxford University Press.; cmt.com - Steve Huey, *All Music Guide*; carthagetexas.com **Mel Tillis** — meltillis.com; opry.com, musicweb-international.com; cmt.com - Jason Ankeny - *All Music Guide* **Pam Tillis** — pamtillis.com; cmt.com **Trent Tomlinson** — cmt.com; gactv.com **Merle Travis** — cmt.com - Bruce Eder, *All Music Guide*; musicguide.com; imdb.com **Randy Travis** — randytravis.com; cmt.com; starpulse.com - Brian Mansfield and Stephen Thomas Erlewine, *All Music Guide*; imdb.com **Travis Tritt** — cmt.com - Stephen Thomas Erlewine - *All Music Guide*; opry.com; sonynashville.com; thephoenix.com **Ernest Tubb** — countrymusichalloffame.com - Ronnie Pugh, Adapted from the Country Music Hall of Fame® and *Museum's Encyclopedia of Country Music*; cmt.com - David Vinopal, *All Music Guide*; songwritershalloffame.org, from the Country Music Hall of Fame® **Tanya Tucker** — cmt.com; starpulse.com - Sandra Brennan, *All Music Guide* **Josh Turner** — cmt.com; billboard.com - Steve Leggett, *All Music Guide*; joshturner.musiccitynetworks.com **Shania Twain** — gactv.com; askmen.com; starpulse.com - Stephen Thomas Erlewine, *All Music Guide* **Conway Twitty** — cmt.com; countrymusichalloffame.com - Robert K. Oermann - Adapted from the Country Music Hall of Fame® and *Museum's Encyclopedia of Country Music*, published by Oxford University Press.; imdb.com **Carrie Underwood** — carrieunderwoodofficial.com; buddytv.com; billboard.com - Heather Phares - *All Music Guide*; people.com; cmt.com; imdb.com **Keith Urban** — starpulse.com - Ed Nimmervoll, *All Music Guide*; askmen.com; cmt.com **Porter Wagoner** — tennessean.com - Peter Cooper; people.com; billboard.com; latimes.com, Randy Lewis; nytimes.com, Douglas Martin; cmt.com **Billy Walker** — billywalker.com; countrymusic.about.com; cmt.com **Ray Walker** — jordanaires.net; elvis.com - interview by L. Kent Wolgamott **Steve Wariner** — opry.com; cmt.com; members.tripod.com; stevewariner.com **Kitty Wells** — kittywells.com; pbs.org; nndb.com; cmt.com - Brian Mansfield and Stephen Thomas Erlewine, *All Music Guide* **Dottie West** — members.tripod.com; musicianguide.com - Elizabeth Wenning; imdb.com; sing365.com **Slim Whitman** — cmt.com - Sandra Brennan - *All Music Guide*; musicianguide.com - by Kevin O'Sullivan **Chuck Wicks** — chuckwicks.com - David Jeffries, *All Music Guide*; cmt.com; gactv.com; buddytv.com; the9513.com; countrystandardtime.com; rcarecordlabel.com **Doyle Wilburn** — cmt.com - Jason Ankeny, *All Music Guide*; musicguide.com; sweetslyrics.com; tv.com **Terry Wilburns** — cmt.com - Jason Ankeny, *All Music Guide*; tv.com; musicguide.com; sweetslyrics.com **Don Williams** — imdb.com; musicguide.com - Elizabeth Thomas; shopping.yahoo.com - Stephen Thomas Erlewine, *All Music Guide* **Hank Williams** — rockhall.com; alamhof.org - Stephen Thomas Erlewine; thehankwilliamsmuseum.com; countrymusichalloffame.com - Colin Escott - Adapted from the Country Music Hall of Fame® and *Museum's Encyclopedia of Country Music*, published by Oxford University Press. **Hank Williams, Jr.** — hankjr.com; cmt.com; sing365.com; biography.com **Kim Williams** — countrymusic.about.com; durango-songwriter-expo.com **Bob Wills** — bobwills.com - *Chronology of Bob Wills' Life* By Dwight Adair; rockhall.com **Gretchen Wilson** — gretchenwilson.com; cmt.com **Lee Ann Womack** — leeannwomack.com; cmt.com - Stephen Thomas Erlewine; msnbc.msn.com **Tammy Wynette** — cmt.com; imdb.com; gactv.com; countrymusichalloffame.com - Mary A. Bufwack - Adapted from the Country Music Hall of Fame® and *Museum's Encyclopedia of Country Music*, published by Oxford University Press **Trisha Yearwood** — cmt.com - Steve Huey, *All Music Guide*; imdb.com; trishayearwood.com **Dwight Yoakam** — starpulse.com; cmt.com; answer.com; imdb.com - Stephen Thomas Erlewine, *All Music Guide*; countrypolitan.com **Faron Young** — cmt.com - Stephen Thomas Erlewine - *All Music Guide*; sing365.com; musicguide.com; ddiekman.tripod.com; imdb.com; countrymusichalloffame.com - Daniel Cooper - Adapted from the Country Music Hall of Fame® and *Museum's Encyclopedia of Country Music*, published by Oxford University Press.

Appendix

Listed below are the country artists with the dates when they first were invited to join the cast of the Grand Ole Opry.
Also listed are the dates when the artists were inducted into Country Music Hall of Fame®.

Roy Acuff — Joined Opry, February 19, 1938 — Hall of Fame, Sept. 15, 1962

Trace Adkins — Joined Opry, August 23, 2003

Duane Allen *Oak Ridge Boys* — Hall of Fame, October 30, 2000

Bill Anderson — Joined Opry, July 15, 1961 — Hall of Fame, 2001

Eddy Arnold — Joined Opry, 1944 — Hall of Fame, 1966

Ernie Ashworth — Joined Opry, March 7, 1964

Chet Atkins — Joined Opry, 1950 — Hall of Fame, 1973

Gene Autry — Hall of Fame, October 15, 1969

DeFord Bailey — Joined Opry, 1925 — Hall of Fame, November 15, 2005

Phil Balsley *Statler Brothers* — Hall of Fame, 2008

Bobby Bare — Joined Opry, August 14, 1965

Dierks Bentley — Joined Opry, October 1, 2005

Clint Black — Joined Opry, January 10, 1991

Joe Bonsall *Oak Ridge Boys* — Hall of Fame, October 30, 2000

Boxcar Willie — Joined Opry, February 21, 1981

Garth Brooks — Joined Opry, October 6, 1990

Glen Campbell — Hall of Fame, November 15, 2005

A.P. Carter *Carter Family* — Hall of Fame, 1970

Maybelle Carter *Carter Family* — Hall of Fame, 1970

Sara Carter *Carter Family* — Hall of Fame, 1970

Johnny Cash — Joined Opry, July 7, 1956 — Hall of Fame, 1980

June Carter Cash — Joined Opry, 1950

Roy Clark — Joined Opry, August 22, 1987

Terri Clark — Joined Opry, May 20, 2004

Patsy Cline — Joined Opry, January 9, 1960 — Hall of Fame, October 15, 1973

Jeff Cook *Alabama* — Hall of Fame, 2005

Cowboy Copas — Joined Opry, January, 1946

Floyd Cramer — Hall of Fame, 2003

Charlie Daniels — Joined Opry, 2007

Jimmie Davis — Hall of Fame, 1972

Skeeter Davis — Joined Opry, August 4, 1959

Alton Delmore — Joined Opry, 1931 — Hall of Fame, 2001

Rabon Delmore — Joined Opry, 1931 — Hall of Fame, 2001

Jimmy Dickens — Joined Opry, September 25, 1948 — Hall of Fame, Ocotber 10, 1983

Ralph Emery — Hall of Fame, 2007

Don Everly — Joined Opry, 1957 — Hall of Fame, 2001

Phil Everly — Joined Opry, 1957 — Hall of Fame, 2001

Lester Flatt — Joined Opry, 1955 — Hall of Fame, October 14, 1985

Red Foley — Joined Opry, April 1946 — Hall of Fame, 1967

Tennessee Ernie Ford — Hall of Fame, October 8, 1990

Jimmy Fortune *Statler Brothers* — Hall of Fame, 2008

Lefty Frizzell — Joined Opry, July 21, 1951 — Hall of Fame, October 11, 1982

Larry Gatlin — Joined Opry, December 25, 1976

Terry Gentry *Alabama* — Hall of Fame, November 15, 2005

Don Gibson — Joined Opry, May 20, 1958 — Hall of Fame, 2001

Vince Gill — Joined Opry, August 10, 1991 — Hall of Fame, 2007

William Lee Golden *Oak Ridge Boys* — Hall of Fame, October 30, 2000

Jack Greene — Joined Opry, December 23, 1967

Merle Haggard — Hall of Fame, October 5, 1994

Tom T. Hall — Joined Opry, January 1, 1971 — Hall of Fame, 2008

Emmylou Harris — Joined Opry, January 25, 1992 — Hall of Fame, 2008

Hawkshaw Hawkins — Joined Opry, 1955

Mark Herndon *Alabama* — Hall of Fame, November 15, 2005

Ferlin Husky — Joined Opry, 1954

Alan Jackson — Joined Opry, June 7, 1991

Stonewall Jackson — Joined Opry, November 10, 1956

Sonny James — Joined Opry, October 27, 1962 — Hall of Fame, 2006

Waylon Jennings — Hall of Fame, 2001

George Jones — Joined Opry, Aug. 4, 1956 — Hall of Fame, Sept. 30, 1992

Grandpa Jones — Joined Opry, March 16, 1946 - Hall of Fame, October 9, 1978

Wynonna Judd — Joined Opry, September 15, 2001

Buddy Killen — Joined Opry, 1950

Pee Wee King — Joined Opry, 1937 — Hall of Fame, October 15, 1974

Alison Krauss — Joined Opry, July 3, 1993

Kris Kristofferson — Hall of Fame, November 9, 2004

Brenda Lee — Hall of Fame, September 24, 1997

Hank Locklin – Joined Opry, November 9, 1960

Charlie Louvin – Joined Opry, February 10, 1955 – Hall of Fame, 2001

Ira Louvin – Joined Opry, February 10, 1955 – Hall of Fame, 2001

Patty Loveless – Joined Opry, June 11, 1988

Loretta Lynn – Joined Opry, Sept. 25, 1962 – Hall of Fame, Oct. 10, 1988

Barbara Mandrell – Joined Opry, July 29, 1972

Neal Matthews Jr. *Jordanaires* – Hall of Fame, 2001

Martina McBride – Joined Opry, November 30, 1995

Reba McEntire – Joined Opry, January 14, 1986

Roger Miller – Hall of Fame, October 25, 1995

Ronnie Milsap – Joined Opry, February 6, 1976

Bill Monroe – Joined Opry, October 28, 1939 – Hall of Fame, 1970

Patsy Montana – Hall of Fame, 1996

George Morgan – Joined Opry, Sept. 25, 1948 - Hall of Fame, Sept. 23, 1998

Lorrie Morgan – Joined Opry, June 6, 1984

Willie Nelson – Hall of Fame, September 29, 1993

Bob Nolan – *Son of the Pioneers* – Hall of Fame, 1980

Randy Owen *Alabama* – Hall of Fame, November 15, 2005

Buck Owens – Hall of Fame, 1996

Brad Paisley – Joined Opry, February 17, 2001

Dolly Parton – Joined Opry, January 4, 1969 – Hall of Fame, 1999

Johnny Paycheck – Joined Opry, November 8, 1997

Minnie Pearl – Joined Opry, Dec. 7, 1940 – Hall of Fame, Oct. 25, 1975

Webb Pierce – Joined Opry, September 1952 – Hall of Fame, 2001

Elvis Presley – Hall of Fame, September 23, 1998

Ray Price – Joined Opry, January 1952 – Hall of Fame, 1996

Charley Pride – Joined Opry, May 1, 1993 – Hall of Fame, October 4, 2000

Jim Reeves – Joined Opry, October 1955 – Hall of Fame, 1967

Don Reid *Statler Brothers* – Hall of Fame, 2008

Harold Reid *Statler Brothers* – Hall of Fame, 2008

Tex Ritter – Joined Opry, June 12, 1965 – Hall of Fame, December 6, 1964

Marty Robbins – Joined Opry, January 19, 1953 – Hall of Fame, 2001

Jimmie Rodgers – Hall of Fame, November 3, 1961 (First person inducted)

Roy Rogers – Hall of Fame, October 10, 1988

Earl Scuggs – Joined Opry, 1955 – Hall of Fame, October 14, 1985

Ricky Van Shelton – Joined Opry, June 10, 1988

Jean Shepard — Joined Opry, November 21, 1955

Ricky Skaggs — Joined Opry, May 15, 1982

Carl Smith — Hall of Fame, 2003

Connie Smith — Joined Opry, June 13, 1965

Hank Snow — Joined Opry, January 7, 1950 — Hall of Fame, October 8, 1979

Tim Spencer *Son of the Pioneers* — Hall of Fame, 1980

Richard Sterban *Oak Ridge Boys* — Hall of Fame, October 30, 2000

Gordon Stoker *Jordanaires* — Hall of Fame, 2001

George Strait — Hall of Fame, 2006

Stringbean — Joined Opry, 1945

Marty Stuart — Joined Opry, November 28, 1992

Gordon Terry — Joined Opry, 1950

Hank Thompson — Hall of Fame, 1989

Mel Tillis — Joined Opry, June 9, 2007 — Hall of Fame, 2007

Pam Tillis — Joined Opry, August 26, 2000

Merle Travis — Hall of Fame, 1977

Randy Travis — Joined Opry, December 20, 1986 — Hall of Fame, Oct. 10, 1977

Travis Tritt — Joined Opry, February 28, 1992

Ernest Tubb — Joined Opry, 1943 — Hall of Fame, October 22, 1965

Josh Turner — Joined Opry, October 27, 2007

Conway Twitty — Hall of Fame, 1999

Carrie Underwood — Joined Opry, May 10, 2008

Porter Wagoner — Joined Opry, February 23, 1957 — Hall of Fame, 2002

Billy Walker — Joined Opry, February 4, 1960

Ray Walker *Jordanaires* — Hall of Fame, 2001

Steve Wariner — Joined Opry, May 11, 1996

Kitty Wells — Joined Opry, 1952 — Hall of Fame, October 11, 1978

Dottie West — Joined Opry, 1964

Slim Whitman — Joined Opry, October 29, 1955

Doyle Wilburn — Joined Opry, 1953

Teddy Wilburn — Joined Opry, 1953

Hank Williams — Hall of Fame, November 3, 1961

Bob Wills — Hall of Fame, October 18, 1968

Tammy Wynette — Joined Opry, 1969 — Hall of Fame, September 23, 1998

Trisha Yearwood — Joined Opry, March 13, 1999

Faron Young — Joined Opry, 1952 — Hall of Fame, October 4, 2000

ACKNOWLEDGEMENTS

My thanks to my wife, Avis, for copy-editing the biographical information. This book would not have been completed without her help. To David Coolidge for proofreading the copy. To Tammy Burrell for her expertise in the layout of the book. To Judy Spencer Nelon for making it possible for me to go backstage at the Grand Ole Opry House and for the one year collection of *Country Weekly*. For the use of their musical instruments on the cover, Debra and Roy Losch. Others who have helped with this book over the past two years are: Steve Brallier, Dennis Disney, Don Reid, Leclair Bryan, Tim White, Debby Delmore, Linda Cottingham, Mignonette Kelsoe, Terry Dorsey, Greg Kelsoe, Michael Dempsey, Michael J. Glynn, George Abiad, Suze Spencer Marshall, John Dowell, Les Leverett, Keena West, Ron Scott, Ronnie Thomas, Jimmie Terry Lemmond, James Akenson, Dale Pickett, Marty Raybon, and Holly G. Miller.

Books by David Liverett

"When Hope Shines Through"
This 240 page book has 110 lighthouse drawings and
106 essays from 90 different writers.

$16.95

"Faith for the Journey"
This 304 page book is an inspirational paperback with
100 church drawings and 103 essays from 98 different writers.

$16.95

"Love, Bridges of Reconciliation"
This 176 page book has 67 bridge drawings
and 72 essays from 68 writers.

$15.95

"Light from the Barn"
This 196 page book is an inspirational paperback with
82 barn drawings and 82 essays from 80 different writers.
$15.95

**"This Is My Story–
146 of the World's Greatest Gospel Singers"**
This 297 page book, published by Thomas Nelson, features biographies
and pen-and-ink drawings of 146 gospel music singers.

$19.95

"Just Beyond the Passage"
This 144 page book is an inspirational paperback with 60 door,
gate, and arch drawings and 60 essays from different writers.
$15.95

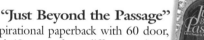

**"They Called Him Sparky:
Friends' Reminiscences of Charles Schulz"**
This 112 page book contains stories about Schulz's life from his early years in
St. Paul, Minnesota. Features several of his *Young Pillars* cartoons.

$14.95

"Those Grand Ole Country Music Stars"
This 248 page book features biographies
and pen-and-ink drawings of 217 country music personalities.

$17.95

Include $4.00 for shipping and handling plus Indiana sales tax where it applies.

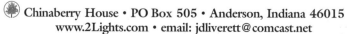

Chinaberry House • PO Box 505 • Anderson, Indiana 46015
www.2Lights.com • email: jdliverett@comcast.net